Nō

AND

Bunraku

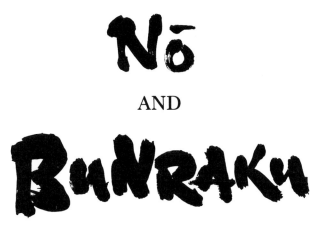

Nō

AND

BuNRAKu

TWO FORMS OF JAPANESE THEATRE

DONALD KEENE

photographs by
KANEKO KEIZŌ

COLUMBIA UNIVERSITY PRESS
New York

Columbia University Press Morningside Edition
Columbia University Press
New York   Chichester, West Sussex

Library of Congress Cataloging-in-Publication Data

Keene, Donald.
[Nō]
Nō ; and, Bunraku : two forms of Japanese theatre / Donald Keene ;
photographs by Kaneko Keizō.
p.   cm.
Reprint (1st work). Originally published: Tokyo ; Palo Alto, Calif. :
Kodansha International ; New York :
Distributed in the U.S.A. by Harper & Row, 1973. Reprint (2nd work).
Originally published: Tokyo : Kadansha International ; New York :
Distributed in the U.S. by Harper & Row, 1973.
ISBN 0-231-07418-2 (cloth).
ISBN 0-231-07419-0 (pbk.)
1. Nō.
2. Bunraku.
I. Kaneko, Keizō, 1933–
II. Keene, Donald. Bunraku. 1990.
III. Title.
IV. Title: Nō.
V. Title: Bunraku.
PN2924.5.N6K38   1990
895.6'2009—dc20   90-2319
CIP

Morningside Edition 1990

CONTENTS

PREFACE TO THE MORNINGSIDE EDITION

THE two books I have written on Japanese theatre—the book on Bunraku of 1965 and the one on Nō of 1966—have a special place in my heart. They were written about ten years after I first began to attend regularly the different varieties of theatre in Japan. I had enjoyed going to the theatre in New York ever since I was a boy and by the time I was in college I had become a confirmed devotee of opera. However, even after I had decided to make the study of Japan my lifework, all I knew about Japanese theatre before I went to study in Kyoto in 1953 came from books that had been published before the outbreak of war in 1941. During the war years it was obviously impossible for me to go to Japan, and even after the war students were not allowed into that country by the army of occupation. I nevertheless wrote my Ph.D. dissertation about one work of the Japanese theatre, the puppet play *The Battles of Coxinga* and its background. I was very rash in writing about Japanese theatre without having once seen a performance, but at the time I reassured myself by recalling that many people had written about ancient Greek drama without knowing more about it than the texts.

This reasoning was mistaken in a critical way: Unlike the Greek drama, which had to be revived after many centuries when its performing traditions had been lost, the three major forms of traditional Japanese drama—Nō, Bunraku, and Kabuki—had been continuously performed ever since they were first invented. Indeed, almost every theatrical art ever known in Japan still survives in some form, despite the changing of tastes over the years. Again and again prophets of despair have declared that the younger generation was uninterested in these relics of the past and predicted that they soon would disappear. I certainly heard such voices when I was first living in Japan, but fortunately prophets of doom are just as likely to be mistaken as incorrigible optimists. The traditions remain unbroken.

When I finally saw a Bunraku play after having written at length about this marvellous theatre of puppets, I realized how imperfect my knowledge had been. It was not that I had made mistakes on the dates when new techniques of puppetry had been introduced or that I had given insufficient attention to the narrative techniques, but that I had no real grasp of what actually happened to the audience once the performance began. Borrowing my information from some prewar study, I wrote that the puppet operators were so skillful that the audience soon forgot their presence. I was merely trusting in other people's opinions; the relatively few photographs I had ever seen of Bunraku certainly did not persuade me that this process really took place. To my astonishment, I discovered that it was really true.

My knowledge of Nō was faulty for a different reason. I had read in class some of the masterpieces of the Nō theatre and thought of them as lyrico-dramatic works. When I tried to imagine what a performance might be like the only images that came into my head were of opera—something other worldly and mysterious like *Pelléas et Mélisande*. The first performance of Bunraku I saw was far more exciting than I had imagined, but the first performance of Nō was a big disappointment because the music seemed so bare and unpoetic. It took me longer to appreciate Nō, but that was normal, considering the length of its traditions and the sensitivity expected of the audience. In the end Nō became one of the greatest pleasures of my life in Japan.

When I was asked to write on these two theatrical arts I eagerly accepted, though I had promised to write other books. (I was later asked to do a book on Kabuki as well, but by that time I really *had* to write the promised books.) The books were produced with the greatest of care in every respect. The photographs of Kaneko Keizō were not only an inspiration to me but, I thought, made it possible even for people who had never been to Japan and had never seen performances of Nō and Bunraku elsewhere to visualize what it was like to be in a Japanese theatre. Some people have told me that they enjoyed these two books more than anything else I have published. If this is so, my indebtedness to Mr. Kaneko's photographs is all the greater.

The cost of producing such books, however, kept the original publisher from reprinting. I had more or less given up hope that the books would again be available when Jennifer Crewe of Columbia University Press suggested to me that it might be possible to publish the two books in one volume. I was delighted to accept this suggestion.

At first I thought I would try to revise the text as completely as possible, but on rereading it seemed to me that the two books effectively transmitted my profound affection for Nō and Bunraku and it would be difficult to change anything without changing the whole. I naturally do not mean to suggest that there have been no advances in scholarship since the books were first published. On the contrary, important books have appeared both in Japan and elsewhere that no serious scholar can ignore. I have included the titles of some of these works in the Bibliography, but I have not attempted to incorporate their findings in my text. I hope, however, that what I have written will still be of interest as an expression of long devotion to two magnificent theatrical arts.

The Classical Theatre of Japan

The text
is dedicated to
NARU HOVHANESS

INTRODUCTION

THE word *nō* means talent and, by extension, the display of talent in a performance. In its earliest forms Nō, an art that today enjoys enormous prestige, may have been little more than a display of acrobatics and circus stunts, but in the course of time the original Nō developed into an aristocratic, almost ritual, art. The remoteness of its style and content from the typical dramatic forms of our own day has often led prophets to declare that Nō could not long survive, that a younger generation accustomed to the pace of films and television could never tolerate the extreme deliberation of Nō. Prophets of doom always sound more authoritative than optimists, but fortunately, they are as often mistaken. Contrary to all the predictions made to me in 1953, when I first saw Nō performed, Nō thrives today as never before, and the audiences consist increasingly of young people, perhaps driven to Nō by dissatisfaction with entertainments supposedly devised for their pleasure.

Nō has often been compared to the Greek drama. The use in both of masks, a chorus, song and stately dances, and poetry of an elevated nature provides some basis for comparison. But there are important differences too. Dramas intended for the huge audiences that filled the Grecian amphitheatres could not help but differ from those intended for a small group of aristocrats at the Japanese court. More important, the conception of drama differed basically. The Greeks, in Aristotle's words, believed that a play must have a beginning, a middle and an end; but the Nō plays tend to be all end, though divided into sections of different musical tempi. The Greek dramas often conclude with the warning that we must not call a man happy until he is dead, even though at the outset of the play the hero seemed to be enjoying great good fortune; but the protagonist of a Nō play has usually died before the play begins, and the end, instead of a warning, is likely to be a promise of deliverance from the tortures he is suffering when he first appears. The Greeks built plays around characters who, though larger than ourselves and confronted by problems far more terrible than any we are likely to face, are recognizably like us; the characters in the Nō plays are hardly more than beautiful shadows, the momentary embodiments of great emotions.

The Greek and Nō dramas, then, are essentially different despite surface resemblances. They are most alike, perhaps, in retaining their appeal to audiences separated by many centuries and infinite numbers of social changes from the periods when the plays were created. Though both dramas were products of particular societies and drew from their myths, their grandeur and lofty disregard of the quotidian enables them to soar eternally. That is why they move audiences today as much as when first performed.

A person equipped with nothing more than a general sensitivity to different forms of art may be deeply moved upon his first visit to a Nō theatre. Yet I believe it is also true that the more one knows about a theatre with traditions as deep-rooted as those of Nō, the greater one's pleasure.

I have written this book in the hope of passing on to others the information I have found helpful in the enjoyment of Nō.

Photographs, it hardly needs saying, are indispensable in any study of a theatrical art, particularly one as unfamiliar in the West as Nō. I have been exceptionally fortunate in my collaborator, Mr. Kaneko Hiroshi. The patience and energy—and skill, of course—demanded by his photographs were never begrudged. Nō is perhaps the most difficult form of theatre to photograph. Long intervals pass virtually without motion onstage, to be succeeded by brief and violent action. The photographer seldom has a second chance if he misses the first time. A Nō play is performed in the season with which it is associated, and often but a single time. If the photographer misses, for example, the moment in *Tsuchigumo* when the monstrous spider throws out his web, he may have to wait a whole year before it is staged again, and it may not be staged by the same group of actors for many years. Again, the photographer who is asked for a picture of Nō being performed at the Itsukushima Shrine at a time when the stage is surrounded by water has a total of about one hour in the course of an entire year. The photographing of the masks, however, poses the greatest problems. They are prized for their ability to shift expression, and the photographer therefore bears the responsibility, through his choice of lighting and angle, for the face that each mask presents to the world.

A problem encountered by anyone preparing an illustrated book on Nō arises from the difficulty of obtaining permission to examine the masks and costumes of the different schools. Mr. Maruoka Akira made it possible to obtain the cooperation of the leading actors; I owe him especial thanks.

I have failed thus far to mention the Kyōgen farces which are equally the subject of this book. This does not reflect any lack of esteem. Indeed, I believe my happiest experiences in Japan were studying and performing in Kyōgen for several years. But Kyōgen is altogether a more genial and outgoing art than Nō and requires little introduction here. I wish, however, to express my thanks to the artists of both Ōkura and Izumi schools for their kind cooperation.

Finally, I must thank the staff of Kodansha International Ltd. for having contrived to satisfy my every request for this book, however unreasonable. Requests for photographs that most publishers in other countries would have refused even to consider—for the costumes of the Kongō school in Kyoto, displayed only at the height of the sweltering summer, or for the rustic versions of Nō performed at Kurokawa in the depths of the bitter northern winter—were cheerfully met and the generosity shown me was a source of real inspiration.

DONALD KEENE

Nō

The conventional way of describing Japanese pronunciation, as rendered in roman letters, is to say that the consonants are as in English, the vowels as in Italian or Spanish. This formula is inexact, but at least it suggests the original pronunciations. All vowels are sounded; thus, the word *kakegoe* is pronounced something like *kah-keh-go-eh*, each syllable being given equal stress.

I have used the transcription Nō to designate the art, though Noh is also familiar.

Throughout the book, Japanese names retain their original order, with family name first and given or adopted name last.

I. THE PLEASURES OF NŌ

Nō BEGINS with a mask, and within the mask the presence of a god. Before a performance of *Okina*, the mask to be worn is displayed in the dressing room and honored with ritual salutations. When the actors have filed onto the stage and taken their places, one called the Mask Bearer offers the mask of *Okina* to another, who prostrates himself in reverence before accepting it. The *Okina* mask is unlike that for any other role; though its features are those of a benevolent old man and not a fearsome being, they are nonetheless a god's, and performing this role, devoid though it is of emotion or special displays of technique, is considered so arduous as to shorten the life of the actor.

Okina, the oldest Nō play, is accorded unusual reverence, but even plays not about the gods partake of the mystery of divinity. Before the actor makes his entrance he gazes at his masked face in the mirror, and though until that moment an ordinary man—whether an outcaste or a nobleman —he himself becomes as he stares at the mask a reflection. Other theatres are often said to be a mirror of life, but Nō is an image in the mirror which life approximates.

The wall at the back of the Nō stage (the *kagami-ita*, or "mirror boards") is decorated with the painting of a huge pine, the Yōgō Pine at the Kasuga Shrine in Nara. Old accounts tell how once an old man was seen performing a dance beneath this pine; he proved to be the god of the shrine. Every year, at the festival of the shrine, the head of the Komparu school of Nō stands beneath the Yōgō Pine so that the god may descend into the actor and make him his reflection. Originally, perhaps, the play merely allowed the god to assume visible form. *Okina* opens with the meaningless but portentous syllables of the god's utterance: the actor, like a medium, pronounces a language he himself cannot comprehend. *Okina* is not in the least tragic. It is a joyous celebration of abundance and long life, but the presence of the god exhausts the actor. Of all Nō plays, *Okina* is probably the most widely performed. At the beginning of the year, on important occasions, at village festivals, *Okina* normally opens the program. It has no plot, is largely unintelligible to the audience, and has little in common with popular stage entertainments, but no one would dream of omitting it; *Okina* is an initiation into the world of Nō.

The solemnity of Nō distinguishes it most conspicuously from other theatres. The Japanese are by no means incapable of comedy. Indeed, interspersed between the Nō tragedies during a complete program are farces called Kyōgen which are filled with humor. The mask of *Okina* itself, a cheerful face, has suggested to some Japanese critics that originally it was a festive work, rather than the stately ceremonial of today. For that matter, the origin of all varieties of Japanese theatre is sometimes traced to the lewd and comic dance performed by the goddess Uzume to lure the sun goddess from the cave where she sulked. But whatever the ancient manner of presentation may have been, a felicitous Nō is today performed with the deliberation and gravity reserved in most parts of the world for sacred rites. The plays are almost all tragic, but even on the rare occasion when the actor says, "How happy I am!" (*Ureshi ya!*) he sounds to the uninitiated spectator like a tortured soul.

The plays were certainly not always acted before spectators wrapped in the hushed awe of a present-day Tokyo audience. Nō performances in rural districts are sometimes as informal as the theatre in China or Southeast Asia. People chatter, eat or doze through the performance, and no one takes it amiss if a well-wisher, sympathizing with the actors on a cold night, steps onto the stage to offer them hot saké. This may have been the normal reception of the Nō plays before court patronage in the fourteenth century gave them an aristocratic dignity. The ritualization of Nō in the seventeenth century imparted to the theatre its present solemnity.

But even if Nō was once lighter entertainment, the plays were performed in a building belonging to a shrine, and the actors, then as today, were participants in a rite. The religion served by the performers is Shinto, the Way of the Gods. This native religion of Japan has its sacred book and a body of theological writings, but most Japanese believe in Shinto not in terms of its formal mythology and the scholars' elucidations, but in terms of gods and demons inhabiting the mountains and waters of Japan. These supernatural beings are innumerable, and include emperors, the ghosts of famous men, animals, trees, and even inanimate objects. The good spirits bring happiness and plenty, but there are also malevolent ghosts. One way to appease the dead, who might otherwise return to afflict the living, was to recite or re-enact their deeds on earth, assuring them that they had not been forgotten. The sacred dances at the Shinto shrine, Kagura, originated in this manner, it appears, and Nō may also have been intended to calm the troubled dead. The dead return to life on the Nō stage to tell again their hours of glory and grief.

We cannot be sure how Nō came to assume its present form or what its relation was to religious rituals. Often we must guess from a survival in some remote village, an older form of Nō than the more polished art in the cities. Sometimes too we can obtain hints by examining the theatre elsewhere. In Thailand, for example, plays are performed today on a row of tiny stages before the great stupa at Nakhorn Pathom—not for an audience (though a few old people and children may be present), but for the gods. The family of a recently deceased person offers the plays, which are staged with the utmost intensity, even without an audience. Perhaps this was true in Japan in ancient times. Nō stages have three steps leading down from the front. These have no function in performances (though, one may be wryly informed, an actor who fell from the stage could use them to climb back). In the past the actors were rewarded after a performance with gifts from the daimyo they served, presented by an official who used the steps for the purpose. But originally, perhaps, the steps were added so that the actors, priests at a Shinto shrine, might pass from the shrine to the stage where they performed not for an audience of mortals but for the gods.

Today, a performance of Nō, like any other theatrical representation, demands not only a stage and actors but an audience, and its purpose is to provide "entertainment." However, the stage, actors, and audience differ so markedly from those in theatres elsewhere that we are apt to be less conscious of what Nō shares with drama in other countries (or with other forms of drama within Japan itself) than of its uniqueness. The entertainment it provides is unlikely to afford a casual visitor much distraction, but it possesses immediately recognizable beauty: the masks, superb examples of the carver's art; the magnificent costumes; the hypnotically eloquent singing of the chorus; the stately movements of the actors. Yet as soon as one enters a Nō theatre one realizes from the austere stage, the respectful hush of the audience, that it is the scene not merely of drama but of ritual. An appreciation of the ritual of Nō may come intuitively and instantly, as Western visitors sometimes discover, or it may be the product of years of study. Nō gives pleasure in proportion to what the spectators bring to their appreciation, whether a sensitivity to any form of beauty, or a specific knowledge of the texts, movement and music. Because Nō makes no concessions, the slowness of pace and unrelieved gravity may weary, but this risk is taken deliberately.

The purpose of Nō is not to divert on the surface but to move profoundly and ultimately, to transcend the particular and touch the very springs of human emotions.

Of all theatres probably Nō makes the greatest demands on the audience. The texts are in medieval language, studded with quotations from even older classics, and would be difficult to follow even if pronounced with the utmost clarity. The actors scorn as mere "theatricality" any suggestion of realism in representation, and the audience is prepared to accept in the role of a beautiful girl a tottering old man with a quavering voice and heavy jowls visible around the mask. A child may perform as a warrior capable of inspiring terror in demons, and no one in the audience laughs at his high-pitched little voice when he reassures his frightened followers that they have nothing to fear. The masks make it possible to believe that an actor with an unattractive face is a god or a beautiful woman; in this sense they provide a realistic touch, but the unvarying expression on Shizuka's face, whether angry, weeping, or resigned to her fate, must be given shades of meaning by the eye of the connoisseur. The appeal of Nō is by no means entirely intellectual or aesthetic; it moves many in the audience to tears, and leaves haunting and poignant remembrances.

A recent critic, reviewing the performance of a sixty-four-year-old actor in the part of Lady Rokujō in *Nonomiya* ("The Shrine in the Fields"), a play based on *The Tale of Genji* and describing the beautiful, elegant princess who desperately loved Genji, wrote, "I have never seen such a deeply-felt performance of *Nonomiya*. . . . The actor succeeded in leaving so profound and penetrating an impression that for awhile afterwards I was quite overcome, and even now I feel something like a lump in the pit of my stomach. It goes without saying that the play produced a different effect than a reading of *The Tale of Genji*, but even in terms of Nō the impression I received was at times different from any other representation I have witnessed. On this occasion Rokujō of course was beautiful, but one was made to think less of the aristocratic dignity of the woman than of her fate. Above all, I was impressed by the strength in Nō itself and in the actor's art to move men's hearts."

This performance of *Nonomiya*, by an actor whose normal appearance and voice in no way suggested a beautiful court lady, was more deeply affecting than a more realistic representation could have been. The text of *Nonomiya* is a masterpiece, but no one by reading the text alone could sense the shattering loneliness of the moment on the stage when Rokujō, standing before the *torii* of the Shrine in the Fields, lifts her foot to step through, a gesture of symbolic renunciation of the world and Prince Genji, only to return her foot to its place, yielding to a final burst of longing. The performance of the actor as Rokujō must reach its climax at this moment, and he is abetted by the harsh, desolate beat of the hand drum (*ōtsuzumi*). The actor must not only transcend his physical limitations but convert them into the elements of a supreme artistic experience. The particular qualities of an actress in the part of Rokujō might obscure the eternal, absolute nature of the princess and her tragic love, but an old man's voice, his movements perfected during half a century on the stage, the stylized beauty of his mask, costume and fan, can emphasize the eternal lines of the story. Additional realism would be as foolish as coloring in the lines of Euclid's propositions, or in as bad taste as the rubies and emeralds with which the barbarous sultans adorned their Chinese porcelains.

It has taken some six hundred years for Nō to achieve its present refinement. We have no way of telling whether actors of former days were more or less capable than those today, but the natural human tendency to glorify the past has induced critics at all times to assert that the performers of their day were no match for those of the past. Zeami (1363–1443), the greatest figure in the history of Nō, was sure that no contemporary actor could remotely touch the abilities of his father, and a writer describing performances he had seen in 1658 declared, "Nō in the old days used to encourage virtue by representing the good and chastise vice by representing the bad, and the movements of the actor's feet and head were never at variance with decorum, but modern performances, in complete violation of the old traditions, have reduced the art to vulgarity."

Each age had brought changes to the performing techniques, generally as a reflection of changing times and tastes rather than of a decline in the actors' skill. Today, at a time when other Japanese traditional arts have lost their popular following, new stages have been built for Nō, and hundreds of thousands of amateurs are learning the singing and dancing. Numbers alone do not prove that Nō is now enjoying its period of greatest distinction, but the size of the audiences means that Nō does not survive merely in a fossilized form, revived rarely and piously on special occasions like the European miracle plays. Though confined to a repertory largely established four hundred years ago, and staged in exact conformance to the traditions of the different schools of performers, Nō is a living art, changing subtly but surely with the times, as interpreted by its outstanding performers.

The Nō repertory comprises a great variety of works, ranging from virtually static celebrations of the glories of a particular shrine to pieces of violent movement in which devils assert their terrible powers. It includes works which are almost purely poetic and symbolic, suggesting the loveliness of plum blossoms or the snow, and others which treat betrayal and vengeance. Usually when critics make generalizations about Nō they are thinking of the poetic dramas associated with the name of Zeami; these plays indeed are closest to the essence of Nō. Many earlier or later pieces show a more pronounced dramatic quality and realism. They form an essential part of the repertory and, on the whole, enjoy even greater popularity than Zeami's masterpieces, but it is not for their sake that the audience goes to the Nō theatre. Though the members of the audience may prefer the stirring *Funa Benkei* ("Benkei in the Boat") to the remote loveliness of *Kakitsubata* ("The Iris"), the slow-moving, poetic works give Nō its meaning and ultimate appeal. Modern audiences, no less than their predecessors, are there to witness a special form of drama, and they respect its demands. They may be less inclined than those of fifty or more years ago to sit through a full program of plays, but they are moved by precisely the same moments: when Rokujō hesitates before the *torii*, or when the ghost of Matsukaze, the fisher girl deserted by a nobleman, disappears for the last time, "leaving only the wind in the pines." The Nō plays are admired because they capture in words, music and dance the tragic climaxes of profound emotions.

Actors today may interpret the parts with greater psychological subtlety than their predecessors, but this is not a violation of the texts, which contain poetic truth of eternal and universal validity, leaving them open to interpretation and appreciation by men of different ages and societies. Every gesture in Nō has centuries of tradition behind it, but the actor has greater leeway in interpreting the roles than in works of more specific content tied to this time or that place. Nō is realistic in its evocations of what a woman experiences when deserted by her lover or what the taste of defeat is to a hitherto unvanquished warrior. This realism, as contrasted with the fantasies of other forms of Japanese theatre, is the glory of Nō. It is found at its intensest in the slow-moving masterpieces of Zeami.

The audience at a Nō performance today consists mainly of connoisseurs. Many have learned the parts as amateurs or have seen performances so frequently they can detect the seemingly slight differences that distinguish a great actor from a merely competent one. Some carry texts of the plays to the theatre and consult them, not in the casual manner of the operagoer skimming through a libretto during the intermissions, but with minute care, noting variations in the performance from the musical notations in the printed text. Some are so engrossed by the musical aspects of the plays that they hardly lift their eyes to the stage, as if the acting were only incidental to their enjoyment. Others watch each gesture raptly, and study the shifting light and shadows on the masks or the details of the costumes. The printed texts are necessary for those who have not studied them in advance, because the deliberately muffled delivery, accentuated by the masks, makes it virtually impossible to understand the lines spoken or sung. Some in the audience, including connoisseurs, doze through whole sections of the plays, awakening instinctively for the climactic moments. The manner of enjoying the performance may differ, but each spectator has shared in the beauty of an art evolved by many men's efforts over the centuries.

Nō, created in the fourteenth century, reached its full growth by the middle of the fifteenth century. It shares much with other forms of expression during the period: it is bare, yet evocative, like the monochrome landscapes; beautiful, yet austere, like the temple gardens; preoccupied with death and the ultimate means of deliverance from life like the literary works inspired by the Buddhism of the time. The movements of the actors owe much to the martial arts that thrived in an age of warfare and to the decorum expected of the Zen priest. The actors' distinctive walk, a bare lifting of the feet from the floor, occurs also in the tea ceremony, another art perfected in the fifteenth century. These arts are all marked by an economy of means used to achieve a maximum effect, a preference for suggestion rather than representation. The Nō plays are staged before the unvarying backdrop of the Yōgō Pine, and in place of the realistic props found in some Western theatres (fountains with real water, doors that slam with a convincing bang), the props for Nō are seldom more than outlines of the objects suggested—a boat, a hut or a carriage. The gestures of the actors are highly stylized: either simplified, as when a hand lifted before the slightly lowered mask denotes weeping, or developed into the pattern of a dance, as when the simple action of noticing something is depicted by the actor's bringing together his opened fan in his right hand to his left hand, slowly lifting the fan diagonally upwards, then lowering his left hand diagonally to the left as his gaze falls on an object. Above all, the masks, by eliminating not only particularities of features but any readily apparent change in emotions, evoke more in the connoisseur than the most expressive actor's face.

Suggestion, achieved through the most restrained means, is not an end in itself; like every aspect of Nō it is intended to achieve beauty. Nō is a supremely aesthetic theatre. Critics and commentators from the time of Zeami have devoted their greatest attention to beauty of effects rather than, say, how an audience can be moved to tears. A Nō play must move the audience, but never by ugliness or violence. The humblest character—a fisher girl or a peasant—wears magnificent robes and speaks great poetry. But even beauty is not the final object. Nō reaches out towards eternity through beauty and the elimination of the temporal and accidental.

The Nō plays are set in the distant past and no attempt is made to give them immediacy. The characters are sometimes historical, sometimes drawn from the fiction of the tenth and eleventh centuries, sometimes the gods of legends, but the subjects and their treatment are so absolute that it is irrelevant to ask whether or not the plays are faithful to the times they portray. The performances too are absolute. The actor's vocal delivery and walk are identical whether he is taking the part of a man or a woman; gestures which might indicate the age or sex of the character are avoided in most plays, and the choice of masks and costumes is governed largely by tradition. Above all, the actor refrains from admixing anything of his own personality in the roles and from allowing any variation to creep into successive performances. Hōshō Kurō (1837–1917), the creator of modern Nō, said that the difference between an amateur and a professional Nō actor was that the professional always played a part in exactly the same manner. The characters depicted in the plays, however vividly they may emerge through the poetry and the movements, exist only as part of the play; it would be absurd to wonder what they were like when younger or in happier circumstances. Their absoluteness makes the plays as valid today as when written; it may be that performances are now closer to the authors' intent than was possible when the whims of courtiers might disrupt a program. In any case, despite their heavy reliance on classical poetry and unfamiliar Buddhist thought, they are immediately affecting both to Japanese and Western spectators, and can be accepted unconditionally by readers capable of enjoying poetry and myth. The powerful effect produced on Yeats and Pound, though they never saw a play performed, suggests the universality of the appeal of the Nō plays as literature.

The plays, indeed, are among the supreme masterpieces of Japanese literature, combining a richness of language and an integrity of emotion. They are so filled with ambiguities, allusions and wordplays that it seems hardly possible their first audiences could catch more than the general drift of many passages, yet they definitely were not armchair dramas. For Zeami the plays were chiefly vehicles for the display of the singing and dancing of the actors. In Europe the great plays, whether or not performed, have been read and esteemed as literature, but in Japan the evaluation of the plays has been intimately connected with performance; unstaged plays have aroused no interest. Paradoxically, the Nō is absolutely dependent on the beauty of its texts, for the deliberate manner of delivering the lines tends to exaggerate their qualities. Of the thousands of Nō plays written during the last six centuries (many, of course, intended for performance on a single occasion only), only some 230 survive in the repertory. Some have retained their popularity despite weaknesses in the text, thanks to the beauty of the music or the dances, but the vast majority are works of literary distinction.

If we attempt to examine the Nō plays in terms of some traditional definitions of drama in the West, we become immediately aware of how unsuited these criteria are. Drama begins with conflict, we are often told, but scholars of Nō have insisted that the Nō plays totally lack conflict because there is only one true personage, the *shite*, or protagonist; the other persons are merely observers of the action and not antagonists. The point is overstated, but it contains truth; most Nō plays lack the confrontation of characters typical of drama elsewhere, and some are virtually devoid of action. *Yōrō* ("Nurturing the Aged") tells of the discovery of a mineral spring with miraculous curative powers, a happy augury for the emperor's reign. The story is felicitous, but hardly dramatic. *Unrin-in*, as currently performed, is concerned mainly with explaining the meaning of certain obscure poetical terms in the tenth-century novel *Ise Monogatari*. Numerous other plays are mainly retellings of the history of a shrine or some other auspicious site, described with no suggestion of conflict.

Another Western view of drama, which stresses the importance of the creation of characters, reached its absurd heights with such nineteenth-century studies as *The Girlhoods of Shakespeare's Heroines*. But even though the *shite* is the only personage in a Nō play, he possesses few individual qualities. More often he is the incarnation of some powerful emotion, whether unforgiving enmity, possessive jealousy, or remorse for some unspeakable deed. In the early plays, before Zeami imprinted Nō with his view of the art, and in the late plays written as the form was disintegrating, more distinctive personalities are depicted, and sometimes there is conflict between the *shite* and another character. Normally, however, the *waki* ("person at the side") is little more than a representative of the audience who asks the questions it might ask, not possessing a personality or even a name of his own. The *shite* may have one or more *tsure* ("companion"), but the *tsure* is usually no more than a shadow. The *shite*, then, is generally the only person in a play, but even the *shite* belongs to another world, not our own, and creation of character, in the sense that the term is used in other forms of drama, is meaningless in Nō.

Some students of Nō, calling attention to the prominence of the final dance *(shimai)* performed by the *shite*, which may occupy a third of the total time of the play, have considered Nō as a form of spectacle and the texts as the means of creating the circumstances and atmosphere necessary for the dance. Certainly Zeami devoted enormous care to the choreography of the plays, and our most lasting impression of such a work as *Hagoromo* ("The Feather Cloak") is of the unearthly final dance of the angel. But some Nō plays are without dancing or are provided with only the suggestion of a final dance. Many are virtually without movement. Indeed, the less movement in a play, the higher its "rank" *(kurai)*. *Sekidera Komachi*, a work of so lofty a rank that in the past century only half-a-dozen actors, all acclaimed masters at the close of their careers, have ventured to perform the role, lasts about two hours; during the first hour and a half the *shite* sits motionless inside the prop, a frame representing a thatch-covered hut. A critic who saw the performance in

1955 reported that the interest of the play was mainly in the motionless hour and a half. Zeami himself wrote that the moments without action were especially appreciated by the audience; the actor, unable to rely on movement or words to distract the audience, had somehow to communicate his underlying spiritual strength. The final dance is extremely important to Nō, and may make reading the plays seem only a shell of the whole work, but the dance itself is not so much a display of agility or brilliance of movement as a continuation in different idiom of the mood created by the motionlessness.

It might be imagined, finally, that Nō resembled opera in being a drama which exists primarily for the sake of music. The music is unquestionably a vital part of Nō. The music and words have always been inseparable, the texts being transmitted orally, each syllable sung or declaimed in accordance with the musical traditions of a school of Nō. But no one ever sang the music without the words, as often happens with opera. Nor do the dances exist apart from the words in which they are framed. The music, played by drums and a flute, or sung, and the dances at the end or elsewhere, spring from the words and are in essence one with them.

A Nō play, then, fits badly into any category established by conventional Western theories of drama. To attempt a definition: it is a dramatic poem concerned with remote or supernatural events, performed by a dancer, often masked, who shares with lesser personages and a chorus the singing and declamation of the poetry. The texts of Nō are most properly discussed as literature, as in Chapter III.

Nō can be performed on any kind of stage, whether a hastily revamped modern auditorium stage or the crude platform built for a village festival, but to be appreciated fully it should be seen in a theatre built for its special use. Some old stages survive, such as the one at the shrine at Miyajima on the Inland Sea, where at certain times of day the tide flows between the audience and the stage, heightening the sense of mysterious distance. At the Nishi Honganji in Kyoto one can sit in splendor like the barons of former days, surrounded by sliding screens covered in gold leaf, and watch from a separate building the performance on the old stage. Between the seats of the nobles and the stage is a gravel-covered area where in former days the "groundlings" sat. In all Nō theatres today the tradition of having the stage in a building separate from the audience is vestigially retained by a massive wooden roof over the stage, even in modern concrete theatres. Though the gravelled area has shrunk to a symbolic foot or so, it too continues to divide the world of the audience from that of the actors.

The audience sits on two sides of the stage, to the center and to stage-right. Most Nō theatres today have seats like those in a Western theatre, but the ground floor of the older ones is divided into boxes where four or five people can sit in Japanese style, warming their hands over a *hibachi* in winter, or perhaps eating lunch from tiered lacquer boxes. The stage itself, some eighteen feet square, is built of polished but unpainted *hinoki* wood. At each of its four corners are pillars supporting the heavy curved roof. Behind the stage proper is an addition about nine feet deep (*atoza*) where the musicians and stage assistants sit; it is distinguished from the main stage by the horizontal direction of the floor boards. To stage-left is another extension, a mere three feet wide, where the chorus sits in two rows. The boards here run parallel to those of the stage. A passageway called the *hashigakari*, of the same width as the *atoza*, leads to the stage from the backstage. The *hashigakari* ranges in length from eighteen to forty-five feet, depending on the size of the theatre. On the side closer to the audience three small living pines are planted at regular intervals. At the far end is a brocade curtain with vertical stripes of contrasting colors which is lifted to permit actors to make their entrance. Two other architectural features are a low door (*kirido*) to the left of the *atoza* and the three steps leading from the stage to the gravel. Underneath the stage, invisible to the audience, are large jars placed to increase the resonance of the actors' voices and the musical instruments.

The beginning of a play is signalled from offstage by a flute. The Nō flute has not the softly melodic quality of the European flute, but sounds shrill and sometimes harsh. Its notes at the start of a performance seem to come from another world, not the Elysian Fields of the celebrated flute solo from Gluck's *Orfeo ed Eurydice* but a world infinitely distant from ours filled with a suffering we cannot comprehend. After the flute has sounded, the brocade curtain is lifted by men holding bamboo poles inserted in the hems, and the musicians enter, gravely walking in single file along the edge of the *hashigakari*, as if unwilling to tread the same boards in the center over which the actors presently will appear. The members of the chorus, eight or ten men, enter at the same time from the *kirido* at stage-left and take their places, sitting in formal Japanese style, their fans on the floor before them. The musicians sit in a prescribed order: the flutist, on the floor, farthest to stage-left; next, the player of the small drum (*kotsuzumi*) on a folding stool; the *ōtsuzumi* drummer, also on a stool; and finally, (in many but not all plays) the bass drum (*taiko*) player, kneeling on the stage a little to the rear of the others. Stage understudies (*kōken*), attired in formal black kimonos, sit at the rear of the stage, rising occasionally during the course of performance to straighten an actor's robe. The *kōken* is normally a distinguished performer capable of taking over from the *shite* if he becomes indisposed or to prompt if an actor forgets his lines.

When the musicians are seated, the flutist again plays, this time joined by the percussion instruments—the hollow thud of the *kotsuzumi* and the sharp crack of the *ōtsuzumi*. These sounds are augmented by the inarticulate, portentous cries of the drummers, suggesting again the immense distance separating the audience from the persons in the play. The brocade curtain, lowered after the musicians had all appeared, is again lifted, this time to permit the entrance of an actor and the beginning of the play.

The roles in a Nō play are known not by the names of the characters, as in a Western drama, but by the category of the role. In addition to the *shite*, *waki*, and *tsure* mentioned above, there are *kokata* (child parts, a variety of *tsure*) and *kyōgen*, generally rustics or menials. In the late Nō plays these distinctions often seem arbitrary. In some, the *waki* is more important than the *shite*, and in a few it is not even clear which part is *shite* and which *waki*. But in the plays of the great period, the first half of the fifteenth century, the *shite* is of predominant importance. The distinction between *shite* and *waki* is heightened in performance by the marked difference in costume (the *shite* wears brocades, the *waki* usually the black robes of a priest); in the use of masks for the *shite*, but never for the *waki*; in the different quality of the singing and recitation; and in the dances, which give the role of the *shite* its authority even if the part has less dialogue than the *waki*'s.

Many plays open with the entrance of the *waki*, often an itinerant monk, who tells us he intends to visit a certain shrine. His walk is deliberate, and his facial expression grave. He may describe his journey, but it is suggested in performance merely by a few steps. Eventually, he goes to the pillar at front stage-left, known as the *waki* pillar, and there awaits the appearance of the *shite*.

Nō plays are in either one scene or two. The difference is not merely in setting or length, but depends also on the nature of the play—whether about a ghost or a more realistic work. Most plays in one scene are about persons who belong to this world. The *shite*, if taking the part of a male character of his own age, may appear without a mask. In plays in two scenes, however, the *shite*'s appearance changes in the second part, and he may even be an entirely different person. In *Atsumori* we see the *shite* in the first scene as a humble reaper, but after the interlude he reappears in the second scene wearing the splendid armor of a general, his "true" appearance; this time, if not before, he wears a mask. In *Funa Benkei*, the *shite* in the first part is the unhappy Shizuka, a beautiful woman whose lover, Yoshitsune, must leave her behind as he sets out on a dangerous journey; in the second scene the *shite* is the terrible, vengeful spirit of Tomomori, a warrior vanquished by Yoshitsune, who rises from the sea to menace his ship. In this case, naturally, every detail of the *shite*'s appearance will be different in the second scene. The *tsure* accompanying the *shite* may also change appearance, but the *waki*, who belongs to this world, remains the same throughout whether in plays of one or two scenes.

The *kokata* performers appear not only in the roles of children, but also as fully-grown emperors, perhaps to avoid any suggestion of disrespect, and in most plays where an inappropriate romantic element might be created if fully grown actors appeared as man and woman in the *shite* and *tsure* parts. Yoshitsune in *Funa Benkei* is played by a boy, but in *Shōzon* a boy takes Shizuka's part. *Kokata*, whether they appear as males or females, are never masked.

The chorus, eight or ten men dressed in matching formal kimonos, sits at the side of the stage throughout the play, taking no part in the action. The function of the chorus is to recite for the actors, particularly when they are dancing. Unlike the chorus in a Greek play, it makes no comment on the action, and is never identified as townsmen, warriors or demons; the chorus, in fact, has no identity, but exists solely as another voice for the actors. Any *shite* actor, from the head of the school down, may appear in the chorus, remaining anonymous in the ranks.

The *kyōgen* parts are taken by actors attired in conspicuously humbler costumes than even the *waki*'s sombre robes. In the two-scene plays they appear during the interlude *(ai)*, generally as a rustic or "a man of the place," who explains to the *waki* the history of some remarkable occurrence. The interval *kyōgen* recitations possess slight interest for modern day spectators, who often go out for a smoke when the performer appears, but originally, when the texts were not yet printed nor so carefully studied, the *ai-kyōgen* actor was probably welcomed by the audience because he explained in a more colloquial, though eloquent, language the story so cryptically related elsewhere in the play. Perhaps also *ai-kyōgen* satisfied a craving for rhetoric, for occasions did not exist for oratory in the days when Nō was created. Today, the *ai-kyōgen*'s chief importance is that it fills the stage while the *shite* is changing costume, though a few are display pieces of narration or have an intrinsic dramatic interest.

In contrast to the *ai-kyōgen*, which rarely are humorous and are considered of such slight literary interest that they are usually omitted from texts of the plays, the independent Kyōgen, presented in alternation with the Nō plays as part of the program, are enjoyed as comedies, the best Japanese literature provides. Kyōgen farces seem to have supplied the necessary compensating humor to the unrelieved tragedy of the Nō plays from the inception of this form of theatre. Kyōgen may even be older than Nō; Kyōgen actors figure prominently in performances of *Okina*. An account of 1464 indicates that Nō and Kyōgen regularly alternated by that time if not much earlier. Although denied the prestige of Nō, Kyōgen has long shared its stage and some of its glory.

A single Nō play now takes from one to two hours to perform, depending chiefly on the length of the dances; even the most extended texts rarely run to ten pages of print. In the past the plays were performed much more quickly than today, perhaps at twice the speed, as we can judge from the number of plays presented as part of a single day's program. One play, however perfect, was never considered sufficient entertainment, and it was the practice instead to perform a series of plays in a prescribed order of categories. *Okina* was set apart, no doubt because it clearly belonged to an older tradition than the rest, and was invariably performed at the start of a program. The other plays of the repertory were divided into five categories: (1) plays about the gods *(waki Nō)*; (2) plays about martial heroes *(shuramono)*; (3) plays about women *(kazuramono)*; (4) plays of a miscellaneous or contemporary character *(genzaimono)*; and (5) plays about demons *(kiri Nō)*. The order of these five categories was determined primarily by their prevailing tempo. Each play was considered to consist of three main sections: *jo*, the introduction; *ha*, the development; and *kyū*, the climax. The pace of the play gradually increases in tempo from the deliberate introduction to the strenuous and sometimes agitated movements of the final dance. A program of Nō plays followed the same pattern. Plays of the first category, though possessing *jo*, *ha* and *kyū* sections, on the whole are slow-moving; their fastest sections are only relatively fast, and can by no means by compared to the *kyū* episodes of plays in the fourth or fifth categories. Plays of the second, third and fourth categories were considered to correspond to the *ha* section, increasing within this category from the generally slower tempo of the plays about warriors to some plays in the fourth category which depict demons in a manner almost indistinguishable from the fifth category, the *kyū* section of the program. The progression of plays was intended to provide the audience with a complete theatrical experience, starting with the stately movements of a religiously-inspired piece about the gods, a suitably elevated opening of the program, gradually increasing in human interest through the warrior play until the woman play, the most lyrical part of the program, was reached. The intensity of the woman's love portrayed in these plays might be pushed to the extreme of madness, as in some fourth-category works, or the human interest might become so dominant as to eliminate the supernatural or lyrical elements, as in the contemporary plays. Finally, the demon plays produced an exciting and satisfying effect at the end of a program similar to that of the presto finale of a symphony. The Kyōgen farces staged between the plays did not break the mood so much as they gave the audience a temporary and welcome respite from the overpowering emotions of the tragedies.

Audiences today are not often prepared to spend the eight or more hours at the theatre that a complete program of Nō and Kyōgen would require. Often a program consists of three Nō and a single Kyōgen. The sedate god plays are performed relatively seldom, and even the woman plays, long termed the "rice bowl" of the actors, figure less frequently on the programs than plays of the fourth and fifth categories. But an over-emphasis given to the more exciting Nō plays tends always to weaken the effect and even defeat the purpose of the art. If the audience is not prepared spiritually by slower, more symbolic works before it sees a play like *Ataka*, the experience will hardly differ from seeing *Kanjinchō*, the Kabuki play derived from *Ataka*. It is not only forgivable but perhaps even necessary that the spectators be bored or made drowsy by a program of Nō. The plays are works of such lofty aspirations that a certain magnitude and even tedium is part of the total effect. If the audience has sat through a full program, its reaction to *Ataka* when presented as the fourth work will not be simple enjoyment of the exciting story and interesting characters; the audience will see *Ataka* as part of the world permeated by the atmosphere of Nō. Dramatic excitement is an element in Nō, and the stories have a concentrated intensity which rivals that of any stage, but Nō is prized above all for what it and no other theatre can achieve.

The special vocabulary of Nō makes discussion difficult for the uninitiated. The term *yūgen* is especially important as a criterion of Nō, but its meaning is not easy to define. Originally *yūgen* meant "dark" or "obscure" with overtones of mystery. It was frequently employed in Japanese poetic criticism of the twelfth century to describe beauty which is suggested rather than stated. There is *yūgen* in this famous poem by Fujiwara no Shunzei:

yū sareba	Evening has come;
nobe no akikaze	The autumn wind from the fields
mi ni shimite	Cuts into the flesh
uzura naku naru	And the quails are calling now
Fukakusa no sato	In Fukakusa Village.

The atmosphere evoked in this poem is lonely rather than inviting, monochromatic rather than colorful, but beneath the externals one may glimpse a deeply-felt beauty. Poets of this school felt that the emotions aroused by more conventionally admired sights were real but limited, but there was no limit to what might be evoked through suggestion. A monochrome suggests more than the most brilliantly tinted landscape; the evening in autumn evoked by Shunzei's poem is eternal and universal, not the happy or sad experience described by one man alone.

The ideal of *yūgen* shifted in meaning during the three centuries between Shunzei and Zeami. The word came to mean "charming" or "graceful" and was used, for example, to describe dancing boys at a shrine or even the traditional court football (*kemari*). When Zeami himself attempted to define *yūgen* by giving examples from the manners, appearance and speech of people he knew, he chose the courtiers, and indicated that *yūgen*, at least at this period of his career, meant "grace" or "elegance." His insistence that Nō be filled with *yūgen* may have meant no more, then, than that it should aim at graceful expression even when representing ugly or frightening characters, unlike harsher and cruder types of theatre. The grace of an old woman or even a demon—let alone a beautiful woman—is certainly apparent in contemporary performances. In part this is due to the use of masks, but in Zeami's day the physical beauty of the actors, especially the boys who performed without masks, must have contributed much to the *yūgen*. Zeami himself, as a boy of eleven, attracted the attention of the young Shogun Yoshimitsu in 1374, and Yoshimitsu's infatuation (as much as his interest in the theatre) occasioned the patronage which the shogunate was to bestow on Nō for almost five hundred years. The plays provide for an unusually large number of children's roles, probably for this reason. Grace and beauty in the appearance of the actors, achieved if necessary by wearing masks, and in the language of the texts made up much of Zeami's *yūgen*.

But it is hard to imagine that Zeami meant nothing more profound by the term. In Zeami's later critical works *yūgen* takes on a darker coloration, and this return to the earlier poetic ideal has remained its prevailing meaning. If a critic says of a woman play that it possesses *yūgen*, he clearly does not mean merely that it is gracefully written or that the actor performed attractively. *Yūgen* in fact tends to reject conventional notions of beauty: if a display of feminine grace on the Nō stage were the highest aim, real women could now take the parts, though they were not permitted on the stage in Zeami's day. But the thought of a woman performing the role of, say, the courtesan Eguchi is repugnant to lovers of Nō who insist that a man in his sixties with a cracked bass voice and large, ugly hands has more *yūgen*. They are right: anyone who saw Kita Roppeita dance the role of the *shite* in *Sagi* ("The White Heron"), a man in his eighties taking the part of a bird, surely sensed the mysterious, indefinable presence of *yūgen*.

It is impossible to tell how Zeami's changing conceptions of *yūgen* may have been reflected in his works; though his criticism is dated, the plays are not. The texts of the plays in any case have been much altered. Zeami himself advocated that plays constantly be modified to suit the tastes of successive audiences. Zeami is now credited with authorship of only some twenty-five of the plays, though formerly he was believed to have written about half the plays in the repertory. Ironically, only one play of the third category, *Izutsu*, is now definitely attributed to Zeami, though the woman plays embody most perfectly his ideal of *yūgen*. Perhaps further research will restore to Zeami some of the masterpieces now labelled "of unknown authorship"; if not, we may become aware of the existence of one or more playwrights no less gifted than Zeami. Even in this unlikely case, Zeami's supreme importance in Nō will remain unshaken, not only because of the place he occupies in the historical development but because of his critical writings.

Zeami says disappointingly little about the composition of his plays even in his critical work devoted specifically to the subject, but his analysis of the art of acting is superb. Zeami's enumeration of the nine levels of actors reveals his philosophical as well as practical grasp of the art:

"*The Art of the Flower of Mystery*. This can be symbolized by the phrase, 'In Silla at midnight the sun is bright.' It is impossible to express in words or even to grasp in the mind the mystery of this art. When one speaks of the sun rising at midnight, the words themselves do not explain anything; thus too, in the art of Nō, the *yūgen* of a supreme actor defies our attempts to praise it. We are so deeply impressed that we do not know what to single out as being of special excellence, and if we attempt to assign it a rank, we discover that it is peerless artistry which transcends any degrees. This kind of artistic expression, which is invisible to ordinary eyes, may be what is termed the Art of the Flower of Mystery.

"*The Art of the Flower of Profundity*. This can be symbolized by the verse, 'Snow has covered the thousand mountains; why does one lonely peak remained unwhitened?' Someone long ago once said, 'Mount Fuji is so high that the snow never melts.' A Chinese, hearing this, criticized the expression as inadequate and insisted that one should say instead, 'Mount Fuji is so deep that the snow never melts.' Anything which is extremely high is also deep. One might also say, perhaps, that there is a limit to how tall a thing can be, but the depth, being limitless, cannot be measured. Perhaps that is why the immeasurable wonder of a landscape in which, though a thousand mountains are buried in snow, one peak alone remains unwhitened can be taken as an equivalent of the Art of the Flower of Profundity.

"*The Art of the Flower of Stillness*. This can be symbolized by the words, 'Snow piled in a silver bowl.' The whiteness and purity of snow piled in a silver bowl is truly a lovely sight: may we not say it represents the Art of the Flower of Stillness?

"*The Art of the Flower of Correctness*. This can be symbolized by the words, 'The mist is bright, and the sun sinks, turning the countless mountains crimson.' The vast panorama of countless mountains sharply defined in bright colors by the light of the sun shining on the world from a perfectly clear sky represents the Art of the Flower of Correctness. The artistic rank of this art is superior to that of Versatility and Precision, and is the rank of an actor who has already mastered a flower of the art of Nō and entered its domain.

"*The Art of Versatility and Precision*. This can be symbolized by the words, 'To tell completely of the clouds on the mountains, the moon on the sea.' The intent to depict completely the vast spectacle of nature is most surely present in the training for the Art of Versatility and Precision. This art is the turning point where the actor either advances to the higher ranks or falls back.

"*The Art of Faint Patterns*. This can be symbolized by the words, 'The Way that can be explained is not the eternal Way.' The actor should first learn to tread the eternal way and then learn of the Way that can be explained. By 'faint patterns' is meant that the actor, still not deeply etched with the art, shows its first beauty. This Art of Faint Patterns is considered the entry into the study of the Nine Levels.

"*The Art of Strength and Delicacy*. This can be symbolized by the words, 'The metal hammer moves, the precious sword glints coldly.' The movement of the metal hammer suggests the strong movements of this art. The coldness of the glint of the precious sword suggests an astringent style of acting, one suited to the discriminating spectator.

"*The Art of Strength and Crudity*. This can be symbolized by the words, 'The tiger, three days after it is born, is ready to devour an ox.' The strength displayed by the tiger in being disposed barely three days after its birth to eat an ox suggests the strength of this art. 'Eating an ox' indicates its roughness.

"*The Art of Crudity and Coarseness*. This can be symbolized by the words, 'The innate faculties of the flying squirrel.' Confucius said, 'The flying squirrel has five talents. It can climb a tree, swim in the water, dig a hole, fly and run. But these five talents are appropriate to the level of the flying squirrel; it performs none of them well.' When art lacks delicacy it can be said to be crude and a distortion of the true qualities."

Zeami's descriptions are elusive but there can be no doubt that he knew exactly what he meant. The highest "flower"—by "flower" Zeami seems to have designated the particular beauty an actor displayed—is that of "mystery." Though not a commonly mentioned aesthetic ideal in Western performing arts (technique, "sincerity," emotional intensity, etc. would be more common standards of excellence), it is not difficult to understand. Perhaps the closest embodiment of this ideal among twentieth-century artists was Greta Garbo, who managed always to remain inviolate, untouched by the vulgarity of the world around her, mysterious and supremely beautiful. The next highest flower is that of the master actor, a superbly accomplished performer, who deliberately admixes an element of imperfection into his art lest audiences become bored with too great, unrelieved perfection: the single unwhitened peak is this coarser element, lending greater allure to the many peaks covered by the flawless snow of *yūgen*. The art of Sarah Bernhardt, to judge from contemporary accounts, had qualities suggesting this "flower." The next flower, that of stillness, may bring to mind the voice of Elizabeth Schumann—absolute purity, lacking the touch of vulgarity that might have made her a supreme artist or destroyed her. "Snow piled within a silver bowl" is perfectly evocative of the stillness and mystery of *yūgen* incarnate.

As one descends further Zeami's nine levels, mystery and purity yield to accuracy and, finally, energy. Zeami insisted that an actor must begin his training not with the crude vigor of the bottom levels but about halfway up the scale, with the "Art of Faint Patterns." He studies the "two arts" (singing and dancing) and the "three roles" (the warrior, the woman and the old person) and improves his acting ability until he can be said to have attained the level of versatility and precision. If he achieves these qualities, he may be able to display the first of the "flowers," that of correctness, the level of the highly competent, professional actor. If he fails to display this flower, he will drop to the lower levels of performers, where he can still be a useful member of a troupe in roles requiring stamina or acrobatic skill. Had he started at the bottom levels, however, without having received the training suited to the higher roles, he would not be qualified to perform even roles of a more superficial nature.

Zeami considered *yūgen* to be the touchstone of his school of acting, but he did not ignore *monomane*, "imitation of things." The actor must perform the three roles convincingly to appear frightening as a demon or pathetic as a beggar. Despite the highly stylized nature of Nō performances, details needed to create a convincing character are not overlooked, as we can tell most easily from adverse comments. Here is how Shūō, the author of the seventeenth-century book of criticism *Bushō Goma*, denounced an actor who had played Shizuka in *Funa Benkei*: " 'I thought I would accompany you wherever you might go, but a feeble comfort, not to be depended on, is the human heart. Alas, there is nothing I can do!' are lines where the character weeps, but this hard-hearted Shizuka showed not the least inclination to weep. The woman does not exist who does not weep when she thinks she may never again see the man she was prepared to accompany to the ends of the earth."

Many similar examples could be found in the criticism written today. The actor playing Shizuka must be sufficiently versed in *monomane* to corroborate every phrase of the text, not with the literalness of the gesture-language of the dances of India, but within recognized, symbolic terms. He must not, on the other hand, forfeit the mysterious beauty of *yūgen* in the interests of convincing realism; an actor who attempted to persuade us he was really Shizuka by imitating a feminine voice, swaying seductively as he walked, or weeping convulsively, would be unspeakably vulgar on the Nō stage. Skill at *monomane* means a mastery of the symbols of the parts. The genius of a particular actor enables him to make these symbols seem exactly appropriate, so that when the blind Yoroboshi appears on the stage the angle of his head at a certain moment (certainly not any gesture of sniffing) exactly suggests that he has caught the scent of plum blossoms, telling him as he wanders in the dark of his blindness that he has reached his destination, the Tennōji Temple. An actor is usually able in the latter part of his career to embody in his performance the combination of *monomane* and the *yūgen* fitting each role; only then can he be called a master actor.

Zeami, like his father Kannami, was at once playwright, actor, and composer, a practical man of the theatre who took into account both his audience and the actors he worked with. His audience consisted chiefly of aristocrats who, he could assume, possessed an expert acquaintance with Nō and a sensitivity to slight variations in performance; they also were familiar with the original literary texts from which the plays derived and with earlier plays on the same subjects. Zeami wrote, "Many of the recent Nō plays have been based on old Nō, and are revised versions set to new music. . . . They stem from seeds which are capable of blossoming brilliantly at any time; it is necessary only to change the words somewhat and add a new flavor to the music so as to accord with the tastes of a different age. The Nō plays of the future should also be written in accordance with their times and prevailing tastes." The plays, then, had to meet the demands of the audience, but this did not mean playing down to their level; Zeami's experience in the theatre convinced him that actors with *yūgen* (rather than those with cruder, more striking talents) enjoyed the most lasting popularity. The author was no less bound by the actors; Zeami declared that "in composing Nō the most important thing is to write parts suited for the available actors." We know little about the actors of Zeami's troupe, but we can infer that *Atsumori* and *Kiyotsune* were written for young actors. An old actor in such parts, as Zeami pointed out, would not convince the audience even if disguised by a mask and youthful attire. But Zeami created his greatest works for older actors. He occasionally used the word *hie* ("chill") to describe the *yūgen* of the old actor. The term, also found in the literary criticism of Zeami's day, seems to have meant an interiorization of *yūgen*, an invisible *yūgen* which is no longer external grace or charm but comes from within. This highest development of *yūgen* has remained the actor's goal, and is still appreciated by audiences more than the most dazzling virtuoso display. Great actors possess this *yūgen*; it is instantly recognized by spectators, even those witnessing Nō for the first time; it never disappears.

Zeami thought that even demons should be represented with *yūgen*, and grudgingly admitted that actors of Kyōgen, which he seems to have held in low esteem, might be said to possess *yūgen* if their comedies amused audiences without descending into vulgarity. Zeami's disapproval of low comedy may account for the remarkably clean humor of Kyōgen, certainly when compared to the European medieval farces. In Zeami's day the plays may have been largely impromptu, with some admixture of obscene or slapstick comedy, but today the texts have considerable literary finish and the lines are delivered with a meticulous attention to clarity of diction which is unique among the Japanese theatrical arts. Kyōgen places little emphasis on singing and dancing, though both are present. The plays are essentially dependent on dialogue and the antithesis of the characters, rather than on the aura given off by a single character as in Nō. The roles are types, rather in the manner of the commedia dell'arte, but the range is severely limited by the conditions which prevailed in Japan at the time. Japan was virtually isolated from the rest of the world, and the occasional Chinese or Korean who made his way to Japan in the fifteenth or sixteenth century was much too uncommon a sight to figure in the farces. This meant that Kyōgen, unlike the European farces, made virtually no use of the comic possibilities of the foreigner—the amorous Frenchman, the reserved Englishman, the uncouth American, and so on. Isolation was not the only reason for the absence of foreigners: the humor of Kyōgen is essentially vertical, depending on the complications in the relations between master and servant rather than on the horizontal relations between two servants, two masters, or two people from different countries. In Kyōgen, moreover, rustics are funny not because of their accents (all persons of the same station tend to talk in exactly the same language) or the use of Japanese equivalents of zounds! or gadzooks! but because they behave inappropriately to their station. (The rustic baron cannot compose poetry decently.) The most frequent comic situation revolves around a foolish master and his clever servant. Invariably, the servant manages to trick the master, who realizes he has been duped only when it is too late. The successes of servants over masters have been cited by some scholars as expressions of protest by the lower classes. A few plays would seem to confirm this thesis, but common sense indicates that a farce would not be funny if it told of a clever master who gets the better of his hapless servant. The shoguns and their courts, the patrons of Nō and Kyōgen, would certainly never have tolerated satire of themselves if they thought it threatened their authority.

Kyōgen, like Nō, have been divided into categories, but they are less rigid. Only plays of the first category, the *waki* Kyōgen, are truly distinct; like the *waki* Nō they deal with gods or with auspicious occasions. The other categories include plays about daimyos, the great lords, and *shōmyō*, the lesser lords; about bridegrooms and sons-in-law; about devils or *yamabushi*, the fierce mountain ascetes; about priests and blind men, and so on.

Some Kyōgen, like *Uri-nusubito* ("The Melon Thief"), are constructed around a single farcical idea, others, like *Tsukimi Zatō* ("The Blind Man Looks at the Moon"), rise above the level of farce to that of a warm humanity. The best Kyōgen, as might be said of the best comedies anywhere, approach the borderline between comedy and tragedy, where we recognize the foibles of the characters but do not necessarily laugh at them. A few Kyōgen cross the borderline and are cruel rather than comic, but these are seldom performed.

The humor of Kyōgen stems mainly from the situations but, as we might expect in a theatre which places such emphasis on vertical relationships, it owes much also to the contrasting manner of delivery of characters belonging to different classes. Phrases which would have to be translated almost identically into English sound utterly different when pronounced by a daimyo or by Tarō-kaja, the servant, and some of the pleasure of Kyōgen comes from hearing the same lines pronounced in the strikingly dissimilar rhythmic patterns of master and servant.

The contribution of the actors to a performance is so overpowering that one tends to forget that Kyōgen must have had authors. Unlike Nō, we know virtually nothing about who wrote the Kyōgen plays, though many have been attributed to the learned priest Gen'e (1270–1350) or to Komparu Shirōjirō (d. 1473). These attributions, repeated to this day, are no longer seriously believed because so little evidence supports them. Perhaps these men supplied the germs of the plays with which they are credited, but the plots are simple, and have unquestionably been much altered by the actors over the years.

Kyōgen, though performed in close connection with the Nō plays, bear little resemblance in plot, unlike the European interlude farces which often specifically derided the action of the tragedies they followed. Some Kyōgen plays require masks, mainly when the actor performs as a god or a devil, but the actors normally appear without masks or makeup. Performing in Kyōgen seems to impart a remarkably warm and amiable quality to the faces of aged actors. This impression may owe much to the imagination of the beholder, but an aged Kyōgen actor performing one of the major roles may well bring to mind Zeami's remark that even the humblest role should be crowned with flowers. The level of Kyōgen is humble when compared to Nō, but within its chosen domain it has developed into an art at once engaging and heartwarming, the other side of the tragic world depicted in Nō and its necessary complement.

II. THE HISTORY OF NŌ AND KYŌGEN

THE EARLY PERIOD

The Yōgō Pine in Nara provided a passage for the descent of Nō from the world of the gods to the world of men, and the dancer at the annual festival still re-enacts the birth of Nō beneath the tree, moving at the will of a god as his creature, a medium possessed of the divine spirit. It would be meaningless to discuss the dancer's skill or his powers of interpretation; he is supposed merely to allow the god to guide his movements. In former days it was customary for an entire village to participate in its festivals. There were no spectators, and any man might perform as the central figure of the festival, the god. Eventually, however, one villager was deemed to excel as the interpreter of the god, his vehicle, and he was chosen from then on to give corporeal form to the unseen divinity. Other villagers believed he would please the god by the beauty of his actions. The first actor, then, may have only gradually become aware that he was a man playing the part of a god; the first spectator was the god. The dancer performed with the hope that the god, satisfied with the representation of his own actions, would grant long life and prosperity.

In time other spectators were attracted, and the performance of the dances or playlets at the festivals came to be the responsibility of the most talented men. Stages were built within the precincts of Shinto shrines facing the main object of worship, and the actors served as celebrants of a religious rite intended to benefit either a whole village or else a particular donor.

We have yet to uncover documentary evidence revealing when plays recognizable as Nō originated. Certainly by the twelfth century *Okina* was being staged. This play contains both Buddhist and Shinto elements, inseparably intertwined. The two religions, though entirely different in origins and sometimes absolutely contradictory in teachings, had early been woven by the Japanese into a single faith. Far from attempting to resolve the differences between the optimistic, this-worldly Shinto and the prevailingly pessimistic, other-worldly Buddhism, the Japanese took from each religion what suited them best, ignoring the contradictions. A desire for long life makes little sense in terms of the Buddhist tenet that this world is a place of trial and suffering preparatory to the true life after death, but the Japanese prayed for long life anyway, guided by the Shinto love of this world. The plays often describe the Shinto gods, but a strong Buddhist coloring runs through them in the language, the allusions to Buddhist texts, and the underlying acceptance of such Buddhist concepts as the impermanence of life. However, the ghosts who play so prominent a part in the Nō plays, returning from the world of the dead to speak to the living, those fearsome presences who must be exorcised so that the living may escape harm, originate in folk beliefs unsanctioned by either Shinto or Buddhism. An ill-defined, shamanistic religion, sharing much with similar beliefs on the mainland of Asia, provided a core around which formal Shinto and Buddhist tenets accumulated.

The union between the two religions was demonstrated by the close association of Buddhist temples and Shinto shrines. The Kōfukuji Temple, which exercised jurisdiction over the Kasuga Shrine (the site of the Yōgō Pine), was the scene of many early dramatic presentations. Priests of esoteric Buddhism known as *shushi* (or "spell makers") performed songs and dances by way of making their magical rites more intelligible to the onlookers. The *shushi* priests, dressed in splendid robes befitting their ecclesiastical functions, attracted spectators as well as worshipers, and their performances acquired dramatic elements. Probably they were the first to present *Okina*. This baffling conglomeration of songs and dances may originally have been a presentation in entertaining form of a Buddhist text, but the meaning is now buried under the accretions of the centuries.

The performances by the *shushi* priests were accompanied by lighter diversions—acrobatics and the like—in which professional actors known as *sarugaku* appeared. These actors belonged to entirely different, secular traditions, though they were likewise attached to the Kōfukuji and other temples for financial support. Their art can ultimately be traced back to *gigaku*, a kind of dancing imported from China in 612 A.D. This oldest recorded Japanese stage entertainment has almost completely disappeared, but more than 220 *gigaku* masks are preserved. Fragmentary records suggest that a *gigaku* performance began with a procession of actors masked as lions, birds, "strongmen," barbarians, and so on, in all a dozen or more parts. The procession was followed by dances accompanied by flutes and drums: in one an actor masked as a bird executed a dance in which he pretended to be pecking for worms; in another a contest was portrayed between the "strongman" and the barbarian for the favors of a beautiful girl, ending in triumph for the "strongman," who leads off the barbarian by a rope tied to his penis. One *gigaku* entertainment that has survived is the *shishimai* (or "lion dance"), a popular feature of many festivals.

The Japanese court, in a mood of enthusiasm for all things Chinese, initially welcomed *gigaku* and commanded that youths be trained in the art. The high point in *gigaku* history occurred in 752, on the occasion of the ceremonies marking the inauguration of the Great Image of Buddha at the Tōdaiji Temple, when sixty *gigaku* performers appeared. Half a century later only two men were still qualified as *gigaku* artists. The court in the meantime had discovered a more decorous entertainment in *bugaku*, stately court dances. Two varieties of *bugaku* were introduced in the seventh century: "left dances" (*samai*), imported from China, included Indian music; "right dances" (*umai*) were of Korean and Central Asian origin. The names "left" and "right" denoted the direction from which the dancers made their entrances. The *bugaku* dances were in some sense representational, depicting a moment of a longer story, such as the triumphal return of a king from battle, but so highly stylized that the surviving dramatic element is negligible.

The *bugaku* dances, still performed at the Imperial Palace and at certain Shinto shrines, impart a distinctly alien atmosphere, largely because of the exotic masks and costumes. The original Chinese or Korean dances have nevertheless been altered by Japanese influences over the centuries. *Bugaku* in turn influenced Japanese dramatic and musical arts, including Nō. The division of each *bugaku* piece into three musical sections of increasingly rapid tempo—the *jo, ha, kyū* of Nō—was perhaps the greatest influence. *Bugaku* was at its full maturity when first introduced to Japan, and because it continued to retain its alien character it became in time a petrified ritual which could only be repeated, not developed. The changes that occurred in *bugaku* were doubtlessly unintentional and even unnoticed. By the end of the twelfth century *bugaku* had become a palace ceremonial.

The variety of entertainment called *sangaku* had been introduced to Japan from China together with *bugaku*. *Sangaku* included feats of magic, acrobatics, juggling, animal shows, etc. A picture of one stunt survives: a dancing girl wearing high clogs crosses a rope strung between poles balanced on the chins of two recumbent men, the girl juggling as she walks. *Sangaku* playlets were on such themes as "The head clerk of a temple slips on the ice and loses his trousers" and "The nun Myōkō begs for swaddling clothes," probably satirical pieces deriding the distraction or incontinence of the Buddhist clergy. Other playlets, like "The clever repartee of a Kyoto man" or "An easterner's first visit to the capital," seem to have been skits contrasting the sophisticated ways of city-dwellers with the artlessness of rustics. We know little more than these outlines, mentioned in a work written about 1160, but they prove that *sangaku* (or *sarugaku*, as it was known in a corruption of the word) included plays with plots and dialogue as well as dances and acrobatics.

From the grab bag of variety entertainments performed by the *sarugaku* players would eventually develop Nō and Kyōgen. The secular *sarugaku* actors, rather like the mimes of medieval Europe, began as clowns and acrobats but in the end presented works of an exalted, religious nature. Even the name *sarugaku*, though written with characters meaning "monkey music," lost its comic flavor when the performers, ever eager to add to their repertory, borrowed the plays of the *shushi* priests and presented them as entertainment rather than as religious instruction. *Sarugaku* also absorbed influences from two other early theatricals, *dengaku* and *ennen*, which shaped it artistically.

Dengaku (or "field music") was the name originally given to the songs and dances performed by country people, at times as part of the harvest celebrations. *Dengaku* of this nature can still be seen at festivals all over Japan. The court nobles in Kyoto, always on the lookout for new diversions from their usual activities, heard of these country dances and invited the performers to the capital. If *dengaku* in the thirteenth century was no more engrossing than its counterparts today, the nobles must have been stupendously bored before they could derive pleasure from such crude and inartistic caperings. Be that as it may, the original *dengaku* dancers—farmers and priests— soon gave way to professional actors who modified the performances to accord with the tastes of more sophisticated audiences. The simple costumes formerly worn in *dengaku* were replaced by elegant robes, and the songs were embellished with poetic language. By the fourteenth century, when the provincial lords also began to sponsor *dengaku*, the staging had become quite elaborate. The expenses incidental to performances were indeed so enormous that the downfall of Hōjō Takatoki (1303–33), the regent for the shogun, has been attributed to his mania for *dengaku*. By Kannami's day *dengaku* and *sarugaku* had become similar arts, much influence passing between the two. *Dengaku* failed to keep pace with *sarugaku*, perhaps because of the historical accident that it had no outstanding performers during the crucial period when Kannami and Zeami were developing *sarugaku* into a great dramatic art.

Ennen, the name of the other early dramatic form which influenced *sarugaku*, means "prolong years." It originated as ceremonies of prayer for the prolongation of some exalted person's life, but as early as 1100 the *ennen* prayers were followed by dances. The dances developed into plays by the fourteenth century. An account of *ennen* performances in 1429 indicates that the plays, in highly poetic language, were staged with ornate sets. *Ennen* influenced Nō by providing a model of how old songs, quotations from religious and secular literature, and a vocabulary including words of Chinese as well as Japanese origins might impart to the texts a dignity and beauty not found in older forms of drama. Probably each innovation in *sarugaku*, *dengaku* or *ennen* was quickly adopted by the others, making it difficult to distinguish among these arts. On the other hand, slight differences in the manner of recitation or dance were elevated into secrets by performers whose livelihoods might depend on their possessing (or seeming to possess) unique traditions. Already in Kannami's day there were four troupes of *sarugaku* actors in the province of Yamato: Yūsaki (founded by Kannami himself), Tohi, Emai, and Sakato, the ancestors of the present Kanze, Hōshō, Komparu, and Kongō schools respectively. Three other *sarugaku* troupes performed in the province of Ōmi, and there were troupes of *dengaku* and *ennen*. In contrast to the rigidly partisan divisions characteristic of the schools of Nō in later times, relations among the different *sarugaku* and *dengaku* players apparently were friendly, and a member of one troupe often studied the acting techniques of another. But even in the early days each troupe took care not to fall behind the others in techniques or in patrons.

Whatever the form of theatre, the most important factor in its development was the patronage of the upper classes. Without the backing of the nobles, *dengaku* would have remained no more than the prancing and artless singing of the country festival; *sarugaku* acquired its dignity only when enabled to abandon the crude realism demanded by the provincial audiences in favor of the poetic beauty appreciated by the court. Not only did the nobility patronize the drama and the actors, but by 1250 nobles themselves were performing in *sarugaku* for their own amusement. The future of *sarugaku* as the exalted art of Nō was determined in 1374 when Ashikaga Yoshimitsu, the shogun, attended performances at the Imakumano Shrine in Kyoto. On that occasion Kannami, then forty-one, appeared in *Okina* as the old man, and his son, later known as Zeami, in the role of Senzai. Yoshimitsu, entranced, lent his patronage to both father and son. Kannami, who had formerly toured the provinces with his troupe, was assured of court protection and was enabled to write plays not for illiterate farmers but for the most discriminating audiences.

YOSHIMITSU AND NŌ

Ashikaga Yoshimitsu was only seventeen when he witnessed the performances at Imakumano, but he was unquestionably the outstanding man in the entire country, not only by virtue of his office—Barbarian Quelling Great General—but because of his remarkable intelligence and ability. Yoshimitsu, the grandson of the founder of the Muromachi shogunate, did not forsake the martial traditions of his ancestors, as so often happened by the third generation, but he possessed also the literary and cultural talents of the courtier. He was an expert *tanka* poet (a number of his poems were selected for the imperially-sponsored anthologies), accomplished in linked verse *(renga)*, Chinese poetry, music, and Zen philosophy. He enjoyed travel, combining the business of consolidating his power over the country with his pleasure in excursions to Mount Fuji, the Inland Sea or the Great Shrine of Ise. As shogun he not only represented the apex of power during the Muromachi period (1336–1568) but ranks among the most powerful men of Japanese history. His success in military affairs was crowned by his reunification of the country in 1392 after sixty-four years of bitter division. Yoshimitsu has nevertheless been treated as a traitor by Japanese historians because his passion for things Chinese induced him to accept the title "King of Japan" bestowed on him by the Chinese court. His treatment of the imperial family, by no means reverent, has also aroused condemnation. Despite his failings, however, Yoshimitsu was a remarkable combination of martial statesman and aesthete.

Yoshimitsu's passion for Nō continued throughout his life. His patronage was extended not only to Zeami but to Dōami, a rival *sarugaku* actor, and to Kyōgen performers. His thorough grasp of poetic tradition and Buddhist language allowed Zeami to enrich his texts with a vocabulary and imagery of startling complexity. Yoshimitsu himself never performed, but he enjoyed theatrical display, as we know from the diary of his visit to Itsukushima, when he embarked wearing a "narrow-sleeved, wide-hemmed costume of a pale blue lozenge pattern tied with a red sash, green leggings and red knee-length breeches." This bizarre attire, the current craze among city dandies, excited comment, but was typical of Yoshimitsu's eccentric taste in dress.

Yoshimitsu abdicated the office of shogun in 1394 and took Buddhist orders the following year, but remained in control of the government. He also maintained his interest in *sarugaku*, an enthusiasm he transmitted to his son, the shogun Yoshinori, creating the tradition that the shogun, whatever his tastes, would protect Nō. Yoshimitsu may have found Nō brick, but he certainly left it marble.

KANNAMI AND ZEAMI

Yoshimitsu had probably already heard of Kannami when he decided for the first time in his life to attend a *sarugaku* performance and commanded that the most accomplished, rather than the senior, actor of the troupe should appear in *Okina*; he wished to see Kannami in the role. Kannami performed with such success that he was elevated to the position of "companion" *(dōhōshū)* to Yoshimitsu, sharing this distinction with other notable artists of the day. Kannami, however, never renounced his earlier audiences; he died in 1384 while on a tour of Suruga, an eastern province. Zeami spoke of his father with the utmost reverence, whether as an actor, composer, choreographer or playwright, but Kannami's greatest single contribution to the development of Nō may have been the incorporation into the plays of *kusemai*, a dance to an irregular, strongly-accented rhythm. *Kusemai* was to figure as the climactic, narrative section of most Nō plays, adding far more complexities of plot than the older dramatic forms permitted. Kannami is credited also with many celebrated works of the repertory, including *Matsukaze*, *Sotoba Komachi*, *Kayoi Komachi*, and *Eguchi*. Some critics claim that Kannami's style was simpler and directer than Zeami's, but little evidence supports this. *Jinen Koji*, it is true, startles at times by its realism, but *Matsukaze* and *Eguchi* reach summits of poetry rarely surpassed by later Nō dramatists. Kannami's plays were often adaptations of older works, and were in turn revised and augmented by Zeami and later men, leaving in the end only elements of Kannami's distinctive style; the eight or ten surviving plays believed to have been written by Kannami show few mutual resemblances, and stand apart also from later works. Scholars have argued that in the earliest Nō only one character, the *shite*, was of consequence, but *Kayoi Komachi* develops from the antithesis between the *shite*, Shii no Shōshō, and the *tsure*, Komachi; and *Sotoba Komachi* includes a theological dispute between the *shite*, Komachi, and the *waki*, a priest. The works attributed to Kannami suggest dramatic possibilities which most later dramatists rejected. Kannami's importance is unquestionable, but because he left no critical or autobiographical writings, most of what we know about him derives from his son's lavish but unverifiable praise.

Far more is known about Zeami. He emerges indeed as a distinct historical figure, though the basic biographical data is missing or incomplete. Our only source of information for his birthdate is the statement made in 1432 that he had reached his seventh *chitsu*, a word meaning decade; the words have therefore been interpreted as signifying that Zeami was then seventy years of age by Japanese reckoning, or sixty-nine by ours, fixing his date of birth at 1363. The six hundredth anniversary of his birth was accordingly celebrated in 1963, only for a new theory to be published which claimed that 1364 was correct. If this is correct, other dates must be shifted accordingly, placing the Imakumano performances in 1375 instead of 1374; but whichever the year, Zeami was eleven when he first appeared before Yoshimitsu.

Eleven is now considered too young for an actor to appear in adult roles, but Zeami believed that this was the time to begin mastering the repertory. "His childish appearance will give him *yūgen*, whatever role he may take. At this age too his voice is charming. These two advantages will make people forget his defects and call attention to the development of his qualities." By the time the actor is sixteen or so his voice has changed and he will have lost the "flower" of the boy performer. "Now that he is taller his charm has disappeared; it is no longer so easy for him to escape criticism because of the beauty of his voice and his physical charm." The emphasis Zeami gives to the beauty of the boy actor reflects the contemporary partiality, especially in samurai society, for young boys. Senzai, the role danced by Zeami before Yoshimitsu, is still assigned to the handsomest actor of a company, who dances without a mask. We know how much Zeami attracted Yoshimitsu from the account written by a nobleman in 1378, which describes Yoshimitsu taking Zeami to see the Gion Festival. Special stands had been erected for the Shogun and Zeami to watch the floats passing down Shijō, the main avenue. "The Shogun was accompanied by a boy, a Yamato *sarugaku* player, who watched the festival from the Shogun's box. The Shogun, who has for some time bestowed his affection on this boy, shared the same mat and passed him food from his plate. These *sarugaku* performers are no better than beggars, but because this boy waits on the Shogun and is esteemed by him, everyone favors him. Those who give the boy presents ingratiate themselves with the Shogun. The daimyos and others vie to offer him gifts, at enormous expense. A most distressing state of affairs."

At nineteen Zeami was already an established actor when he succeeded in 1384 as head of the troupe, following his father's death. Zeami seems, however, to have fallen into a slump afterwards; in *Kadensho* ("The Book of the Transmission of the Flower") he describes in terms that suggest autobiography the ridicule which the public often directs against an actor between the ages of seventeen and twenty-four, a period when his youthful charms have disappeared but his powers as a full-fledged actor have not yet emerged. During this critical period the actor must summon up all his resolve to keep from abandoning Nō altogether, in despair.

Zeami apparently recovered from his depression during his middle twenties, when he achieved recognition as an outstanding performer. He wrote, "By this period the actor's voice has settled completely, and his body has assumed its adult proportions. . . . People begin to notice him and to comment on his skill. He may be awarded a prize in a competition, even against actors of considerable ability, the public being delighted by the freshness of the talent he displays on that occasion. The public and the actor himself may then begin to think he is truly accomplished, but this is most detrimental to the actor. His is not a true 'flower'; he is merely in the prime of his youth, and the audience has been momentarily captivated by his charm. The true connoisseur will recognize the difference." The actor, in order to avoid serious harm to his career, must not let himself be deluded by flattery, but study all the harder the techniques of older actors, particularly *monomane*, "the imitation of things."

Zeami, in his middle thirties when he wrote *Kadensho*, described this as the culminating period of the actor's career. If he has still not won public recognition, he clearly has not acquired a genuine "flower," and his abilities will presently deteriorate. Zeami insisted on public recognition as the gauge of an actor's talents; the actor's function is to please the audience, and it alone will ultimately judge his merits. Zeami believed that the actor who had established a solid reputation by his middle thirties might preserve his "flower" even when his physical beauty began to fade in his forties. A truly remarkable performer, like Kannami, who appeared on the stage just a few weeks before his death in his fifty-second year, may still dazzle an audience though his repertory and range of color are now drastically limited by his age. (Zeami would probably have been astonished to see contemporary performances in which an actor in his sixties still takes the parts of beautiful young women.) Zeami likened the talent of the aged actor to flowers still blossoming on an aged tree with few remaining leaves.

In 1399, the year before writing *Kadensho*, Zeami appeared in festive performances of Nō attended for three days by the new shogun, Yoshimochi. The great success he scored on this occasion clearly established him as the leading *sarugaku* actor. It was a logical moment for him to take stock of his art. Most of Zeami's opinions concerning acting techniques were admittedly derived from his father; his purpose in writing *Kadensho* was, in fact, to preserve for his descendants the teachings of Kannami. The emphasis on *monomane* found throughout this work reflects Kannami's experience as an actor who habitually appeared before a public which demanded believable representation. Zeami in this work reveals himself as a practical man of the theatre whose desire to please his audiences took precedence over interpretative or aesthetic matters. He wrote, for example, that if persons of quality happen to arrive early for a performance it is improper not to begin immediately; if, on the other hand, exalted persons arrive towards the close of a performance their presence will so affect the audience that the usual order of plays must be altered.

Zeami contrasted the *sarugaku* styles of Yamato, which emphasized *monomane*, and of Ōmi, which gave priority to *yūgen*, considering elegance to be the basic element of Nō. This statement suggests how much Zeami's own art in his maturity was to be indebted to the Ōmi school; indeed, Zeami acknowledged that he owed much to Inuō (later known as Dōami), the leading Ōmi player. Inuō had first been introduced to Yoshimitsu by Kannami, and never forgot this kindness. His relations with Zeami were close, especially after Kannami's death, and the two men were almost equally respected as artists by Yoshimitsu. During the performances of Nō staged before the Emperor Go-Komatsu in 1408, on the occasion of his visit to Yoshimitsu's mansion at Kitayama, Zeami appeared on the eleventh of April and Inuō a week later. This was the apogee of Zeami's career as an actor. A month later Yoshimitsu fell ill, and on the thirty-first of May he died, in his fifty-first year. This event came as a severe blow to Zeami: Yoshimitsu had not only been a generous patron of Nō but its most discerning critic. Komparu Zenchiku, Zeami's son-in-law, wrote of Yoshimitsu that he had seen all the actors from Yamato and Ōmi, and could distinguish their qualities, "rejecting the crude and vulgar and insisting on *yūgen*." Yoshimitsu, we are told, "searched into the old and understood the new . . . He was scrupulously fair when it came to the arts." *Sarugaku* might have remained a folk entertainment but for Yoshimitsu's financial and artistic support, which enabled Zeami to develop it into a complex and elevated art.

Yoshimitsu's successor, Yoshimochi, bestowed his patronage chiefly on a *dengaku* actor named Zōami. We can gather from Zeami's description that Zōami was unusually accomplished; he wrote that he all but wept with emotion at Zōami's performance, which he likened to the "flower of stillness." Yoshimochi's appreciation of Zōami is easier to understand than his coldness towards Zeami. During the decade from 1413 to 1423 Zōami and *dengaku* reigned supreme in Kyoto. A dozen or more benefit performances of *dengaku* attest its popularity; not a single *sarugaku* benefit occurred during those years. Zeami, in his fifties, wrote some of his finest criticism, including *Shikadōsho* ("The Book of the Way of the Highest Flower," 1420) and *Nōsakusho* ("The Book of Nō Composition," 1423). In these works Zeami seems less interested in the elements of a successful performance—the "flower" of the actor, the intrinsic interest of a play, or the novelty of presentation—than in the unchanging aesthetic values of Nō. He emphasizes the importance of the combination of song, dance and *yūgen*, the latter term having now shifted in meaning from "charm" to "mysterious beauty." Undoubtedly Zeami also composed Nō plays while writing these essays, but we cannot tell which works fall in this period.

In 1422 Zeami, having reached the age of sixty by Japanese reckoning, became a Buddhist priest and withdrew as head of his company, leaving the position to his son Motomasa, about thirty years old at the time. Zeami had one other son, Motoyoshi, for whom he wrote *Nōsakusho* and who in turn recorded Zeami's sayings in *Sarugaku Dangi* ("Conversations on *Sarugaku*," 1430). We can assume that he entertained high hopes for both sons. Motomasa quickly established himself as a superlative actor in Zeami's tradition, and his future seemed assured when a threat unexpectedly arose in the person of Zeami's nephew Motoshige. The latter's spectacular rise to fame began in 1427 when he was selected by Gien, the abbot-prince of the Shōren Temple, to appear in a benefit performance of Nō. On the death of Yoshimochi without heir in 1428, this same Gien, Yoshimochi's brother, returned to the laity to assume the office of shogun under the name Yoshinori. He too was hostile to Zeami and Motomasa and, as Motoshige's protector, was determined to make him first among the *sarugaku* actors. In August, 1428, at Yoshinori's command, Motoshige performed Nō at the Muromachi Palace. Neither Zeami nor Motomasa was invited. In 1429 Motomasa and Motoshige both appeared in plays staged on the riding grounds of the Muromachi Palace, spectacles distinguished by the use of "real horses and real armor," a far cry from the symbolic use of props that distinguishes Nō today. Ten days later Yoshinori issued an order forbidding Zeami and Motomasa from appearing at the palace of the Retired Emperor; from then on Motoshige gave the New Year's performances for the Retired Emperor. In 1430, again by order of Yoshinori, Motomasa was dismissed from his post as Master of Music at the Kiyotaki Shrine and replaced by Motoshige. Motomasa, dismayed by these repeated indications of Yoshinori's hostility, left Kyoto to live in the hinterland of Yamato Province. Towards the end of the same year, 1430, Zeami's second son, Motoyoshi, gave up the stage to become a priest.

These events were terrible blows to Zeami, but the worst was yet to come: in 1432 Motomasa suddenly died. A month later Zeami wrote a final tribute :

"'To the roots the blossoms return, to old nests the birds hurry back; will the spring go the same way too?' This expression of love for the blossoms and envy for the birds must surely have been written by a man of feeling. I have known such inconsolable grief for the beloved son I have lost that I have envied the mindless blossoms and birds; the color of the blossoms and the songs of the birds have brought me only pain and uncertainty. I realize now, however, that the emotion involved must be the same.

"On the first day of the eighth moon my son Zenshun died at Anonotsu in Ise Province. It may seem foolish of me not to have resigned myself long ago to the fact that the young do not necessarily die after the old, but the blow came so unexpectedly that it quite overwhelmed my aged mind and body, and tears of grief rotted away my sleeves. Zenshun, though I say it of my own son, was an incomparable master of acting. Long ago my late father established our family name in this art, and I too, succeeding him, labored selflessly for it. Now I have reached my seventh decade. It seemed to me that Zenshun's talents surpassed even those of his grandfather, and I recorded for him all the secret traditions and mysteries of the art, remembering the text which says you must tell a man the truth while you can, for otherwise you may waste his talents. But all that I wrote down is now the dream of Rosen, and I have no choice but to let these teachings, which nobody will master and which will benefit no one, turn to dust and smoke. If I preserve them for posterity now, whom will they help? The sentiments described in the poem, 'Now that you are not here, to whom shall I show these plum blossoms?' are true indeed. But my grief is unendurable when I think that the destruction of our art is at hand, and that I must witness such a disaster with my own eyes, in the meaninglessness of the lingering last years of my life. Alas! Confucius was heartbroken at the death of his son, and when Po Chü-i was preceded in death by his son, they say he vented his hatred on the medicine still left by the boy's pillow.

"Zenshun came into this phantom world. For a moment we became father and son. Now, in grief over parting, I have scattered words aimlessly as leaves tumbling from a bough, truly a sign my grief is too much to bear. 'Did I ever dream it? That while I, a withered tree, linger in this world, I should see the fall of a flower in full bloom?'

9th moon, 4th year of Eikyō [1432]   Shiō [Zeami]

" 'If I did not think my life had a term, how could I know any end to the tears shed by this aged body?' "

Zeami's despair was eventually mitigated by the achievements of his son-in-law Komparu Zenchiku (1405–1468), his artistic successor and the heir to his teachings, but his despondency over Motomasa's death darkened this whole period of his life. Motomasa was not only a superb actor, as we know from Zeami's testimony, but a gifted dramatist. His surviving works include *Sumidagawa* and *Yoroboshi*, among the most affecting plays of the repertory; the unhappy circumstances at the end of his life may account for their strong element of pathos. After his death the headship of the Kanze school went to Motoshige (now known as Onnami), probably at Yoshinori's insistence. An account of the benefit performances staged in Kyoto in May, 1433, before Yoshinori and members of the imperial court suggests the lavish scale on which Yoshinori supported Onnami's art.

One further disaster awaited Zeami: in 1434 he was banished to the island of Sado. Yoshinori's reasons for exiling Zeami are not known, but his hatred must have been implacable indeed to send a man in his seventies to a distant, lonely island. Zeami probably remained on Sado until 1441 when a general amnesty was declared after the assassination of Yoshinori. Zeami's exile was lightened by the solicitude displayed by Zenchiku. After his return to Kyoto, Zeami apparently lived with Zenchiku until his death in 1444, at the age of eighty. While on Sado, Zeami wrote *Kintōsho*, a series of prose-poems describing his exile. One account reports that seven plays written by Zeami at the time were responsible for his securing pardon. The story is dubious, but it indicates at least that some plays may date from the last years of Zeami's life.

NŌ AFTER ZEAMI

The brutal assassination of Yoshinori while he was watching a performance of *sarugaku* is indicative of the unrest which seriously threatened the government. Yoshimitsu's authority had been absolute, but the strength of the shogunate was constantly eroded during the fifteenth century. Frequent uprisings against authority occurred throughout the country, the climax occurring with the Ōnin Rebellion of 1467 to 1477, when most of Kyoto was destroyed. After the rebellion the rule of the shogunate was largely a fiction.

The Nō theatre was a fitting form of drama for these chaotic times. The presence of ghosts and the world of the dead (as if they had displaced the living not only in importance but in reality) reflects the Buddhist conviction that this world is a place of foulness and corruption, a temporary dwelling before we move on to the more lasting realities of the life after death; it also suggests the agonizing uncertainty of a world where destruction was the rule and the heritage of the past had been reduced to ashes. In the first year of the Ōnin Rebellion, Ichijō Kanera, the Prime Minister and a great noble, was forced to go begging for food after his house and library, the repository of centuries, were wantonly destroyed. In such times it is not surprising that men turn to comfort promised beyond the grave.

Buddhist thought, though important in the works of Kannami and Zeami, becomes dominant both in the plays and essays of Komparu Zenchiku. Few details are known about Zenchiku's life, partly because he performed mainly in Nara, rather than in the capital, but records bear witness to his friendship with the leading Buddhist priests of the day, including the celebrated Ikkyū (1394–1481). One essay by Zenchiku is purely theological, a criticism of a certain Buddhist sect, and the others make frequent use of Buddhist terminology, explaining in metaphysical terms the nature of Nō. The search for a meaning beyond appearances, rejected as illusory, is found also in the works of Shōtetsu (1381–1459), a Buddhist priest and the best poet of his day. For him *yūgen* was that ultimate reality: "What we call *yūgen* lies within the mind and cannot be expressed in words. Its quality may be suggested by the sight of a gauzy cloud veiling the moon or by the autumnal mists swathing the scarlet leaves on a mountainside. If one is asked where *yūgen* can be found in these sights, one cannot say; a man who cannot understand this truth is quite likely to prefer the sight of the moon shining brightly in a cloudless sky. It is quite impossible to explain wherein lies the interest or wonder of *yūgen*." Clouds and mists, veiling the bare truths of a landscape, lend ambiguity and mystery, and suggest more than a brightly illuminated scene. The poet himself may not be able to explain the ultimate meaning of his words, but the sensitive person will detect and respond to something lying beneath the surface; what each man finds is likely to be different. If the sceptic dismisses the mystery as nothing more than the emperor's new clothes, or prefers crimson leaves radiant in the sunshine to glimpses of them through mist, one obviously cannot convince him that he is wrong.

The need that Zenchiku and Shōtetsu experienced to believe in the existence of some ultimate meaning behind the terrible spectacle of the world induced them to seek beauty which might be sensed if not described. Their preference for suggestion and mystery was shared by the masters of the tea ceremony, and by the landscape architects who created gardens bare of flowers or trees. Zen philosophy gave direction to their aestheticism. Zeami's critical writings showed an increasingly marked Zen coloration; with Zenchiku it became dominant. The aesthetics of Nō may owe more to Zenchiku than to Zeami: the bare stage, the insignificant props, the movements of the actors, recalling at once the Zen priest and the warrior. The overpoweringly sombre tone of the plays certainly brings to mind not Zeami's "flowers" but the gloom of a monochrome, flowerless world.

Zenchiku's successors, however, turned to realistic or dramatic themes with few symbolic overtones. The plays of Miyamasu treat mainly martial subjects; the characteristic works of Nobumitsu (1435–1516), like *Dōjōji* or *Momijigari*, are "demon" plays filled with violence; those of Kanze

Nagatoshi (1488–1541) often have such large casts as to make them resemble Kabuki more than Nō. Zenchiku's grandson, Komparu Zempō (c. 1474–c. 1520) wrote one play, *Hatsuyuki*, in the *yūgen* manner, but his characteristic vein was straightforwardly dramatic. Even at the court of the shogun in Kyoto the dramatists, unable to hope for a patron like Yoshimitsu, were obliged to entertain with works which pleased by their novelty and dramatic excitement. With the collapse of the shogun's power in the sixteenth century, the Nō troupes had no choice but to rely on popular support, and the general public was ever more insistent on dramatic action.

Even in the sixteenth century, however, Nō did not reject altogether its unique qualities in favor of theatrical excitement. It remained prevailingly a repertory theatre, and the different troupes continued to stage the works of Zeami and Zenchiku. Surviving records indicate that the individual plays most often performed were *Yuya, Kureha, Takasago*, and other relatively static works, though plays of the fourth and fifth categories as a whole were by far the most frequently staged. Evidently the public still appreciated the solemn beauty of some plays, though the bulk of the programs was given over to dramatic pieces.

Kojirō Nobumitsu's background as a *waki* actor probably accounted for the prominence of *waki* roles in his plays; in *Chōryō* and *Rashōmon* the *waki*'s part is more important than the *shite*'s, and in *Shōzon* by Nobumitsu's son Nagatoshi, the last important Nō dramatist, the distinction between *shite* and *waki* has become so arbitrary that the nomenclature varies today according to the school.

During the sixteenth century the schools of Nō emerged as distinct and sometimes hostile groups, each jealously guarding its particular traditions. The Kanze school had virtually monopolized performances given in the shogun's presence, but after the death of the Shogun Yoshihisa in 1489 and of the former Shogun Yoshimasa in 1490, the Ashikaga family lost control of the court. A relaxation of the rules of precedence enabled the other three schools of Nō—Hōshō, Komparu and Kongō—to participate in court performances. In 1493, for example, the Kanze and Komparu schools staged rival presentations at the shogun's palace, and in 1497 the Komparu and Kongō schools were pitted against each other. The Kongō and Hōshō schools hardly figure in the earlier history of Nō, but with greater opportunities to perform they now began to gain prominence.

Kongō Ujimasa (1507–1576), a colorful as well as talented performer, was known by the nickname of "Nose Kongō," apparently because of his large nose and nasal voice. The nickname occasioned the legend that he was once so determined to dance with the head of a certain Buddhist statue for his mask that he broke the head from the statue and made its face into a mask. He performed wearing this mask, only for a terrible boil soon to form on his nose; eventually the tip rotted away, giving Ujimasa his sobriquet. Legends aside, Ujimasa was a tempestuous figure, profiting by the new freedom in the world of Nō to assert himself and his school. In 1541 he had a bitter quarrel with the head of the Komparu school over precedence at the Kasuga Festival. He had his way, but two years later an even more violent dispute broke out, which aligned the Komparu, Kanze and Hōshō schools against the Kongō, forcing Kongō Ujimasa to yield. The Komparu and Kongō schools, though enemies on this occasion, generally resembled each other in their conservative style of performance. They were called *shimogakari*, which meant the style of Nara, in contrast to the *kamigakari*, or style of Kyoto, favored in Kyoto and practiced by the Kanze and Hōshō schools.

During the sixteenth century, Nō attained its greatest popularity with the general public, especially as performed by amateur actors. The imperial court, though poverty-stricken, was also devoted to Nō, but its tastes no longer swayed the actors. The scanty remaining evidence concerning Kyōgen in this period indicates that the farces had become established as an integral part of Nō programs, and that the texts, though still unrecorded, were gradually acquiring a fixed form, though improvisation had hitherto been the rule. Performances of Nō and Kyōgen by women were popular; they seem to have been received with equal enthusiasm in tragedy and comedy, suggesting that the audiences made little differentiation between Nō and Kyōgen, treating both with an irreverence which would have dismayed Zeami. New plays continued to be written, in response to a demand for novelty, but they failed to remain in the repertory. Despite its flourishing condition Nō had ceased to be a living dramatic form.

HIDEYOSHI AND NŌ

At the end of the sixteenth century Nō found a new patron in Toyotomi Hideyoshi (1536–1598), the self-made ruler of all Japan. After over a century of civil warfare, Hideyoshi succeeded in reuniting the country and establishing an effective government. Once secure in his position, he felt he must prove that he was not culturally inferior to the nobles and priests; the best way, he decided, was to study Nō. He chose the Komparu school, probably under the influence of Shimatsuma Shōshin (1551–1616), a priest and amateur actor who left some invaluable studies of Nō. Hideyoshi became passionately fond of the art, and other daimyos were obliged to study Nō in order to stay in Hideyoshi's good graces. In 1593, while Hideyoshi was in Kyushu waiting for the start of the invasion of Korea, he spent his time learning Nō, memorizing fifteen roles in the course of fifty days; before long he was confidently performing them before the public. On receiving word of the birth of his son, Hideyoshi hastily returned to Kyoto, and as part of the festivities himself performed for three days before the Emperor Go-Yōzei. Hideyoshi appeared in sixteen plays, including *Okina*, *Matsukaze*, and *Eguchi*. Tokugawa Ieyasu performed *Nonomiya*, and on the second day joined with Hideyoshi in a newly composed farce, *Kubihiki*.

Hideyoshi's passion for Nō reached its climax in 1594 when he performed at the imperial palace, not only in various classical works including *Sekidera Komachi*, the most difficult play of the entire repertory, but also in five new dramas written at Hideyoshi's order by his biographer Ōmura Yūko (d. 1596) to celebrate Hideyoshi's accomplishments. *Yoshino-mōde*, a "god" play, describes Hideyoshi's visit to the cherry blossoms of Yoshino. The *waki*, a courtier, explains at the beginning that Hideyoshi has ruled the country as he sees fit for three years and conquered Korea. Lately, moreover, he has won martial glory against the Chinese, desisting from warfare only at their earnest request. He has returned to the capital and built a great castle at Fushimi, and now has come to Yoshino to admire the cherry blossoms. In the second scene of the play the god of Yoshino appears and announces he will protect Hideyoshi on his return to the capital. *Shibata*, a warrior play, relates Hideyoshi's exploits in defeating Shibata Katsuie; the *shite*, the ghost of Shibata, describes how he triumphantly led his forces into Ōmi Province and seemed about to win a great battle when "Hideyoshi himself came riding up against us, and the tens of thousands on my side, slashed down by his sword, fled the field, unable to withstand him." The *shite* of *Kōya-mōde*, a "woman" play, is none other than Hideyoshi's mother. She appears first as a nun, but in the second scene reveals herself as a bodhisattva of song and dance, and informs us that she owes her salvation to the prayers of her filial son. Hideyoshi himself is the *shite* of *Akechi-uchi*, and the play concludes with a paean of praise for his martial prowess. *Hōjō* has virtually an identical plot. *Toyokuni-mōde*, written by another dramatist after Hideyoshi's death, is a fitting conclusion to the series of plays, presenting him as the god Toyokuni Daimyōjin. The *tsure* is Yūgeki, a Chinese general, who comes with tribute offerings for the god, declaring that Toyokuni Daimyōjin is worshiped not only in Japan but in China too.

The Nō plays written for Hideyoshi are typical of the man, but they suggest also the exuberance of the Momoyama period—the end of the sixteenth century—when Japan, after long years of warfare, enjoyed a rebirth of secular learning and pleasures. The military men threw themselves eagerly into cultural pursuits. The study of *The Tale of Genji* in particular developed into a craze, and Nō based on this novel (like *Aoi no Ue*) enjoyed the greatest popularity. The plays about Hideyoshi reflect his enormous pride in his cultural attainments. It would have been extraordinary in any theatre for an actor to perform as himself in a heroic drama, but the Nō theatre especially avoided any taint of contemporary realism; the dramas of Zeami and his successors were set in the past, either a remote, dateless antiquity or else the period of the twelfth-century wars. Hideyoshi's Nō plays describe events that had just occurred, pointing the way to the highly topical Kabuki and Bunraku plays of the seventeenth century.

We know of other startling changes in Nō from the letters of European missionaries in Japan at the time, who mention dramas on Biblical themes, apparently cast in the form of Nō. The addition of contemporary and foreign subjects and the use of dramatic forms which ignored the traditional division of parts into *shite* and *waki* and tended to make the chorus superfluous made it seem that Nō was about to break with the past and develop into a form of drama closer to that of Europe. In fact, however, precisely the opposite occurred.

TOKUGAWA NŌ

At the close of the sixteenth century the great cultural ferment created a demand for more theatrical entertainment. Two new forms of theatre, Kabuki and Bunraku, better suited to the general public than Nō, came into being and usurped the audiences from the older drama. There were hardly any benefit performances of Nō under Hideyoshi, a sure sign that it was fast becoming an upper-class entertainment, normally not open to the general public. After the death of Hideyoshi in 1598 the Nō actors were forced to look for new patrons. They turned not to the public but to Tokugawa Ieyasu. As soon as Ieyasu's castle in Edo (the modern Tokyo) was completed in 1606, the Kanze and Komparu troupes hurried to the scene, eager to perform for the Shogun. The Kongō and Hōshō schools followed the example, and in 1608 all four schools gave performances in the castle.

From this time on, Nō served as the official music of the Tokugawa regime. The shoguns, devoted to Confucian doctrines, considered rites and music to be essential elements of government, and just as *bugaku* had provided the ceremonial music for the emperor's court, the gravity and stately movements of Nō won favor at the shogun's court, which was run according to the decorum imposed by the Confucian code. The performances of Nō, especially at the New Year, were elaborate rituals believed to be capable of affecting the prosperity and welfare of the state. Skillful actors, because they contributed to the stability of the régime, were therefore provided with stipends in rice or money by the government and ranked as samurai. They lived far more luxuriously than most samurai because their incomes were frequently swelled by presents from the daimyos and other pupils. The gifts received after the first performances of the year might be so generous as to provide the leading actors with their living expenses for the entire year. However, the rulers were not only munificent patrons but exacting critics. They tolerated no idleness, let alone mistakes. An actor who committed a lapse during a festive performance was immediately and unsparingly punished; in extreme cases, actors were condemned to commit ritual disembowelment or were sent into exile for faulty performances. The severity of the punishments was not only inspired by aesthetic standards but by the belief that mistakes in the execution of the ritual music might lead to national calamity.

The outstanding actor of the early seventeenth century, Kita Shichidayū (1586–1653), had served Hideyoshi and fought against the Tokugawa at the battle of Osaka. So renowned was he as an actor, however, that his offense against the Tokugawa family was pardoned by the Shogun Hidetada. He was even granted permission to found a school of Nō bearing his name, the first new school since the time of Kannami. The Kita school, though derived from the Kongō, is still distinguished by its martial quality in performance. Shichidayū was by far the most popular actor at the shogun's court: in the year 1629 alone Hidetada requested him to appear in eleven special performances as against only one by another actor. In 1631, when Hidetada was stricken with a mortal illness, all five schools performed Nō by way of prayer for his recovery. The death of Hidetada deprived the Kita school of its protector, and the jealousy of the other schools threatened its existence. In 1634 Shichidayū's performance of *Sekidera Komachi* was denounced as being unorthodox and at variance with tradition, grave charges in a Confucian society. The Shogun Iemitsu, acting on the advice of the heads of the other schools, condemned Shichidayū to six months' imprisonment. He was released after special intercession in his behalf by the powerful daimyo Date Masamune, but seldom performed afterwards.

The shogun's government frequently showed its concern about Nō by directing admonitions to the actors. In 1647, for example, these commands were issued:

"Actors must not neglect the performing techniques handed down in the various schools. They should not indulge in inappropriate arts but devote themselves exclusively to preserving the traditions of their profession. They should in all things obey the directions of the head of the school; in the event of a lawsuit, they should request the head of the school to petition the authorities. Any misdemeanor on the part of the head should be reported at once to the authorities.

"On the occasion of command performances of *sarugaku*, the actors will be informed on the previous day. They should assemble at the residence of the head of the school, rehearse the works to be performed thoroughly, and make sure that there will be no mistakes on the following day.

"As repeatedly directed, actors should refrain from any display of luxury and should practice strict economy at all times. Their houses, clothing, food, etc. must be in keeping with their station and modest. Actors are forbidden to abandon their family careers and to learn the military or other arts unsuited to their station. . . .

"Actors should not accumulate unnecessary possessions beyond the costumes and equipment used in *sarugaku*.

"When invited to appear before nobles and other persons of quality they should not eat with their hosts.

"The Komparu school for generations has enjoyed renown. However, the present head of the school, though adult in years, in still immature as an artist. He should henceforth devote himself energetically to his art. Older actors of his school should help and guide him. Any further negligence on his part will be considered a misdemeanor."

It is hard to imagine any other government issuing an official edict of this nature, but the Tokugawa régime considered that it was just as important to its stability that actors perform the official music properly as for priests to offer prayers in an orthodox, acceptable manner. The necessary atmosphere of decorum and dignity implied a suitable magnificence of accoutrements, and the government, though insistent that actors refrain from luxury in their private lives, never prohibited extravagance in the Nō costumes, which became miracles of weaving and dyeing.

Initially, at least, the shogun's government welcomed the enthusiasm exhibited by the daimyos for Nō, preferring this peaceful avocation to warlike pursuits that might endanger the state. When the daimyos themselves began to perform Nō, however, the government felt obliged to issue admonitions, though appearing in Nō was obviously not as serious an offense as playing the samisen or singing popular songs. The daimyos continued to learn Nō without major interference. At the time of the revival of Nō in the late nineteenth century, several nobles ranking as daimyo appeared prominently in performances. Throughout the Tokugawa period, samurai of lesser rank were also active in Nō. Some performed at the Imperial Palace in Kyoto, where professional *sarugaku* actors were still treated as outcastes.

Nō was open to the general public from time to time in the form of benefit performances *(kanjin Nō)*. In the Muromachi period such performances had genuinely been for the benefit of a temple or shrine, but in the Tokugawa period they came to be purely commercial ventures on the part of the actors. Most benefits required only the permission of the local magistrate, but there were also special "once-in-a-lifetime" benefits for outstanding actors, performances staged for the townsmen, who may have felt that attending Nō placed them higher up the social ladder than going to see Kabuki or Bunraku. In most respects these benefits were performed with the same degree of ceremonial as if before the shogun, but the press of the crowd was sometimes so intense that the stiff, formal holiday attire of the spectators was in danger of being ripped to shreds. Elderly people sent substitutes to hold their places, and these men, dressed in nondescript clothes, would cheerfully shout greetings to the shogun and other high officials when they arrived— "There's the chief!" "Best in Japan!" Such informality normally would have been unthinkable in the rigid society of Tokugawa Japan, but the theatre, like the gay quarters, was immune from the usual hierarchical demands, and the guards stationed inside the theatre made no attempt to suppress the rowdy spectators.

Because of the ritual nature of Nō during this period the repertory remained virtually static. Many plays were written, perhaps two thousand, but generally for a particular occasion and never repeated. None of the two hundred or more surviving plays of the period has been deemed worthy of a revival. The Tokugawa Nō plays, bound both in language and plots to the traditions of a departed age, are usually no more than pastiches of the mannerisms of Nō without any emotional involvement. The subjects were remote, the dramatists (unlike those of Hideyoshi's time) too timid to treat contemporary subjects. The best may actually be not inferior to some works in the current repertory, but the latter have at least the advantage of being genuine.

The elevation of Nō to the status of court ceremonial meant also that its dramatic appeal need no longer be considered. The dialogue, originally close to the tempo of speech, came to be pronounced in a deliberate, protracted manner, and the sung parts were delivered in muffled, almost unintelligible tones. The dances too were greatly prolonged, and moments when nothing occurred on the stage, save for an occasional beat of the drum and a strangled cry from the drummer, came to occupy as much as a quarter of the length of the play. The *monomane* elements were largely sacrificed. But, it may be argued, the slow, ritualistic presentation may have accorded better with Zeami's ideals than the livelier performances of his own day.

The extreme solemnity of Nō probably whetted the appetite of the spectators for Kyōgen as comic relief. During the Muromachi period Kyōgen was so unimportant that it was scarcely noticed by the diary writers who supplied detailed accounts of Nō; they treated the Kyōgen plays with the silent disdain of the learned film critic of today discussing a program of avant-garde masterpieces which happens to include a Donald Duck cartoon. During the Tokugawa period the Kyōgen actors ranked lowest among the performers associated with Nō, below the flutists and drummers, but thanks to the general patronage of the art as a ceremonial, Kyōgen acquired a measure of dignity. The texts were established for the first time and, inevitably it would seem, three distinct schools—Ōkura, Izumi and Sagi—insisted on their own versions. The new dignity did not destroy the humor of Kyōgen. On the contrary, a comparison of the oldest surviving texts with the definitive versions compiled later in the seventeenth century reveals that the comic features were sharpened and the satirical elements—the fun poked at pompous but foolish daimyos and the like—made more effective.

It may seem strange that the daimyos should not only have tolerated but enjoyed comedies in which they were the butt of the humor. Probably even in the Muromachi period they felt no class solidarity with the parvenu daimyos depicted so irreverently, finding them as absurd as the court of Louis XIV found the *petit marquis* of a Molière farce. In the Tokugawa period the members of the shogun's court could view with amusement and utter detachment the daimyo in *Kombu-uri* who, after forcing his servant to carry his sword, is compelled by the servant to sing like a peddler hawking his wares. It was inconceivable that any daimyo of the seventeenth century would be on terms of such familiarity with a servant.

The transcribing of the Kyōgen texts in the seventeenth century inhibited the improvisation which had always been part of its humor. It also petrified the humor: though far easier to understand than Nō, the language of Kyōgen had become archaic by the Tokugawa period and no longer could express effectively the amusing experiences of daily life. Most of the two hundred or so surviving Kyōgen plays depict Muromachi life, though revised versions of old works and, more rarely, new plays continued to be staged in the traditional manner.

The Kyōgen actors shared some of the glory surrounding Nō during the Tokugawa period. They had patrons among the daimyos and pupils even in the imperial court, but the comic relief they lent to a program must have been tolerated grudgingly by the sterner Confucianists of the court. The actors took their art extremely seriously, and if given less than due credit when they performed in the forbidding atmosphere of the shogun's presence, they came into their own before the crowds at a benefit performance.

The last and most spectacular of the gala benefits occurred in 1848, the "once-in-a-lifetime" performances given by the head of the Hōshō school. The shoguns, from the days of Yoshimitsu, had favored the Kanze school, but with the eleventh shogun, Ienari (1773–1841), the Hōshō school gained preference, and subsequent shoguns continued this patronage. Permission was granted to Hōshō Yagorō to stage benefit performances on fifteen clear days. The series began on March 6, 1848 but did not reach the fifteenth day until June 13, the rainy spring having interfered with the outdoor performances. An elaborate theatre seating five thousand spectators was constructed in Edo. The audiences consisted of an extraordinarily varied cross-section of Japanese society. The gentry and their wives paid three pieces of silver for the privilege of sitting in upstairs boxes protected from the public gaze by curtains of purple silk dyed with their family crests. The commoners paid two pieces of silver to sit below; but even upstairs, in locations with poor views of the stage, townsmen sat crosslegged in breeches and striped cloaks alongside country bumpkins in cotton kimonos and old women wearing aprons. The audience was at liberty to drink saké, but keeping one's head covered or stripping to one's underwear was strictly prohibited. The crowd downstairs included low-ranking samurai, lady shampooers, Confucian scholars, doctors, fortune-tellers, Shinto priests, poets and many others, all jammed together indiscriminately. Upstairs, the daimyos and their consorts observed the plays "set out in a row, like a display of penny dolls."

The audience was by no means respectful. When Hōshō Yagorō made his entrance, instead of the solemn silence we expect today there were cries of, "Here's the man from Hatago!" (the quarter of Edo where Yagorō lived), and when the actors left the stage at the end of the play they were encouraged by shouts of, "Thanks for your trouble!" The spectators directed comments not only at the actors but at the gentry upstairs. No matter how interesting the Nō or Kyōgen in progress, the arrivals and departures of ladies of quality were greeted with a barrage of wisecracks, sometimes of a decidedly improper nature. A contemporary account relates, "The tumult inside the theatre was indescribable. Everyone was making so much noise all at once that it was impossible to understand what was being said." Clearly, the audience was enjoying not only the plays but the rare opportunity to give vent to their high spirits in the presence of the grandees of the country. The actors no doubt found it a strain to perform before such spectators, but they endured the discomfort, remembering that the purpose of the benefit performances was to make money. In this they succeeded admirably. Enterprising merchants also seized the opportunity to profit by the crowds; concessions were given out for tea, saké, *sushi*, cushions, and even for the disposal of waste matter in the public toilets. Hōshō Yagorō earned twenty thousand *ryō*, and the government itself considered the event of such importance that the reign-name was changed to Kaei ("celebration of eternity") in commemoration.

The benefit performances each day consisted of *Okina*, one Nō from each of the five categories, a final, congratulatory Nō, and five Kyōgen. Hōshō Kurō, who was to emerge as the leading actor of the Meiji period, appeared as the *shite* on each day of the series, though only a boy of eleven in

1848. He succeeded as head of the school in 1853, the year that Commodore Perry's ships arrived off Edo, and performed at New Year both in 1854 for the Shogun Ieshige and in 1858 for his successor Iemochi. These were the last command performances of the shogunate, though Hōshō Kurō continued until 1861 to appear occasionally on the stage inside the castle.

MEIJI NŌ

Nō had been associated with the shogunate ever since the days of Yoshimitsu. With the overthrow of the shogunate in 1868 the actors were forced to decide whether to remain loyal to their old masters, now retired to Shizuoka, or to profess allegiance to the imperial government. Whichever course they might choose, there seemed little chance of ever performing again. Nō, like the Tokugawa régime which had so long supported it, was now in disgrace. Most actors gave up their profession, some to become farmers or shopkeepers, others to work with their hands. A few actors, notably Umewaka Minoru in Tokyo, struggled to preserve Nō. People were suspicious of Minoru, but he persisted, performing on a makeshift stage until he could secure a better one. Minoru with great difficulty persuaded Hōshō Kurō to revoke his decision of 1871 to retire from the stage and become a farmer. Kurō, an exceedingly cautious man who was hypersensitive about his dignity, finally consented in 1875 to appear on Minoru's stage when he realized that even under the new régime, with its passion for novelty and foreign things, there were still people capable of appreciating his art.

The subsequent revival of Nō, at a time when most old traditions were summarily rejected, was paradoxically due to the desire to emulate Western countries in offering suitably dignified entertainments on state occasions. The first performances of Nō after the Restoration were held in 1869 in honor of the visit of the Duke of Edinburgh. The Duke had to be entertained, but Kabuki was judged to be too vulgar for so exalted a guest, and Nō (despite its being in disgrace) was chosen instead. When Iwakura Tomomi, a court noble and high-ranking officer of the new government, visited Europe and America in 1871 he noticed similarities between Nō and opera, the usual entertainment provided state visitors abroad. A member of Iwakura's party commented, "I was never interested in Nō until I saw historical dramas abroad and thought how much they resembled Nō." The turning point in the modern history of Nō occurred on April 4, 1876, when the Emperor Meiji paid a visit to Iwakura Tomomi's residence and witnessed a program of Nō. Iwakura had decided, in the light of his experiences in Europe, that Nō was the appropriate entertainment to offer his sovereign. Performances for the Emperor were followed by another program intended for the Empress and the Empress Dowager, and a further program for the imperial princes and princesses. Umewaka Minoru, who had been entrusted with the performances, was able to find room for Hōshō Kurō in the program, though this had not originally been planned. His determination to draw Kurō back to the stage succeeded, and the collaboration of these two great actors made possible the revival of Nō.

The patronage of the imperial family protected Nō from any criticism of its association with the discredited shogunate. In the past, when the court was still in Kyoto, imperial approval had eagerly been sought by actors though it did not benefit them financially. The Emperor Kōmei, Meiji's father, had been especially fond of Nō and Kyōgen, but the actors who performed for him were rewarded not with robes or gifts of money, but with tastefully costumed little dolls. The Emperor Meiji's mother, the Empress Dowager Eishō (1833–1897), became after the Restoration the chief patron of Nō. In 1878 Meiji built for her pleasure a stage in the Aoyama Palace. Hōshō Kurō in later years described his experience at the inaugural performance: "I was to perform by command the difficult role of *Dōjōji*. The date for the opening had already been set when Ōkubo, the Minister of the Interior, was assassinated, and the inauguration of the stage was consequently delayed several times, finally being set for the fifth of July. I was in a state of extreme agitation for the weather was naturally very hot at that time of year and the role was demanding . . . When

I appeared on the stage I could see the Emperor's seat, but the heat and the demands of the role made me forget everything else. By the time I reached the *rambyōshi* section I had forgotten even the heat. At last came the interval, when I entered the bell. Once inside, I breathed a sigh of relief, only to begin feeling dizzy in the oppressive sultriness. I started to change my costume, wiping with a towel the waterfall of sweat pouring from me, when I discovered that someone had thoughtfully left a fan inside the bell. I used it to stir up a little breeze, put on my robes, turned myself into a serpent, and appeared once again on the stage." The performance, which lasted for nine hours, was judged an eminent success.

The visit of General Grant, the former President of the United States, in the summer of 1879 again provided an occasion for the presentation of Nō to a foreign visitor. Grant was the first head (or former head) of a foreign country ever to visit Japan, and the Japanese were understandably worried about how to entertain him. Grant, in the end, was treated to both Nō and Kabuki. At the conclusion of the Nō he witnessed at Iwakura's residence Grant is reported to have said, "So noble and beautiful an art is easily cheapened and destroyed by the changing tastes of the times. You must make efforts to preserve it." It is difficult to imagine the grizzled old soldier Grant being so powerfully impressed by the remote beauty of Nō, even with the assistance of the translation hastily prepared for the occasion, but his words were taken to heart by Iwakura, who decided that an organization was needed for the preservation of Nō. The Nō Society (*Nōgakusha*) which he founded built the first permanent Nō stage for the general public. In April, 1881, in the presence of the Empress Dowager and two hundred of the highest ranking nobles, the stage in Shiba Park was officially opened. On the third day, when the general public was admitted, over seven hundred persons attended. Umewaka Minoru's son (later known also as Umewaka Minoru) recollected his first stage appearance at the time, when he was four years old. "I was only a child and had no impressions worth mentioning, but I can still remember how beautiful everything seemed. On one side sat the Empress Dowager Eishō, her long hair hanging over her kimono, wearing a scarlet *hakama*, and with her were more than twenty court ladies, all in the same costume, sitting in a row. On the other side was the Empress Shōken. She and her attendants were all in Western costume, looking so beautiful they almost blinded me."

Public performances of Nō became frequent. The five schools, which had gladly appeared on the same stage in Shiba Park when their fortunes were low, before long found the financial support to build theatres for their exclusive use, and the differences between the various schools, which had not been so great as to prevent Umewaka Minoru of the Kanze school from appearing with Hōshō Kurō of the Hōshō school or Sakurama Bamba of the Komparu school, the third great actor of the period, from appearing on the Hōshō stage, were exaggerated. Rivalry over pupils, essential now that the government gave no direct support, further accentuated the differences. The Kanze school, the richest and most important, attracted a disproportionate number of students, perhaps sixty percent of the total, followed by Hōshō with another twenty percent or so; the remaining ten percent was divided among Komparu, Kongō and Kita, small schools whose existence at times has been threatened by the preference for more fashionable styles of Nō. Even the small schools, however, have produced outstanding performers such as Sakurama Kintarō (Komparu), Kongō Iwao (Kongō), and Kita Roppeita (Kita).

NŌ IN RECENT TIMES

The popularity of Nō continued to grow after the death or retirement of the great actors of the Meiji era, confounding the many prophets who had predicted that the younger generation would not respond to so outdated an art as Nō. Like other forms of traditional drama, Nō was favored by the wartime governments, anxious to foster belief in the importance of "pure" Japanese culture uncontaminated by foreign influences. New plays of a patriotic nature, like *Miikusabune* ("Imperial Warship") were composed and widely performed between 1942 and 1945, but quickly forgotten. Almost all the Nō stages in Tokyo were destroyed in 1945 by bombing, and for a time immediately afterwards all schools shared the one remaining stage, under conditions reminiscent of the early Meiji period. Renewed prosperity enabled most schools to build their own stages again.

Nō is today supported chiefly by people living in all parts of the country who study the singing, but not the performance, of the texts. The tuition fees they pay make it possible for Nō to be presented in the theatres, and when they visit Tokyo they naturally wish to see the plays they have learned by heart. We can judge how much they influence the programs from the fact that between 1949 and 1960 the Kanze school performed *Funa Benkei* 208 times and *Hagoromo* 193 times, though some masterpieces were seldom staged. *Teika* was performed only twenty-seven times, *Koi no Omoni* and *Eguchi* thirty-five times.

Performances by amateurs who have mastered the roles are also common and include some by women. Although no formal prohibition was placed on women appearing in Nō in the seventeenth century, when Kabuki was deprived of its actresses, they disappeared from the stage, and today people generally consider their voices and figures totally inadequate for even the most feminine roles. Nevertheless, women persist in their studies, and some day they may achieve recognition.

The study of Nō as a literary and theatrical art dates mainly from the Meiji period when such scholars as Yoshida Tōgo (1864–1918) discovered the texts of Zeami's criticism and other essential documents. Only since the 1930's, however, have truly scientific studies taken the place of the aimless compilation of facts or recollections which previously passed for criticism. The secrecy with which texts are still surrounded by some Nō masters has impeded basic research into the evolution of the texts, but this situation cannot long persist.

Performances today are at a high level. It is true that in some details the standards of the past cannot be equalled; for example, it has become prohibitively expensive to replace the covering of the drums for each performance, the practice in former days. Again, the actors' preference for the Western haircut means that sometimes in roles without masks they look incongruously modern. But these are minor flaws when compared to the devotion and scholarly attention which the roles receive. The reverent hush in the Nō theatre, as we have seen, is a relatively recent phenomenon. Certainly the manner of enjoying Nō must have been different when people brought food and drink to their boxes and divided their attention between the stage and their stomachs. Some today regret the changes, recalling wistfully easier-going days, but artistically they would seem to be in the right direction, pointing to a return to the ideals of Zeami and, indeed, to the solemn beginnings of Nō.

III. NŌ AND KYŌGEN AS LITERATURE

THE TEXTS of the Nō plays have often been likened to brocade woven of brilliant bits of silk to form a magnificent fabric, a simile which suggests how liberally the texts were embellished with scraps from the literature of the past. The *tanka*, the classic verse form, in particular gave the poetry of Nō its distinctive tone. Ever since the tenth century, when the anthology *Kokinshū* ("Collection of Ancient and Modern Poetry") was compiled, the *tanka* had been revered as the noblest form of Japanese poetry, and a thorough knowledge of the *tanka* in the dozen imperial anthologies was assumed of educated men. Zeami urged aspiring Nō actors not to dissipate their talents on other arts, but he made an exception for the *tanka*, the source of so much beauty in the Nō.

The *tanka* had even been credited with supernatural powers. The preface to the *Kokinshū* asserts that the *tanka* can move the gods and demons. We find echoes of this belief in the plays. The central theme of *Shiga* is that the *tanka* promotes the security and happiness of the people because it enjoys the protection of the gods and Buddhas. In *Utaura* a knowledge of the *tanka* is declared to be a means of knowing the future, for poetry reflects the minds of the gods. Zeami often quoted famous *tanka*, sometimes a whole poem, sometimes only a verse or two, confident that his audience would catch the allusions. Quotation of the old *tanka* not only confirmed the mood of a scene by its reference to similar feelings described in the past, but enhanced the text with the magical aura of divinely-favored words.

The bits of silk making up the brocade of the texts did not consist entirely of *tanka*. The play *Atsumori*, for example, quotes not only four *tanka* but phrases from the preface to *Kokinshū*, poems in Chinese by Po Chü-i and others, Buddhist works, *The Tale of Genji* and, above all, *The Tale of the Heike*, the thirteenth-century novel which inspired the play. The number of quotations should not suggest that *Atsumori* is a mere tissue of allusions, a pastiche composed of famous tags from the old classics. Only a small part of the text can be traced to earlier literature, and even these borrowings usually consist of a few key words rather than extended passages. The texts are original works given added depth and complexity by the use of quotations and allusions.

Zeami in his critical writings was concerned mainly with analysis of the art of acting, but he also mentioned on occasion his conviction that the texts themselves were of paramount importance. Unquestionably he took enormous pains with the literary effects of his plays. Zeami's style is marked not only by his reliance on quotations from literary works but by extraordinary complexity in the expression, far beyond the requirements of the theatre. Zeami's use of wordplays, especially the *kakekotoba* or "pivot word," which shifts in meaning depending on the words preceding and following, was another aspect of his constant attempt to supply additional layers of meaning to his words. Zeami did not invent the *kakekotoba*, but he used it with greater effect than any of his predecessors. This passage from *Hanjo* by Zeami contains four *kakekotoba*:

YOSHIDA:	*konata ni mo*	I too have a keepsake
	wasuregatami no	Impossible to forget:

koto no ha wo	The words we spoke.
Iwade *no mori no*	But if, like azaleas hidden
shita tsutsuji	In the silent wood of Iwade,
iro ni idezu wa	You do not speak,
sore zo to mo	You show nothing in your face,
mite koso shirame	How am I to understand?
kono ōgi	Seeing it, I shall know:
	Your fan.

HANJO:	*mite wa sate*	Seeing it?
	nani no tame zo to	What use would that be?
	yūgure *no*	What good can it do
	tsuki wo idaseru	Importuning me so
	ōgi no e no	For a fan with a picture
	kaku *bakari*	Painted to reveal
	nani no tame naruran	The twilight moon?

In this passage Yoshida asks the courtesan Hanjo for the fan he gave her as a pledge of his love, a fan showing the moon at twilight. The translation resorts to double meanings for the *kakekotoba*, but it is unfortunately impossible to suggest in English the force of the Japanese puns. *Wasuregata* means "difficult to forget" with the preceding phrase, but the added syllable *mi* yields another word *katami* ("keepsake") when used with the next phrase. Similarly, *iwade* with the preceding phrase means "not speaking," but with the following phrase is the proper noun Iwade, the name of a forest. *Yū* means "to say," but the suffix *gure* forms the word *yūgure* (twilight). *Kaku* means "to paint" but also "so." Each wordplay enriches the texture with relevant meanings, and affords a compression parallel to the economy of the Nō theatre itself; it is like a magnificently attired actor moving in intricate patterns against the starkly austere setting.

Another feature of Zeami's style is his use of *engo*, or "related words." *Engo* are words chosen from among possible synonyms for their overtones, with the intent of creating a unity of echoes even when the surface meanings are seemingly unrelated. A similar use of language can be found, say, in the thirtieth sonnet of Shakespeare:

> When to the *sessions* of sweet silent thought
> I *summon* up remembrance of things past . . .

Although the main theme is grief over the passage of time, the pervading echoes are those of the courtroom. In Nō the underlying imagery may give a unity to the text: in *Hachinoki* the dominant images are related to snow and purity; in *Obasute* to the moon; in *Eguchi* to a river. The use of this unifying imagery makes it far easier for the Nō actor, with the limited means of representation at his disposal, to project the essential mood of a play.

The most impressive feature of Zeami's style is the power of the imagery. The art of Nō demands a transformation of violent and jagged emotions into a prescribed, unruffled form. In this respect it may remind us of the tragedies of Racine; the surface elegance is broken only occasionally, but those moments stand out with electrifying intensity. Zeami's most powerful work, *Kinuta*, is dominated by the hollow sound of clothes being beaten on a fulling block, evoking the loneliness of long autumn nights. The woman in the play, incensed at her husband's failure to return to her, calls for a fulling block on which to pound out her grief:

inga no mōshū	Tears of remembrance
omoi no namida	For sins committed
kinuta ni kakareba	Fall on the fulling block;
namida wa kaette	The tears turn to flames,
kaen to natte	And choked by the smoke.

mune no kemuri no	Of the fire in my breast,
honō ni musebeba	I shriek, but my voice
sakedo koe ga	Does not escape my lips.
ideba koso	The fulling block is soundless,
kinuta mo koe naku	The pine wind too, unheard . . .
matsukaze mo kikoezu	Only the shouts of hell's tormentors,
kashaku no koe no mi	Horrible their cries!
osoroshiya	

In this passage Zeami used with superb effect the Buddhist terms *inga* ("cause and effect"), *mōshū* ("deep-rooted delusion"), *kaen* ("flames"), and *kashaku* ("tormentors"), words that not only possess powerful religious overtones but by their very sounds, unlike the softer syllables of pure Japanese, give sharp contours to the lines. The intensity of the imagery—tears that turn into flames, mute shrieks of anguish, the cries of the fiends of hell—imprints the passage with the controlled violence of Nō at its most dramatic.

A whole play could not, of course, be maintained at this level. Sections are in prose, declaimed in a conventionally stylized manner; most sentences end with the mournfully prolonged vowels of the copula verb *sōrō*. Other sections, though in poetry, are in a low key, conforming to the prescription that the *jo* section of a play be slow and serene. The structural requirements of the plays, as established by Zeami himself, also tend to confine the poetry of greatest intensity to a few sections, generally at the close of the *ha* division of the work.

An analysis of a typical play of the *waki* (first) category, *Takasago*, by Zeami, may illustrate the structure and the uses of different kinds of poetry.

The play opens as the *waki*, a Shinto priest, embarks with his companions on a journey. They sing the *shidai*, a passage in three lines of 7+5, 7+5, and 7+4 syllables, the first two lines being identical:

ima wo hajime no	*tabigoromo*	Now first we wear our travel robes,
ima wo hajime no	*tabigoromo*	Now first we wear our travel robes,
hi mo yuku sue zo	*hisashiki*	How long are the days of travel ahead.

After singing this passage the *waki* speaks the *nanori*, a passage in prose identifying himself, and relates his intention of making a journey. He and his companions now sing the *michiyuki* (travel song) in seven or eight lines of 5, 7+5 syllables, etc., ending with the statement of their arrival at Takasago. The poetry is in the restrained tone appropriate to the *jo* section, which concludes at this point.

The *ha* section opens with the appearance of the *shite* and *tsure*, an old man and an old woman. Their entrance song, known as the *issei*, consists of lines in 5, 7+5, and 7+5 syllables.

takasago no		At Takasago
matsu no harukaze	*fukikurete*	A spring breeze in the pines blows as dusk falls,
onoe no kane mo	*hibiku naru*	And the temple bell on the peak echoes the close of day.

Next come passages known as *ninoku* (second stanza) and *sannoku* (third stanza), each a line in 7+5 syllables:

nami wa kasumi no	*isogakure*	The waves are hidden at the misty beach,
oto koso shio no	*michihi nare*	Their sound tells of the ebb and flow of the tide.

The scene having been set, the *shite* describes his situation in the *sashi*, usually a passage in about ten lines of 7+5 syllables each:

tare wo ka mo	Whom shall I take

shiru hito ni sen takasago no	As my friend? Even the pine
matsu mo mukashi no tomo narade	Of Takasago is not a friend of old;
sugikoshi yo yo wa shirayuki no	The years on years I have lived through
	are forgotten, but the snows
tsumori tsumorite oi no tsuru no	Keep piling, piling; the aged crane
negura ni nokoru ariyake no	In his nest, a spring moon lingering
haru no shimoyo no okii ni mo	In the frosty dawn, awakens:
matsukaze wo no mi kikinarete	I hear nothing but the familiar pine wind,
kokoro wo tomo to sugamushiro	But making its song my friend, as I lie
	on my rush mat,
omoi wo noburu bakari nari	I tell my griefs, my only solace.

Apart from the extra line in five syllables, a common variation, this *sashi* is quite regular. But what complications are involved in the poetry! The passage opens with a *tanka* from an imperial collection, quoted in a slightly altered form: "Whom shall I make my friend? Even the pine of Takasago is not a friend of old." The next line contains a *kakekotoba, shirayuki*, meaning "I do not know" (or "do not remember") with what precedes, but "white snow" with the following words *tsumori tsumorite* ("piling, piling"), alluding to the white hair of the speaker, so old that he no longer has any friends and has even forgotten the past. "The aged crane" is used metaphorically for an old person, but leads also to "nest." These different images coalesce: piled-up snow lies in the nest of the aged crane; the aged crane wakes in a nest lit by the moon lingering in the frosty sky of a spring dawn; the crane becomes a metaphor for the old man who, wakening at night, hears the wind through the pines and makes this poetic sound his friend; and finally, the old man is comforted by expressing his grief in poetry.

Granted that some in the audience could follow these complexities, most spectators probably caught no more than the general drift. The clusters of images, blending imprecisely in their minds, produced an impression of beauty.

Takasago is a calmly majestic play, suitable to the category of god plays. The *sashi*, which occurs at the opening of the *ha* section, was not the place for displaying powerful emotions; nevertheless, Zeami's poetry builds a gradual intensification of interest. The first part of the *ha* section concludes with the singing of the *sageuta* (three or four lines of 5, 7+5, 7+5 syllables) and the *ageuta* (up to ten units of 7+5 syllables). At this point the *shite* encounters the *waki* for the first time.

The second part of the *ha* section begins with exchanges of dialogue in prose between the *shite* and *waki* about the Takasago Pine. The prose rises into poetry that continues the dialogue. Now the chorus enters for the first time, singing a passage in nine lines. This *ageuta*, often sung on auspicious occasions, begins:

shikai nami shizuka ni te	The waves of the four seas are calm,
kuni mo osamaru toki tsu kaze	The land at peace; favorable winds
eda wo narasanu mi yo nareya	Disturb not the branches in this holy era . . .

The third part of the *ha* section, the central episode of the whole play, describes the glory of pines and of poetry. It begins with the *kuri*, a short passage in no fixed meter. A *sashi* follows, also in free rhythms, and then the *kuse*, a long section describing how each sight of nature inspires poetry. All three passages are sung by the chorus with occasional interpellations from the *shite*. The irregularity of the meter reflects the importance of the music and dance in this part.

The *kuse* is followed by the *rongi*, a dialogue between chorus and *shite* in regular meter, terminating with the *shite*'s departure from the stage. A Kyōgen actor, identified as "a man of the place," appears, and after a few brief exchanges with the *waki*, recites the history of the Pine of Takasago. In some plays the *ai* section merely repeats in simpler language information already given; probably it was necessary for spectators who failed to understand the plot from the difficult sung passages.

After the *ai* is completed, the *kyū* section of the play begins. Usually this occupies only a page or two in print, but in performance it often takes twenty or more minutes mainly because it contains the final dance of the *shite*. The *kyū* section usually (but not in *Takasago*) begins with the *waki*'s song of waiting, seven or eight lines in 5, 7+5, 7+5 meter, followed by the second appearance of the *shite* to a *sashi* of three lines in 5, 7+5, 7+5 syllables. In *Takasago* the *shite* reveals himself as being in reality the god of the Sumiyoshi Shrine. Next ensues a dialogue between *shite* and chorus on the miraculous nature of the god, followed by the *shimai*, the final dance. A last *rongi* (dialogue) between *shite* and chorus, generally in about fifteen lines, ends most plays; in *Takasago* it is an expression of awe and delight over the revelation of the god Sumiyoshi.

Hardly a single play fits this formula exactly. Zeami himself cited *Yumi Yawata* as a model work, attributing its regularity to its sacred character. But even though the elements of most plays are somewhat at variance with the ideal pattern, perhaps to avoid monotony, their overall construction generally corresponds closely to that of *Takasago*.

Plays of the first category are the least rewarding dramatically. *Takasago* is one of the most interesting examples; a more typical work, like *Shirahige*, requires the *shite* to sit motionless in the middle of the stage through most of the performance as the chorus recites events associated with a shrine.

Plays of the second category, the warrior plays, are distinctly more dramatic. Because they belong to the slow section of the program, they do not approach the violence or emotional intensity of plays about warriors presented later in the program; of the sixteen *shuramono* (warrior plays) in the current repertory, thirteen are by Zeami, a sure indication that these plays are more likely to be poetic than realistic depictions of martial deeds.

Many warrior plays were derived from *The Tale of the Heike*, that repository of stirring or pathetic incidents from the wars between the Taira and the Minamoto. Zeami declared in his critical writings that texts based on this work must be faithful to the original, but his own are free, not only in language but in emphasis. *Atsumori*, for example, retains little of the original dramatic tension; the source is in fact more theatrical than the play. In *The Tale of the Heike* we are told how the Minamoto captain Kumagai challenges a fleeing enemy general to an encounter. They fight, and Kumagai fells his opponent. Tearing off the man's helmet, he discovers a boy of sixteen, a noble, and decides to spare his life, remembering how grieved he had been that day when his own son, also sixteen, was wounded. In polite, almost deferential language, Kumagai asks the boy his name, but the boy insolently recommends that Kumagai show his severed head to men on his side. The superbly dramatic dialogue is broken by the approach of other Minamoto soldiers. Kumagai, resigned now to killing Atsumori, the young man, promises to pray for his repose. He kills the boy and strips his armor, only to find a flute, a further reminder of the boy's aristocratic lineage. In the end Kumagai abandons his career as a soldier to become a priest.

In the play *Atsumori*, Kumagai appears as the *waki*, the priest Renshō. He tells of his intention to pray for Atsumori's repose at Ichinotani, the site of the Heike defeat. There he encounters some reapers and hears one play a flute. This reaper remains after the others go and tells the priest that he is of Atsumori's family. After the interlude the young man reappears as a ghost in armor, this time identifying himself as Atsumori. He relates the disasters that struck the Taira family, and recalls how he played his flute the night before the battle. Finally he relives his mortal struggle with Kumagai, but at the moment that he raises his sword to strike, in the gesture of a *shura*, a still resentful ghost, he sees that the priest Renshō is praying for his salvation. "Pray for me again, oh, pray for me again," are the concluding words of the play.

Comparing the two stories we see that almost every element of pathos or drama in *The Tale of the Heike* has been deleted from the play. Atsumori's youth, his resemblance to Kumagai's son, his insolence in response to Kumagai's solicitude, Kumagai's regret when forced to kill Atsumori—all are eliminated, leaving only the story of a man unable to forget his defeat at an enemy's hands.

Of course, the audience was familiar with the story as told in *The Tale of the Heike*, but Zeami's play does not depend on this knowledge; instead, he chose to delete everything particular about the two men in the interests of achieving a stylized, universal tragedy. One man kills another; by this act he brings salvation to both. Kumagai's remorse over killing Atsumori leads to his taking Buddhist orders, and this act in turn ultimately brings Atsumori salvation. The attention of the author of *The Tale of the Heike* was focused on the dramatic contrasts between the two men: the grizzled warrior and the boy-soldier, the rough frontiersman and the flute-playing aristocrat, the compassionate old man and the insolent youth. In the play, however, the central theme is Atsumori's release from the torment of being a *shura*. His ghost has lingered on earth in the guise of a reaper because, unable to attain salvation, his attachment to the world makes him relive again and again the moments of his final battle. Only his flute, the symbol of his youth and noble aspirations, brings solace to this tortured spirit. When Renshō promises the unknown reaper to pray for his soul, Atsumori appears in his true form. He repeats the motions of his mortal encounter with Kumagai, raising his sword with the cry, "Here is my enemy!" But at that moment he is saved. He cries, "We shall be reborn on the same lotus!"

Zeami chose not to dwell on the contrasts found in *The Tale of the Heike*. Atsumori's inability to renounce his memories of this world does not stem from his youth, his courtly accomplishments or his pride; only when he recognizes that Renshō is not his enemy can he be saved. The play, though telling of warriors, neither glorifies nor condemns the military life. Zeami wrote that plays dealing with soldiers of the Heike wars must be elegant: "In plays of this type especially, a brilliance of effect is desirable." In *Atsumori* the boy's youthful beauty and the music of his flute impart *yūgen*, as in *Tsunemasa* the music of the *biwa* or in *Tadanori* the cherry blossoms on the strand of Suma give a haunting beauty to the stories of defeated warriors. The more powerful *Kanehira*, on the other hand, has little of this quality:

hakujin hone wo	Horror of naked blades
kudaku kurushimi	Smashing on bone,
gansei wo yaburi	Scenes of eyes gouged out,
kōha tate wo nagasu yosōi	And shields floating on crimson waves
yanagui ni	Like scattered blossoms
zanka wo midasu	Breaking against a weir.*

Kanehira belongs to the world of the *shura*; the characters are proud of their hours of glory and need no priest to pray for their salvation. *Kanehira* is more exciting than *Atsumori*, but it fits poorly into the *jo* section of a program, and its lack of *yūgen* suggests that Zeami, despite traditional attributions, was not the author.

Plays of the third category, the woman plays, contain the most beautiful poetry. Love, when treated in this category, has a bittersweet fragrance, though apt in plays of the fourth category to be an obsession powerful enough to derange a woman. The story of Lady Rokujō, derived from *The Tale of Genji*, is described touchingly in the third-category play *Nonomiya*, where we see her at a lonely shrine in the fields awaiting her last meeting with Genji; in the fourth-category play *Aoi no Ue*, Rokujō's love for Genji is depicted as the demonic instrument of the death of Aoi, Genji's wife. The poetry in each case creates the mood. In *Nonomiya* we find:

nonomiya no	My carriage is bright
aki no chigusa no	With the thousand autumn grasses
hanaguruma	Of the Shrine in the Fields.
ware mo mukashi ni	The wheels turn; I too
meguri kinikeri	Have returned to the past.

The hollow sound of the drum accompanying the poetry suggests with unspeakable pathos the autumn, season of memories. When Rokujō, passing under the *torii*, the boundary between life

*Translation by Stanleigh H. Jones, Jr. in Keene, *Twenty Plays of the Nō Theatre*, p. 275.

and death, disappears, perhaps at last to gain release from the love of Genji which binds her still to the world of the living, we sense almost painfully the lonely, mysterious beauty of *yūgen:*

nonomiya no	Even the moon
tsuki mo mukashi ya	At the Shrine in the Fields
omouran	Must remember the past;
kage samishiku mo	Its light forlornly trickles
mori no shitatsuyu	Through the leaves to the forest dew,
mori no shitatsuyu	Through the leaves to the forest dew.
mi no okidokoro mo	This place, once my refuge,
aware mukashi no	This garden, still lingers
niwa no tatazumai	Unchanged from long ago,
yoso ni zo kawaru	A beauty nowhere else,
keshiki mo kari naru	Though transient, insubstantial
koshibagaki	As this little wooden fence
tsuyu uchiharai	From which he used to brush the dew.
towareshi ware mo	I, whom he visited,
sono hito mo	And he, my lover too,
tada yume no yo to	The whole world turned to dreams,
furiyuku ato ni	To aging ruins;
tare matsu	Whom should I pine for now?
mushi no ne wa	The voices of pine-crickets
rin rin toshite	Trill *rin, rin,*
kaze bōbō taru	The wind howls:
nonomiya no yosugara	How I remember
natsukashiya	Nights at the Shrine in the Fields!

The sin of attachment, which draws ghosts back to memories they cannot relinquish, is most affectingly evoked in the woman plays, where the memories are not of vengeance, but of love. In *Izutsu,* Ariwara no Narihira's childhood sweetheart recalls their early happiness together, contrasting those days with his later deceit. She puts on Narihira's court robe and cap and, going to the well-curb *(izutsu)* where as children she and Narihira compared heights, looks at her reflection in the water.

mireba natsukashiya	She looks—how sweet the memory,
warenagara natsukashiya	Sweet the memory, though of herself,
bōfū hakurei no sugata wa	This ghost in her dead husband's form:
shibomeru hana no	A withered flower,
iro nōte	Color vanished,
nioi nokorite	Perfume only lingering.
Ariwara no tera no kane mo	The bell of the Ariwara Temple too
honobono to akureba	Tolls dimly in the dawning.
furudera no	Over the old temple,
matsukaze ya	The wind through the pines,
bashōba no	The rustle of plantain leaves,
yume mo yaburete	Broken easily as dreams;
samenikeri	Awakened,
yume wa yabure	The dream is broken,
akenikeri	The day has dawned.

The texts are replete with ingenuity—plays on words, thoughts that shift in direction, sounds echoed from one line to the next, adjectives modifying both the word they follow and the word they precede—but they do not represent virtuosity for its own sake; the complexity should suggest the shifting flow of thoughts of the characters themselves. The poignancy achieved in the poetry, rather than any display of femininity in performance, gives the woman plays their heart-breaking beauty.

The fourth category includes the widest variety of works, ranging from plays hardly distinguishable from the poetic dramas of the third category to realistic plays almost devoid of poetry. *Hagoromo*, which tells of a goddess who must perform a celestial dance as the price of a fisherman's returning her robe of feathers, is sometimes classed in the fourth category, presumably because the presence of the fisherman lends a realistic note, but it by no means resembles the bulk of the *genzaimono*, or contemporary plays. *Jinen Koji* by Kannami, an early *genzaimono*, tells of a girl who has sold herself to white slavers so that she can make an offering to the memory of her dead parents. The priest Jinen Koji, discovering what has happened, rushes after her, arriving at the shore of Lake Biwa just as the men are rowing off their boat, with the girl lying in the bottom, bound and gagged. Jinen induces the men to return the girl, but in exchange they demand that he perform the songs and dances for which he is famous. The one thing common to *Hagoromo* and *Jinen Koji* (and to many other plays of the fourth category) is that the dances are identified in the play as such, and are not heightened, abstract expressions of the emotions described in the poetry.

Another important group of plays belonging to the fourth category are those dealing with mad persons. "Madness," however, is by no means uncontrolled lunacy; it embraces such emotions as the overpowering grief of the mother in *Sumidagawa* who searches the country for her kidnapped child, or the jealous despair of the woman in *Kinuta* who fears that her husband has deserted her. These women are obsessed rather than mad, but "madness" in Zeami's day, like the divine madness of the Greeks, was associated with poetry and music; the other characters in *Sumidagawa* ask the distraught mother to display her madness, as if excess of grief had made her entertaining.

Plays of the fourth category usually recount a story rather than attempt to create a poetic atmosphere. Audiences have always responded more readily to such works than to those of more remote beauty, and as a group they are highly popular. *Aoi no Ue*, *Hachinoki*, *Dōjōji*, *Ataka* and *Sumidagawa*, though entirely dissimilar in mood and plot, all engage the audience less by their beauty of language than by their theatrical effectiveness. Yet for all their comparative theatricality, they are far removed, say, from Kabuki. The plot of *Ataka* is virtually identical to that of the Kabuki play *Kanjinchō*, but it remains stylized and aloof where *Kanjinchō* is warmly human; nothing in *Ataka* has the quality of the touching moment in *Kanjinchō* when Yoshitsune, aware how painful it must have been for Benkei to strike him, his master, extends his hand towards Benkei in a gesture of affection and understanding. However dramatic a Nō play may be, its symbolic possibilities can be preserved only if a distance is kept between the play and the audience. An unadorned play like *Shunnei* is likely to drop from the repertory even if its plot is interesting.

The final components of a Nō program, the devil plays, are closely related to those of the fourth category, but their tempo is faster, as we should expect in the *kyū* section. The *shite* is often a demonic being who appears in the second part wearing an enormous red or white wig that cascades over his brilliant costume, and the frenzied movements of his dance are accentuated by the ferocity of his mask. The props too, unlike the customary bare outlines of a house, tree or gate, may be solidly constructed platforms ornamented with gold and silver trees. In the first part of these plays the *shite* is likely to appear in some pleasant guise—as a gentlewoman in *Momijigari*, a priest in *Tsuchigumo*, or an old woman in *Kurozuka*—but in the second part the demon reveals his true form, and stamps wildly, swinging a mallet. The lively tempo of the play creates a cheerful impression on the audience, despite the frightening presence of a demon, and brings the program to a satisfying close.

The demon plays were written mainly by playwrights of the century after Zeami. Though effective as theatre and sometimes moving as poetry, they fail to touch the exalted utterance of the greatest Nō plays. It has been said of *Funa Benkei*, nevertheless, that "of the two hundred works in the current repertory, it ranks as a masterpiece of the kind one can count on the fingers of one hand." It rates this praise especially because of its brilliant variety of effects. In the first scene Benkei persuades Yoshitsune to dismiss his sweetheart Shizuka, who has accompanied him on the flight from the capital. The actor playing Shizuka must suggest the grief of this ill-starred woman; but in the second scene the same actor, taking an entirely different part, must rage with masculine vigor as Tomomori, a defeated Heike warrior who rises from the sea to menace the fugitives in their boat. Between the two sections of the play an unusually absorbing *ai-kyōgen* is played by the boatman who ferries Yoshitsune, Benkei and the others across the Inland Sea. He battles with tremendous waves stirred up by Tomomori's ghost, giving vent to realistic cries and gestures that contrast with the stylization of the rest of the play.

The demands of sixteenth-century audiences for action and lively presentation probably account for such works as *Shōzon*, *Chikatō* and *Kasui* by Nagatoshi. The former two works each have nine characters, *Kasui* has thirteen. *Shōzon*, the tale of a plot against Yoshitsune's life thwarted by Benkei, is devoid of poetry, and is performed by some schools with such acrobatics as somersaults and perpendicular backward falls. *Chikatō* has four principal characters, each given a display scene, rather in the manner of an Italian opera. *Kasui*, a work not currently performed, has many changes of scene, and its plot shifts from the fable of a dragon princess who dries up a river in order to compel the Chinese court to provide her with a husband, to the more realistic scene of the courtier who volunteers to marry her, to a strange episode in which a great drum sounds of itself, presaging war, and finally to a battle scene in which the Chinese emperor, aided by the Dragon King, is victorious. The dances in these plays are no longer natural outgrowths of the poetry but arbitrary insertions, and the texts themselves are as conventional as they are flat. *Hatsuyuki* by Zempō, more poetic than most plays of the period, contains these uninspiring lines:

are are miyo ya	Oh, oh, just look!
fushigi ya na	How strange it is!
are are miyo ya	Oh, oh, just look!
fushigi ya na	How strange it is!
nakazora no kumo ka to	What seemed to be
mietsuru ga	A cloud high in the sky
kumo ni wa arade	Is not a cloud:
samo shirotae no	White as glossy silk,
Hatsuyuki no	Hatsuyuki,
tsubasa wo tarete	Lowering its wings,
tobikitari	Has flown back.
himegimi ni mukai	Its form as it dances,
samo natsukashige ni	Ever so affectionately,
tachimau sugata	Facing the princess,
ge ni aware naru	Makes a truly touching
keshiki ka na	Sight to behold.

The plays by Nagatoshi and Zempō mark the end of the creative period of Nō. It should be noted, however, that many plays are of unknown authorship, and we cannot even assign them an approximate date. *Nonomiya*, *Hagoromo*, *Utō*, *Kumasaka*, *Yuya*, *Kantan*, *Tsuchigumo*, *Hachinoki* and *Kagekiyo* are among the plays which traditionally were ascribed to Zeami but now, in the absence of firm evidence of authorship, are listed as "other works." But if *Nonomiya*, *Yuya* and the rest were actually by another dramatist, he surely ranks (despite his anonymity) as Zeami's equal. It seems improbable that so great a genius could have remained completely unknown. It may be that the reaction against unproved attributions has been excessive, and future discoveries will enable us to credit Zeami with masterpieces whose authorship is now uncertain. His genius was not likely to have occurred twice.

KYŌGEN

The name Kyōgen, written with characters meaning "wild words," seems to have originated in a Chinese phrase which derogatively described all literature as being no more than "wild words and fancy language." The phrase came to be used in a Buddhist sense, with the implication that even frivolous writings may provide the impetus to salvation. It figures in some plays as a designation for the art of Nō itself. In *Tōgan Koji* the lines occur, "One can enter the true path of giving praise to the Buddha and setting the wheel of his Law in motion by means of 'wild words and fancy language.' Let us celebrate this flower of the human heart." The farcical Kyōgen plays may have been dignified as being a path that leads to enlightenment in order to justify their innocent frivolity.

By Zeami's day both *ai* and independent Kyōgen formed part of Nō programs. Zeami mentions that performances offered at shrines customarily included three Nō and two Kyōgen. The alternation of Nō and Kyōgen became the general rule. Kyōgen actors, in addition to appearing in *ai* and in the farces themselves, performed in Nō, usually in minor roles, as servants, messengers and the like. Generally the dialogue for these parts consists merely of such phrases as "I obey your commands," but occasionally, as in *Hanjo* (where the brothel proprietress is performed by a Kyōgen actor) the roles have dramatic importance.

The different functions of Kyōgen actors on the Nō stage indicate how intimately the two arts were related. Kyōgen, however, was normally considered only a minor element in the program. Zeami's prescription for Kyōgen actors suggests he held them in low esteem: "A Kyōgen actor performing in the *ai-kyōgen* of a Nō play should refrain from attempting to make the audience laugh. His function is to relate the plot of the Nō and to address himself to the audience in such a way that they will feel he has actually seen and heard the events he describes."

The subordinate position of Kyōgen is further suggested by the fact that the texts were not recorded until the beginning of the seventeenth century. The first substantial collection, published in 1660 under the name *Kyōgenki*, included fifty plays. This edition and a much augmented later version are now dismissed as being mere explanations of the plots with snatches of dialogue, and not accurate transcriptions of the texts. But though inferior and misleading, these are the oldest versions we have; a 1578 collection, the earliest Kyōgen document, consists merely of brief summaries. The lack of authentic texts dating back to the sixteenth century forces us to depend on the oral traditions of the three schools—Ōkura, Izumi, and the now defunct Sagi. In principle, each Kyōgen teacher carefully transmits the texts word-by-word to his pupils, but minor variants exist even within a single school, and a comparison of the texts of the three schools reveals enormous differences, not only in the dialogue but even in the structure of the plays. Probably these variants are very old: the bare outlines of the plot may originally have been the actors' only guide, the dialogue being left largely to improvisation. For this reason it is foolish to search for authors of the plays. Undoubtedly someone, whether an actor or a dramatist, first conceived the plots, but the lines developed naturally over the years, successful passages being retained and others dropped, rather than originating like Nō in a single writer's imagination.

The Kyōgen plays vary so markedly in literary quality that some scholars believe it is possible to trace a progression from early, unsophisticated works to the later masterpieces. The oldest Kyōgen were probably in the tradition of *Okina*, festive plays depicting the villagers' hopes for a prosperous new year. *Sannimpu* ("The Three Farmers"), for example, describes the happy journey of the three farmers to the capital in order to pay their taxes, no hardship in a year of peace and plenty. Such works contain more singing and dancing than the more satirical Kyōgen, and the humorous elements are minor. Congratulatory Kyōgen are sometimes referred to as *waki* Kyōgen, by analogy to the *waki* Nō, because they are presented first in a program.

The later Kyōgen are marked by greater ingenuity of plot, cleverer situations and a sharp decrease in musical or choreographic elements. The parts are often referred to as the *shite* (or *omo*) and *ado*, corresponding to the *shite* and *waki* of Nō, but there is little subordination of one part to the other; in a play like *Shūron* where a priest of the Amida sect and a priest of the Nichiren sect try to outsmart each other, it is essential that they be equal antagonists. Though secondary characters tend to be stereotypes with little individuality, they certainly assert themselves far more vigorously than the *waki* or *tsure* of Nō. As dramas the Kyōgen are therefore closer to Western theatre than most Nō plays; in recent years a few medieval European farces have even been adapted to the Kyōgen stage. The later Kyōgen partake of the universal nature of farce, though never descending to the crudities typical of many Western examples. They lack the refined wit of high comedy, but they afford the actors maximum opportunities to display ringing voices and agile bodily movements.

A Kyōgen actor may appear in any part, regardless of his age, physical appearance or voice, but some prefer the part of Tarōkaja (the servant), others the termagant wife, and still others the more pathetic roles. Most parts are performed without either masks or makeup. An actor taking the part of a woman merely ties a towel around his head in an approximation of a female head-dress, but neither in voice nor in movements does he suggest femininity. Child actors may perform not only as children but in roles of indeterminate age; their high-pitched monotones do scant justice to the lines, but the childish gravity they display in reciting and dancing endears them to the audience.

Masks are used chiefly when actors appear as non-human beings—animals, demons or gods—but there are also comically ugly masks for both male and female roles. Unlike Nō, where the mask may represent the "true" appearance of the characters, Kyōgen masks are often put on as a means of deception; a character may pretend to be a god (as in *Ishigami*) or a demon (as in *Oba ga Sake*) in order to frighten another person into obeying his wishes. Masks are used only in about one-eighth of the plays of the Kyōgen repertory.

The style of the Kyōgen texts is infinitely less complicated (and less distinguished) than that of Nō. Except for occasional songs, sometimes in mock imitation of Nō, the texts are in prose, each sentence generally ending with the copula verb *gozaru*. Whole passages may be the same from play to play, and there is much repetition in the dialogue. Audiences are not bored with such repetitions; on the contrary, they provide pleasingly familiar elements close to the essence of Kyōgen. The daimyo, for example, usually summons his servant Tarōkaja with the words: *Yai, yai, yai, Tarōkaja, oru ka yai?* The translation, "Hey, Tarōkaja, are you there?" certainly gives no idea of the effect of the Japanese. Translation is even more inadequate when it comes to Tarō-kaja's response, a long *Haaaaaah*, rising about two octaves, and translatable only as "Yes."

Kyōgen possesses little of the literary merit of its tragic counterpart, Nō. It occupies a position somewhere between a comedy of masks and true comedy, but relies most heavily for its effects not on the texts but on the manner of presentation—the intonation, the stylized movements of the actors, and the delightful cadences of the sentences ending in *gozaru*. A few of the plays boast plots ingenious enough to survive even in translation, and many others are enjoyable because of the glimpses they afford into the lives of the common people of the sixteenth and seventeenth centuries, but Kyōgen needs a stage for even a fraction of its pleasures to be adequately conveyed.

IV. BACKGROUND OF THE PERFORMANCES

TRAINING OF THE ACTOR

A Nō actor's training begins in his infancy and may continue until his last tottering appearance on the stage. As a small child he hears from the next room the sounds of his father rehearsing or of pupils being instructed, and he absorbs the words and intonation of Nō almost as easily as those of normal conversation. By the time he is five he makes his debut, delighting the audience with his piping in high monotones of lines whose meaning undoubtedly escapes him. He will have learned by rote every word, every gesture he so awkwardly (but winningly) performs, patiently guided by his father. Only the son of an actor is likely to receive this training from the cradle which, connoisseurs of Nō insist, is indispensable to a truly professional actor. Indeed, the pedigree of an actor of Nō or Kyōgen is so vital a consideration that it is almost unthinkable that an outsider could achieve eminence. Conversely, the actor who can boast the finest pedigree in his school may succeed to the headship even if he himself is an indifferent performer.

Gradually the boy actor moves from token appearances to *kokata* parts which require skill in both recitation and dancing. By the time he is thirteen or fourteen he may assume his first *tsure* part. It sometimes happens today, as often in the past, that a boy who has become the head of his school because of his pedigree rather than his superior talent will take *shite* parts even at ten or twelve. Save in rare instances of genius little more can be expected of so youthful a *shite* than a display of boyish charm.

Some boys, the sons of *waki* actors, are trained in the *waki* roles, resigned from childhood to the fact that no matter how proficient they may become as actors they can never hope to become the star of a play; by tradition, actors of the *shite* and *waki* schools do not cross the lines of their specialities.

At sixteen a promising young actor may be entrusted with his first *shite* role. Usually he begins by performing as a young warrior, particularly in the later Nō plays. Energy and agility (reminiscent of the flying squirrel at the bottom of Zeami's Nine Levels) are considered far easier for an actor to project than the elusive qualities of roles with little movement; the crown of an actor's career, as we have seen, is the performance of the almost motionless roles of old women. The actor gradually progresses up the scale towards roles requiring inner rather than outer display.

The young actor's training is demanding and sometimes painful. Hōshō Kurō kept as mementos of his favorite pupils their practice-books stained with the blood from nosebleeds induced by intense rehearsals. Instruction is mainly oral, though the pupil keeps the text open before him. The teacher sits before a little desk, his pupil facing him at his own desk on which the text rests. The teacher pronounces a line and the pupil, guided more by his teacher's voice than by the notations on the text before him, repeats the line again and again until the teacher is satisfied. The method of instruction in Kyōgen is entirely oral, practice texts not being available. The teacher explains neither the meaning of the words nor the mood they are intended to convey, but insists instead on exact, unquestioning conformity to his own delivery. The pupil parrots the teacher, never attempting to "get inside" the sense of the exceedingly involved poetry. The teacher aids the pupil's recitation by beating time with a small leather baton, but he never suggests that, say, the pupil "give more feeling" to his delivery. When the pupil comes to perform the dances and other movements of the roles, he is shown precisely the number of steps to take at a given moment or the prescribed manner of opening a fan, but not how he is to preserve the flow of movement necessary to a graceful performance. The pupil imitates exactly, avoiding any suspicion of making a fresh attempt to penetrate a role. Only once he has proved that he has mastered the routine techniques will he be initiated into the secret traditions, and only long afterwards will he perhaps interpret the roles slightly differently from his predecessors.

The insistence on imitation and the absence of systematic instruction in performing the texts have resulted in even mature actors at times being ignorant of precisely what they are singing or representing. In extreme cases, as we know from the biographies of distinguished actors, a veteran performer may be unacquainted with the plot of a play in which he has appeared countless times, never having deciphered the language. The Nō actors seem to embody in their voices and gestures the profound beauties of the texts, but their understanding of the parts may be physical rather than mental, and they may lack the intellectual capacity to appreciate why audiences should wish to spend their time and money to attend Nō. Iwakura Tomomi once dismissed with aristocratic disdain all Nō actors except Hōshō Kurō as "monkeys" in the tradition of *sarugaku* ("monkey music"), but even Hōshō Kurō, whose whole life was consecrated to preserving the true traditions of Nō, once expressed amazement that anyone should prefer watching a Nō play to a wrestling match. The lack of intellectual involvement, far from lowering the level of performances, has accounted for the faithful preservation of tradition. The danger today is that young actors, far better educated than their predecessors, will be distracted from a unique concern with Nō into dabbling with other dramatic styles, or may attempt to modernize and rationalize an art which has thus far withstood the assaults of change.

Some changes, however, may become necessary. Sitting in Japanese style on the wooden boards of the stage, surely never comfortable for anyone, has become agonizingly painful for the younger members of the chorus, whose daily lives (unlike those of actors of the past) are spent mainly in rooms with chairs. When at a New Year performance *Okina* is followed by *Takasago*, the chorus and the drum *(taiko)* player must remain in a kneeling position for three hours, a feat of endurance increasingly distasteful to the younger generation. Again, the arbitrary division of the roles into *shite* and *waki*, the latter even following texts of the plays which differ in details from those performed by the *shite*, has been preserved by family traditions for centuries, but ambitious young actors now seem disinclined to become *waki* and play a perpetual second fiddle to the *shite*. Eventually it may be necessary to open all roles to talented actors, and to provide some more comfortable way of sitting for the chorus.

Even more serious than changes dictated by the physical comfort or vanity of the performers are the objections, usually unspoken, against the organization of each school around an *iemoto*, or head. The *iemoto* system, established during the Tokugawa period, was favored by the government, which found it convenient and philosophically desirable to deal with the actors (like other members of the society) in a hierarchical manner, issuing its commands to the head of a school who, like the head of a family, was responsible for the transmission and execution of the order. The system is by no means absolute today, but the head of the school still possesses privileges and obligations that strike the younger generation as being "feudalistic." The head of the Kanze school, for example, is entrusted with the scrolls which explain secret traditions of performing each part. When an actor is qualified to have the secrets imparted to him, the head of the school, with the utmost display of decorum, opens the scroll and reveals only so much of it as is necessary for the particular part. The head of each school normally represents it at cultural festivals sponsored by the government, even if he happens not to be the most distinguished performer of the school, inevitably giving it a bad name among outsiders. The head of the school sometimes also disciplines actors, as a father might discipline a wayward child; two Kyōgen actors who appeared in a Kabuki play were temporarily forbidden to perform in Kyōgen because they had "abandoned their profession." It is hard to imagine an opera director refusing to permit a singer to appear on his stage because the singer had ventured for a few weeks into the domain of musical comedy, but the *iemoto* of Nō and Kyōgen is a father who worries about his children's marriage, drinking habits or lapses from the true path of the art. Needless to say, disciplinary action by the *iemoto*, however benevolently intended, is now often resented.

If the head of a school happens to be its outstanding performer, as for many years Kita Roppeita was not only the finest actor of the Kita school but of the entire world of Nō, the *iemoto* system will not weigh excessively on the actors, who will feel grateful for the prestige the *iemoto* lends to his disciples. Even at its worst, the *iemoto* system has tended to prevent economic hardships among the actors by providing each man with opportunities to perform and a fair share of pupils. The maintenance of the artistic integrity of a school would certainly be infinitely more difficult if no central authority exercised vigilance against departures from orthodoxy and offered the only criticisms which an actor genuinely respected. The five schools—Kanze, Hōshō, Komparu, Kongō and Kita—provide a welcome variety of performance, but the fortunes of the smaller schools are governed by the strength of the *iemoto*'s determination to maintain the traditions. The two largest schools, Kanze and Hōshō, play so dominant a role that the other schools sometimes have difficulty in assembling a competent chorus.

THE SCHOOLS OF NŌ

The five schools have preserved their traditions with a pride commensurate with their long histories. Actors have been known to declare that they never witness Nō presented by another school, either because they fear they may corrupt the purity of their interpretations, or simply because they are totally uninterested in divergent interpretations. The connoisseur of Nō has no trouble in distinguishing among the schools, as a Western music critic will easily identify the mellowness of Central European strings, the clarity of French woodwinds, or the overall brilliance of an American ensemble. To anyone less than an expert, however, *Matsukaze*, regardless of the school, like a Schubert symphony regardless of the nationality of the orchestra performing it, is more likely to leave an impression because of its intrinsic beauty or because of the skill of the performers, rather than by the fidelity it displays to a particular tradition. But the parallel between schools of Nō and European orchestras is far from exact; the variations in the tonal quality of orchestras are apt to be unintentional or even accidental, but the differences among the schools of Nō are so jealously preserved that, the story goes, families will refuse to give their daughters in marriage to men who have studied—even as amateurs—the wrong school of Nō!

The first difference marking the schools is the texts. Textual variants can be found for each play, especially in the prose parts. In extreme cases whole scenes are dissimilar. In presentations of the *shimogakari* (Komparu, Kongō and Kita) schools, *Dōjōji* opens with dialogue accompanying the hanging of the great temple bell, but this scene is omitted from the Kanze and Hōshō presentations. The title of the play may differ according to the school: thus, the work called *Kurozuka* by four of the five schools is called *Adachigahara* by the Kanze school. In some instances, though the title is pronounced identically irrespective of school, the characters used for the sounds differ. *Yuya* is written with characters meaning literally "bear field" by most schools, but the Kita school uses characters meaning "hot water valley."

The repertories also vary from school to school, Kanze boasting the most plays, Komparu the fewest. In 1878 Hōshō Kurō removed thirty plays at a stroke from the repertory of the Hōshō school, some because he considered them inferior, others because their special demands made it impossible for the *iemoto* to guarantee they could always be performed. (*Futari Shizuka*, for example, requires two actors whose build and style of acting will permit them to appear as doubles.) The different schools formerly clung to certain plays as their special possessions, and if another school wished to acquire one of them for its repertory an exchange would be made. This system has now broken down; a work like *Motomezuka*, formerly performed. only by the Hōshō and Kita schools, has been borrowed freely for their repertories by the other schools.

Variations in the text are emphasized by special acting traditions called *kogaki* ("small writing"). The *kogaki* employed in the performance of a play is written in small print after the title in the programs, indicating some departure from standard practice. The *kogaki* were probably devised originally so as to prevent spectators from becoming bored by overly familiar representations of the plays; so well were they acquainted with each work that even a slight shift of emphasis could surprise and excite. Sometimes the variation provided by a *kogaki* consists merely of the *shite* wearing a white instead of a red wig for the part of a demon. This seemingly inconsequential difference is elevated to the importance of a major aspect of the performance. An actor deemed insufficiently senior to wear a white wig would be severely criticized. The *kogaki* are learned by the actor only at the appropriate stage of his career and on payment of the regulation fee. Their importance stems from the conviction that altering any element in a play involves a changed conception of the entire performance. For example, *Takasago* is generally performed without any stage prop, but some *kogaki* require a pine tree. In this case, the *shite*, coming to the line, "I shall rake the dust under the tree," must perform the gesture of raking fallen pine needles. The *kogaki* of some schools prescribe a rake rather than a broom for the *shite* in keeping with this change.

Such variations in performance are less important than the stylistic differences among the schools, apparent to the connoisseur. The Komparu school is considered to preserve the old style of performance most faithfully; one authority characterized its singing as "melodic in an old-fashioned way with a placid delivery." In contrast, the Kanze singing has been called "delicately melodic with a nuanced delivery," and the Kita singing "martial in its delivery." The Kongō school is noted for its vigorous, sometimes acrobatic, dancing, in contrast to the extreme restraint of the Hōshō school. The wealth of a school may accentuate its style of performance: the Hōshō school can costume ten *tengu* (demons) for a performance of *Kurama Tengu*, but the Komparu and Kita schools would be hard-pressed to costume more than two or three *tengu*. A school may also follow a particular interpretation of the unspoken implications of a play. In *Yuya*, for example, the mistress of Munemori begs permission to return home, where her aged mother is supposedly dying. Munemori at first refuses, insisting that she accompany him when he visits the cherry blossoms at Kiyomizu, but eventually he relents. She joyfully takes leave, hurrying off to her mother's sickbed. In one school, however, the actor playing the girl is supposed to suggest by almost imperceptible variations in accent that she is less concerned about her mother's health than about rejoining a boyfriend at home. The text does not readily support this interpretation, but its novelty may appeal to spectators looking for something new to admire in a work they know only too well.

Differences of school in Kyōgen are easily apparent even to the casual spectator. Not only do the texts differ markedly, as noted, but the intonation of the lines is totally dissimilar, that of the Izumi school resembling modern Japanese more closely than that of the Ōkura school. Differences in the repertory are also considerable.

THE MASKS

Masks are the lifeblood of a performance of Nō. A great actor may move us even if the mask he wears is inferior, but a beautiful mask can make his performance immortal. Some masks have been registered as national treasures and are displayed in museums, but as the late Kongō Iwao wrote, "The true value of a mask is revealed only when worn by a performer on the stage. There a superior mask can become a part of the actor's body by dint of his superior artistry; it is alive and his blood courses through it. The true beauty of a mask may be sensed at just such moments, and it is just such masks that teach us the spirit of Nō."

It is not easy for an actor to make the audience believe that the mask he wears is part of his flesh. His success is the culmination of efforts begun as a boy of twelve or thirteen. This was the age when, prior to the Meiji Restoration, he would undergo the "coming of age" (*gembuku*) ceremony, and it is still the age when a mask is fitted to the boy's face for the first time, generally the sacred mask of the old man in *Okina*. This is his initiation at once into the world of adults and of Nō. The young man is permitted afterwards to perform with any mask, excepting only those of the middle-aged woman or the old person. At first he is likely to perform roles in which he previously appeared without a mask, like the youthful god in *Makura Jidō*. He is trained to keep the mask steady, avoiding jerky movements or abrupt (and therefore ugly) raising and lowering of the head. By fifteen or so he is ready to put on a young woman's mask, not as a *shite* but as a *tsure*. The *tsure* roles are generally not especially difficult, but it is no small task to wear the mask in a manner evocative of feminine beauty. The apertures in the eyes of the mask are merely holes which permit the actor at best a glimpse of the customers in the balcony. If he wishes to discover where on the stage he stands he has only the nostril-openings in the mask to look through. The young actor has all he can do to keep from bumping into the others onstage even without attempting to suggest by his use of the mask feminine loveliness.

By twenty the actor, having overcome the initial difficulties of wearing a mask, will take the part of a *shite*, appearing as a young woman and wearing a *ko-omote* mask. At the same time he may appear as a young warrior in such plays as *Tsunemasa* or *Kiyotsune*, wearing the *chūjō* mask. Next he moves on to roles requiring the *heita* mask—the powerful, mature warriors of such plays as *Tamura* or *Yashima*. In his thirties he will study female *shite* roles of the fourth category, wearing the *shakumi* mask in *Fujito* or *Sakuragawa*. He may then progress to the roles of gods and demons, wearing the appropriate masks, to the great female *shite* roles of the third category, and finally, when past sixty, to the parts of old women, wearing the *yase-onna* mask in such works as *Sotoba Komachi*.

The progression from one category of role to the next implies increasing difficulty in interpreting the roles but also increasing beauty in the masks used. It might seem more logical for a young man to appear as the beautiful Matsukaze rather than a man in his fifties—probably in Zeami's day a young actor in fact took the part—but it is assumed today that an actor could not evoke the full poetry of the role unless he had spent many years on the stage. He could not, for that matter, employ the mask to the full effect, adumbrating the shades of emotion by causing shadows or glints to fall on his mask. He would also be unworthy of wearing a mask of the highest dignity (*kurai*). Not only do the masks differ in dignity according to their category (whether for a young general, a young woman or a devil), but also according to the quality of a particular mask within the same category. Sometimes this is a matter of artistic excellence: many masks, particularly of the Muromachi period, rank as masterpieces of carving, and to perform with such a mask is not only an honor but a responsibility. The story is told of Hōshō Kurō's visit to Kyoto with his disciple Matsumoto Nagashi. The young man was to appear in *Tenko*, and Kurō asked the head of the Kongō school if he might borrow a *koujijō* mask for the occasion. The mask offered him was so magnificent that Kurō refused it, saying that young Matsumoto was not yet sufficiently accomplished to merit such an honor.

Even among masks of approximately equal artistic value a difference in "dignity" may arise because one is almost imperceptibly older, severer in expression or more dreamlike than another. The different schools are known for their preferences in these matters: the Komparu actors prefer *ko-omote* masks of a childlike innocence, the Kongō actors a slightly more sensual face, and at the other extreme, we find the almost voluptuous expression on the *ko-omote* masks used by the Kanze school. When Hōshō Kurō appeared twice within a short time in *Sumidagawa*, an admirer remarked that one interpretation had seemed quite astringent, the other almost youthful. Kurō, pleased to find such acuteness of appreciation, took out the two *shakumi* masks he had worn, one aged, the other youthful. The different interpretations of the role had grown from a week or more studying each mask. The slightly different "dignity" had inspired different performances. That is why an actor desires several masks of the same category. As Kongō Iwao put it, if an actor has only one *magojirō* he can express only one level of dignity *(kurai)* in the role, but if he has five *magojirō* masks he can perform five different interpretations of *Matsukaze*. The *kurai* of the mask also determines the costumes used, and it is said that unless the musicians and the members of the chorus know the *kurai* of the *shite*'s mask they cannot perform.

The actor's greatest problem in the use of the mask is giving it expression. The female masks especially are virtually blanks as far as the expression goes. Scholars have argued over whether this "intermediate expression" was intended to represent feminine beauty at its most evocative, or to be a straightforward depiction of a lovely face in a moment of repose, or a symbolic representation of the essential nature of a woman's character; but the researches of Gotō Hajime indicate that the neutral expression of the female masks much antedates the age of Zeami, when the ideal of *yūgen* might have inspired symbolic delineation of the features. No doubt the "intermediate expression" was adopted for masks in order that the actor might suggest without changing his mask the joy or grief of the character. Certainly the female masks are so used today. A lowering of the mask *(kumorasu)* casts shadows suggestive of grief, a raising of the mask *(terasu)* lightens it, giving an expression of happiness. Needless to say, the use of the mask is far more subtle than a mere raising and lowering. In *Nonomiya*, for example, at the lines "Whom should I pine for now? The voices of pine-crickets trill *rin, rin . . . ,*" the actor, who must not resort to any obvious gesture of listening, lowers his gaze to the chirping insects, then gently moves his head laterally in the gesture known as "seeing a voice." The effective use of any mask is difficult, but in comparison to the delicacy required in *Matsukaze* or *Nonomiya*, the warrior plays are relatively uncomplicated in expression, the masks less demanding. The ascending order of the roles is also an ascending order of difficulty in using the masks, culminating in the great plays *Sotoba Komachi* and *Sekidera Komachi*, in which the actor must convince us by the way he uses his mask that beneath the skin of the aged crone there is still a beautiful woman.

Some roles, especially in the *genzaimono*, are performed without mask. In these cases it is hardly an exaggeration to say that the actor's face becomes a mask, that there is hardly more individuality in the face of a great actor performing without mask as Benkei in *Ataka* than in a warrior mask. The Kyōgen actor appearing as Sambasō in *Okina* who repeats again and again the meaningless, incantatory syllables *yo hon ho*, by the end of the performance becomes as impersonal an embodiment of good fortune as the masked old man Okina himself. In the parts performed without mask the *kurai* comes from the innate personality of the actor. The effect is the opposite of the masked roles where the actor endeavors to infuse a carved piece of wood with expression; here the actor must drain the expression from his face into his voice and body. In either case the effect achieved is a stylized and evocative beauty remote from the representational effects of actors on other stages.

Though the roles without masks may be as demanding as those performed with masks, the mask is the symbol of the Nō actor, and the moment when he puts on a mask before a performance marks the transition from his daily existence to the special realm of his art. Before the actor places the mask on his face he stares at it intently, holding it at the two small holes of the ears, the only part of the polished surface which should be touched. The actor's face is padded with wadded cotton wrapped in soft paper so that the mask will fit snugly and securely. The mask is attached to his head by ribbons passed through the ear-holes. The color of these ribbons varies with the mask: white for *okina*, red for *kokushiki*, purple for a woman's mask worn by a *shite*, dark blue for a woman's mask worn by a *tsure*, and so on. The ribbons from the left and right ears must be attached with equal tautness if the actor is to see at all. Originally, it seems, the ribbons holding the mask to the face were concealed by the wider bands attached to the wig, but today the wig is fastened below, leaving the mask ribbons exposed.

The masks are made of *hinoki* (Japanese cypress), a wood easily worked yet durable. The bark side of the wood is fashioned into the inside of the mask; in this way any resin which might seep to the surface will not harm the mask. Ideally, the *hinoki* wood for the masks should come from trees felled in the Valley of Kiso, floated down the Kiso River to Tokyo, and kept there for five or six years in mingled fresh and sea water before being cut into the blocks used by the mask-carver. Wood of this quality is scarce today, but the best available is always used, for the Nō mask is a work of art.

Most masks are about eight and a half inches in length, the width varying somewhat according to the variety. They are too small to cover the actor's entire face, but generally leave a disillusioning sallow or reddish fringe of jowls around the lovely contours of the painted wood. The smallness of the mask may have originated in an aesthetic ideal of a small head on a large body, though Japanese more often have large heads on small bodies. Audiences in the past, seated at a distance from the badly lighted stage, were undoubtedly far less aware of the actor's jowls than we are today from our seats a few feet from a stage brightly lit with fluorescent lamps.

Aesthetic ideals apparently also gave rise to the extraordinarily high foreheads of the masks of young women. The proportions of the forehead are accentuated by the shaved eyebrows and the false eyebrows painted almost at the hairline. The Muromachi fashion for a high forehead and shaved eyebrows, curiously coincidental with the similar fashion in Europe of the time, is perpetuated in the masks, along with the severe part of the hair in the middle. New masks have been devised and the prevailing tastes of later ages have found unconscious expression, but for the most part the masks, like the Nō itself, adhere to models created in the fifteenth century.

The earlier masks, as we know from examples preserved in temples and shrines, showed far greater variety. Some are startlingly realistic, the faces of men and women one might encounter today. No doubt these masks reflect the plebeian origins of Nō. Unlike *gigaku* or *bugaku*, Nō in the thirteenth and fourteenth centuries was a popular entertainment, performed at inconspicuous temples in the hills—anywhere an audience could be attracted—as well as at the great monasteries. The plays surely lacked the exalted manner of Nō in its full glory, and the countrified expressions on the masks suggest little of *yūgen*. Indeed, the masks may originally not have been intended to afford greater beauty than the commonplace face of the actors; they may have been intended instead to make the actors resemble the characters they portrayed, whether a girl, a middle-aged woman, a general or a demon. The old masks usually have a definite expression. Those for young women have smiling mouths and eyes crinkled with merriment, indications that the plays themselves were not the melancholy vehicles now associated with the name Nō. The features, it should be noted, are distinctly Japanese, unlike the *gigaku* and *bugaku* masks, which were faithful copies of prototypes from the Asian continent. The techniques of carving the early Nō masks may have been borrowed from those of the *bugaku* masks—*bugaku* was widely performed when the Nō masks were being created in the thirteenth and fourteenth centuries—but the faces are entirely dissimilar. Even the devils represent peculiarly Japanese conceptions rather than the leonine *bugaku* features. The old masks are true products of the lively theatricals performed before Nō acquired its unique dignity as a court entertainment and the categories of masks were formalized.

The masks today may roughly be divided among the three roles mentioned by Zeami—the old person, the woman, and the warrior—plus the demons. Within each category numerous variations occur. The young woman, for example, may be a girl between sixteen and twenty, as in *Yuya* (*ko-omote* mask), or between twenty and twenty-five, as in *Eguchi* (*magojirō* mask); she may be possessed by a demon like Rokujō in the first part of *Aoi no Ue* (*deigan* mask), or a divine being like the angel in *Hagoromo* (*zō no onna* mask); she may be brooding like Kiyohime in the first part of *Dōjōji* (*Ōmi onna* mask) or griefstricken like the mother in *Sumidagawa* (*shakumi* mask). Each school maintains different traditions and sometimes different names for the masks. The individual actor, moreover, is at liberty to experiment somewhat in the choice of mask for a role in the interests of a slightly altered emphasis. A few masks are used for a single role only, like that for Yorimasa, a man aged but still warlike; for Shunkan, emaciated and deeply embittered; or for Yoroboshi, a blind young man of haggard appearance. (The masks for the roles of blind persons have long, downcast slits for the eyes instead of the usual tiny apertures, paradoxically affording the best visibility to the actors!)

The most distinctive masks are those of the demons. *Beshimi* masks have mouths tightly shut in a frown, and lines in the face denoting strength cluster around the forehead and cheeks. The effect, however, is more comic than frightening, and the mask is used for *tengu*, the rather genial demons. By contrast, the small *beshimi* (*ko-beshimi*) masks, much closer to normal human features, are marked with evil unrelieved by exaggeration. Most terrifying are the different varieties of *hannya*, a horrible grinning mask with horns, the incarnation of feminine possessiveness. The name *hannya*, ironically, means "wisdom" (from the Sanskrit *prajna*), but here it probably comes from the maker, Hannyabō.

The names of sixteen celebrated mask-makers have been preserved from Muromachi times, some mentioned in Zeami's writings. Prized masks today are almost all attributed to these men, but clearly many attributions are legendary, and others refer to a workshop rather than to an individual. The profession of mask-maker was recognized only in the Tokugawa era. Until then, we may gather, masks were often made by priests or general artisans rather than by special artists. Many superlative masks are undoubtedly old copies of even older works. Such makers as Kuoji, Tokuwaka, Himi, Echi and Shakuzuru are solemnly credited with many extant masks, but probably no more can be said about these revered names than that they represent characteristic styles. Certainly the degree of sophistication in the carving of many masterpieces does not accord with the early dates—some in the Kamakura period—assigned to these men. Kongō Magojirō (1538–64), whose name was taken for the female mask typifying the Kongō school, is one of the earliest mask-makers we can date.

Three *ko-omote* masks attributed to the legendary Ishikawa Tatsuemon acquired special fame as prized possessions of Hideyoshi. The masks, known as the "snow," "moon," and "flower" *ko-omote*, were left by Hideyoshi to the head of the Komparu school, the Shogun Ieyasu, and the head of the Kongō school respectively. The "moon" mask was lost in a fire, the "flower" mask has been disfigured by clumsy restoration, but the "snow" mask, now owned by the Kongō school in Kyoto, is a particularly lovely *ko-omote*, considered by some experts to be the most perfect mask of all.

Kyōgen masks, far fewer than those for Nō, fall into four main categories: Shinto and Buddhist divinities, spirits, human beings, and animals. The deities include the god of good fortune, Bishamon (a Buddhist protective divinity), Lightning, and Dragons; the spirits include Buaku and Usobuki, two typical Kyōgen figures; the human beings include Grandpa, the Ugly Woman (Oto), and the Nun; the animals consist of the fox, the badger, the monkey, the ox, the dog and birds. Buaku, a comic villain, wears a grotesque version of the Nō mask *beshimi*: the eyes droop, the cheeks are extraordinarily broad, the teeth protrude and bite the lower lip. The *usobuki* mask has pursed and twisted lips and great goggling eyes; it is used to represent the spirit of a mosquito (in *Kazumō*) or of a cicada (in *Semi*) or of a mushroom (in *Kusabira*) or, occasionally, a pathetic-looking robber (in *Uri-nusubito*). Normally the Kyōgen actor does not resort to using a mask in order to indicate that he is playing the part of a woman, but for comically ugly women the *oto* mask is used. Oto has a bulging forehead and cheeks, a nose squashed almost flat, and a comically twisted mouth. The Nun's mask is sometimes an older version of *oto*, sometimes amusingly lachrymose in expression.

The Kyōgen masks are far from realistic, but just as the Nō masks seem to symbolize the essential traits of a role, the Kyōgen masks exaggerate and distort them. Ugliness, timidity and even ferocity become funny thanks to the masks.

The masks, whether Nō or Kyōgen, are never worn without a wig or head covering. In Kyōgen a towel or a simple hood (*zukin*) will serve as covering, but the Nō masks require a wig in one of three lengths: *katsura, tare* or *kashira. Katsura,* not generally used for male roles, are black wigs parted in the middle, covering the ears and pulled back. *Tare* are longer, falling to the shoulders; they are always worn with a *kammuri* or head ornament, which may be a hat, a crown, or another kind of headgear. Some *tare* are white rather than black, and are used for aged gods or warriors. The third variety of wig, *kashira,* hangs down in back as far as the hems of the robe or even to the floor, in front to the actor's chest. The *kashira* exists in black, white and red: black is for a wide variety of male roles, white for aged persons, red for demons. The wigs are fastened to the head by a broad, decorated cloth band, the ends of which hang down behind. Some wig bands are exquisite examples of weaving and embroidery. The colors used with a particular wig are determined by the role. An expert, if informed of the mask, wig, wig band and headgear used for the *shite's* part, should be able to name the play.

THE COSTUMES

The brilliance of the Nō costumes relieves the performances from any impression of excessive severity that might be created by the astringent bareness of the stage, the harsh cries of the musicians, and the formal gestures of the dancers. In Zeami's and Zenchiku's day the costumes were probably far less elaborate than today, and possibly even in bad taste by modern standards; we can infer this from the description of a costume worn in *Bashō* ("The Plantain Tree"), which was to be suitably ripped here and there to suggest the easily torn leaves of the plantain tree.

The oldest surviving Nō robes, dating from the reign of the Shogun Yoshimasa in the fifteenth century, may have been woven for the Shogun himself, as their sober but elegant taste indicates. One owned by the Kanze family, a jacket (*happi*) of dark green material woven with gold thread in designs of paired dragonflies, is a lovely but unassertive robe. We can imagine Yoshimasa removing his jacket and throwing it to the actors in admiration, rather in the manner of a Spaniard throwing some article of clothing into a bull ring by way of homage to a toreador. The presentation of robes by way of reward goes back at least as far as Zeami's day. By the seventeenth century it came to be a gesture of affluence on the part of daimyos towards the actors they maintained. During the Tokugawa period the robes attained a degree of elegance and luxury unparalleled in theatrical costumes elsewhere. Some were woven or embroidered in silks with breathtakingly bold patterns of plantain leaves, enormous butterflies, wisteria sprays, or ships riding the waves; others were covered with finely figured designs in geometric or floral patterns; still others had patches of contrasting, brilliant colors and designs. The robes were woven in heavy brocades or translucent gossamer silks, and the blend of the colors, whether on the surface of the robes, between one layer and the layer underneath, or between the surface and the lining, was in flawless, though sometimes daring, taste.

The Nō costumes are without exception splendid, whether the actor appears as a princess or a fishergirl, a general or a priest, but the colors and designs are modified according to the roles. The costumes for the female roles are divided between those with and without "color" (*iro*). By "color" was meant red, associated with young women and worn with the *ko-omote, waka-onna* or *magojirō* masks in such plays as *Matsukaze* or *Yuya.* Roles performed with the *shakumi* or *fukai* masks (like the mother in *Sumidagawa* or the jealous wife in *Kinuta*) are costumed in robes without "color." Color is not, of course, used in costuming old women, though there are a few exceptions: the *shite* in *Sotoba Komachi,* though a woman of a hundred years, wears a touch of red in her sash or cloak to suggest that something of the beautiful woman lingers about her. If red is used for the outer robe the color is usually echoed in the wig band, the sash and even in the fan. These hardly visible touches of color help to create a unified impression. On occasion, as when a young god is portrayed, a brilliant red sash, contrasting with the white or pastel color of his robe, produces an effect of youthful vigor.

The colors of the under-kimonos, visible at the neckline, are also important indications of the "dignity" of the role. The colors may be single, double or triple, each variation signifying a difference in character. White, red, light blue, dark blue, ultramarine, light green, russet, yellow-brown and brown are the chief colors used. White is the most dignified, green and brown the least dignified. Red stands for youth, high spirits, good fortune; light blue for a quiet temperament; dark blue or ultramarine is used for strong roles; light green is generally reserved for menials, and the browns for old people. The use of white under-kimonos in a play of the third category marks the role as of the highest "dignity"; more commonly, the neckline will show one white and one red under-kimono. In *Shōjō* two red under-kimonos are worn by the auspicious red-maned demon, and as acted by the Kongō school the demon is further graced by red *tabi* on his feet. Because red is somewhat less dignified than white it is the invariable color of youthful female *tsure*, of some male *tsure*, and of all *kokata*. The *waki* usually wears a light blue under-kimono. A combination of one white and one light blue under-kimono adds dignity to a role.

Each actor before appearing onstage chooses the costume for the part according to the emphasis he desires to give the role, the mask to be worn, and the holdings of his school. Strong traditions dictate the costumes to be worn for certain roles: the snake-lady in *Dōjōji* always wears a robe with a lozenge pattern suggesting a snakeskin. Nevertheless, the actor enjoys some leeway in his shading of most roles. When a play is revived after long absence from the Nō stage the costuming is particularly important. At the revival of the rarely-performed *Ochiba* ("Fallen Leaves") by the present Kongō Iwao, the entrance of the *shite*, wearing a *chōken* (long-sleeved jacket) of a mingled green and brown, evocative of fallen autumn leaves, created an unforgettable impression. This superb garment was a modern reweaving of a *chōken* originally presented the school by the Shogun Yoshimasa.

The articles of clothing worn, including the many varieties of headgear, reveal the function and dignity of the persons. No less than twenty-eight costumes have been distinguished for the male roles performed without mask. Twenty or so distinct types of attire for female *shite* and *tsure* exist, and there are comparable numbers for all other parts, including the Kyōgen. The Nō robes, originally derived from the costumes of the court and military nobility (and the priesthood), were later modified so noticeably that they came to constitute a distinct variety of dress seen only on the stage. A typical robe worn by men and women alike is the *mizugoromo*, a kind of cloak. The *mizugoromo* occurs in white, black, gray, violet and most pastel shades, depending on the role. Most often it is unpatterned and woven of raw silk into a thin gauzy material. When worn in a male role a sash is tied over the *mizugoromo*, but in female roles it is held together by a silken cord. Each detail of the costuming is governed by usage, down to the type of fan carried and whether or not it can be tucked into the sash of the *mizugoromo*. Details of the costumes are discussed elsewhere in connection with the accompanying photographs.

The mask and costume used by an actor in a particular role reveal almost as much about his interpretation of the part as his singing and dancing. The mask and wig give him the face of his choice, the voluminous robes, all but blotting out the outlines of his own figure, give him the shape prescribed by aesthetic ideals, and the most glorious colors ever used to adorn the human form surround him in beauty. The eyes of the spectators are dazzled by the sight of the *shite*, but the purpose of the mask and costume is not so much to attract attention and praise as it is to allow the spectator, undistracted by ugliness, to take these exquisite passages into a realm of absolute beauty.

V. MUSIC AND DANCE IN THE PLAYS

MUSIC

For the hundreds of thousands of amateurs who study the singing of the texts Nō is primarily a vocal art and the actors are above all singers. Amateurs who devote themselves to the *shimai*, the climactic dances in the plays, may disagree about the importance of song, but they recognize equally that music is essential to their dances. The scholar of literature, it is true, may read the Nō plays as if they were verse dramas, not thinking of the music he is missing, but a performance without music would be unthinkable. The stranger to Nō may nevertheless find that the music, though hypnotically impressive, lacks the variety common to most other music for the stage, a variety stemming both from alternations of mood and tempo and from the distinctive styles of different composers. The music in Nō lacks obvious contrasts of mood, and it would be almost impossible to identify the composers. Its importance also seems to be thrown in doubt by the tolerance of the poor voices of many actors. The great Hōshō Kurō went so far as to deplore the tendency, prevalent in his day, for actors to rely on the beauty of their voices to win acclaim; this, he insisted, was contrary to the emphasis on interpretation characteristic of Nō. Even at their most lyric, the songs of the *shite* rarely attain an independent existence as melody; only in the sections sung by the chorus is it easy to detect the melodic element, which sounds—to the non-musician at least—rather like the Gregorian chants. The man witnessing Nō for the first time may find the music to be the most elusive aspect.

The difficulty of Nō music comes both from its complexity and its dissimilarity to familiar Western music. The texts used by the actors are marked with dots, curved and angular lines, and letters of the Japanese syllabary, each indicating the manner in which a particular syllable is to be delivered. A rise or fall in the voice, a shift from declamation to recitative or to full voice, can be prescribed, but these markings (dating back to the sixteenth century) give only the relative pitch and length of the notes, not absolute values. A mark indicates that a sound is held twice as long as the preceding one or that it is higher in pitch, but not the note that might be played on a piano. Neither is the tempo of the successive notes stated except vaguely, in recommendations that a passage be "quietly" rendered and the like. The annotations serve as a guide or reminder to students of Nō, but they must turn to their teachers for instruction. Even then they will discover that ultimately the singing of a role, like the dance, depends on the actor's understanding of its "dignity" (*kurai*), and his ability to suggest by means of vocal techniques unknown in the West the inner natures of the characters he portrays.

The simplest parts of the play are those in prose, sometimes a third or more of the whole. These passages, which bear almost no musical notation, are declaimed in a style marked by regular cadences; in particular, the second note after each pause in a sustained utterance is delivered at a noticeably higher pitch. In some schools the pattern of declamation depends on whether the actor is representing a man, a woman or an old person; in others no distinction is made. Despite the mournful prolongation of the words the prose parts are in general intelligible to the audience. They are delivered without musical background.

It is rather misleading to speak of the "accompaniment" for the sung parts. The "name saying" (*nanori*) at the start of the play is sometimes "accompanied" by a flute, but the flute neither blends with nor opposes the singer's vocal line; its music proceeds virtually independently, decorating or heightening the passage, but not commenting on it. Even the drums "accompanying" the singer may not play at his tempo. Indeed, one feature of all Nō music is its irregularity; the range required of the singer's voice being extremely limited and the musical patterns established by long tradition, slight differences in tempo or accent assume great importance, and the mood evoked by the musician's hand against a drum or by his inarticulate cries evokes the poetry better than would an accompaniment which merely echoed or reinforced the vocal line.

Two styles of singing Nō are distinguished, *yowagin* (weak) and *tsuyogin* (strong). Different styles of singing apparently existed even in Zeami's day, but the present distinction of "weak" and "strong" dates only from the late seventeenth century. Previously, *yowagin* was used exclusively. *Yowagin* can be rendered with reasonable accuracy in Western musical notation, but *tsuyogin*, closer to declamation, hardly goes beyond two distinguishable tones. In contrast to the rich melodic patterns of some passages delivered in *yowagin*, in *tsuyogin* "accent, dynamic stress, tone color, and a special vocal technique are more important than melodic movement itself."* *Yowagin* predominates in most plays, especially in scenes of heightened emotional content, but *tsuyogin* occurs in auspicious or festive plays like *Takasago*.

The vocal music includes sections like the *issei* or *kuri* in free rhythms, and others in fixed rhythms, such as the entrance song (*shidai*) of the *waki*, the travel song (*michiyuki*), and passages of dialogue between the *shite* and chorus. There are three basic rhythmic structures: the first, a majestic, regular beat called *ō-nori*, links each beat to a single syllable; the second, the fast *chū-nori*, links one beat to two syllables; and the third, the *hira-nori*, distributes the twelve syllables of a normal line of Nō poetry (consisting of two verses of seven and five syllables respectively) among eight beats. Of these three rhythmic patterns the last, the *hira-nori*, is by far the most common. Its pattern tends to fall into two sections: the first fits a seven-syllable verse into four and one-half beats, the second fits a five-syllable verse into three and one-half beats. This is done by giving the first, fourth and seventh syllables double the duration of the others. The final beat is usually a pause, plus the beginning of the next beat. The counting of the beat therefore begins not at "one" but at "eight," taking over from the end of the previous section. Many variations exist, but adequate discussion involves technicalities beyond a layman's competence. The rhythms of Nō in any case are flexible, not metronomic; indeed, musicians avoid metronomic regularity as carefully as some Western musicians cultivate it.

Nō gives pleasure to many solely as music, but to the actors the music is the natural outgrowth of the sounds and meanings of the words and of the overall "dignity" of the play. The melodies, whether in such purely instrumental sections as the opening flute solos or in the sustained passages of choral singing, are rarely unique to a particular play, though the combinations form peculiarly appropriate patterns. There is never any improvisation in the performance—every sound, to the last cry from a drummer and the part of his drum he strikes, is noted in the score—but flexibility in the rhythm and tempo enables the actor to impart to his singing an individual interpretation of the roles.

The statements by the great actors on their preferred way of singing the roles afford some clues to their interpretations. Kanze Sakon (1895–1939) wrote about the *waki* part in *Takasago*: "The *waki*, being a minister of state, should sing forcefully and clearly, without faltering. His entrance song, this being a Nō play of the first category, should be delivered with greater forthrightness

*From the excellent article "Japanese *Noh* Music" by Tatsuo Minagawa in *Journal of the American Musicological Society*, Vol. X, No. 3, (1957).

than a normal entrance song. In general, the actor should attempt in singing the *waki* role to preserve a smoothly flowing line." Sakon went on to describe the entrance song *(shin no issei)* of the *shite* and *tsure* in the same play: "The *shite* enters, accompanied by the *tsure*, and sings the entrance song. This passage, as the first song by the *shite*, determines the *kurai* of the piece and is therefore most important. It should be sung loudly and firmly with a relaxed but solemn feeling. The actor must not impart to it sticky, heavy or listless feelings."

The manner in which the music may affect the actor's performance is indicated by remarks of Umewaka Manzaburō (1868–1946) concerning the "woman" plays: "By the time the *waki* has made his entrance the "dignity" of the play should already have been established. Of course, a clear distinction must be made between the music accompanying the *waki*'s entrance song and that found in a god play or a warrior play. This distinction is all the more essential for the entrance of the *shite*; the musicians must exercise sufficient care so that there will be plasticity in the accompaniment. Any lack of understanding on the part of the musicians will make it extremely difficult for the actor even to step out on the *hashigakari*, let alone to travel along the *hashigakari* to the stage. If the musicians let the tempo get out of hand, the *shite* will be forced to race down the *hashigakari*, for he has no choice but to move his feet ahead in step with the *ya ha* of the accompaniment."

Specific recommendations on the manner of singing Nō are apt to be unintelligible to the layman, and even the devoted student of Nō can hardly be guided much by the constant injunctions to maintain grace and dignity. The present head of the Kanze school, Kanze Motomasa, suggests the great emphasis given today to the psychological analysis of a play like *Kagekiyo*: "Even if I were to attempt to treat each problem involved, I could not hope to explain everything. The student has no choice but to follow his teacher's instructions. He should practice the opening passage again and again until satisfied." Motomasa added, "If a student has been able to analyze exhaustively the character of Kagekiyo, he has already succeeded eighty percent with the opening song. Of course, the musical line here is one of unusual difficulty even within the entire repertory, and any belief that analysis of the character alone suffices would lead to serious mistakes. But if the student combines with an adequate command of the melodic line a complete understanding of the role, then practices beyond all normal demands, he will probably pass as a fair singer of *Kagekiyo*."

The delivery of the Nō actor cannot be judged by the standards of Western singing, for no attempt is made to delight by the beauty of sound alone. The different voices—tenor, baritone or bass—are not distinguished intentionally, and certainly there is no exploitation of the extremes of the voice, whether the ringing high notes of the tenor or the growling depths of the basso. A hoarse, quavering or thin voice is not considered a flaw in an older actor, and a younger actor will also be forgiven an inadequate voice if he manages somehow to convey the inner meaning of the texts. The Hōshō school insists that singers produce a "lower voice" together with their normal tones, a complexity in vocal production intended, no doubt, to parallel the complexities of meaning in the text, which easily results in a strong vibrato. The voice, regardless of school, is produced in the back of the throat, altering the quality of the vowels and contributing to the obscurity of the words. A novice taking his first lesson from a teacher of the Komparu school is likely to be informed that it is a feature of the singing of this school to open the mouth wide but never show the teeth; what this does to the diction can be imagined. The peculiarities of the delivery certainly interfere with intelligibility, but the spectators (who either know the texts by heart or consult printed versions) expect the actors to interpret the words rather than enunciate them. The voice itself becomes a special kind of musical instrument, no less than the drums and flute.

Of the instruments used in the Nō ensemble the flute is closest to its Western equivalent. It is some fifteen inches long, made of bamboo, and has seven apertures in addition to the mouth-hole. The flute is the only instrument capable of sustaining a melody, but the thin, sometimes shrill notes are apt to produce an effect of disembodied sound rather than the sweetness associated with the Western flute; the two are as dissimilar as the mad women in Nō and the unhappy heroine of *Lucia di Lammermoor*, who goes mad to a flute accompaniment.

The *kotsuzumi* and *ōtsuzumi* are unlike any Western instrument. Each is shaped like a diabolo, the *kotsuzumi* being covered with coltskin, the *ōtsuzumi* with ox or horsehide. The drums, made of lacquered cherry wood, are kept in tune by six hempen cords fasted to holes in the metal rims at the two ends. The *kotsuzumi* is about eight and a half inches long, the *ōtsuzumi* nine and a half inches; but it is less the difference in size than the difference in the skins drawn over the drum-frames that makes the two drums sound so dissimilar. The *ōtsuzumi* produces a loud and resonant crack, the *kotsuzumi* a more delicate thump. The *kotsuzumi* is grasped by the cords with the fingers and palm of the left hand and held on the right shoulder, where the drummer strikes it with the fingers of his right hand. The quality of the sound depends on the tension of the cords and the place on the skin struck, whether the center or the edges. The *ōtsuzumi* is grasped in the left hand by the cords and placed on the left knee, where the drummer strikes it with the fingers of his right hand. The index, middle finger and palm of the hand are protected by leather coverings against the smart from the taut skin. Unlike the *kotsuzumi*, the *ōtsuzumi* cannot be tuned in performance; this means that the only differences in sound possible are loud and soft, but the expert can recognize whether or not a new drumskin has been used for each performance, as tradition prescribes (but as economic realities rarely permit).

The *taiko*, a large drum, is used in perhaps a third of the plays. It is beaten, like a Western drum, with sticks held in both hands. The *taiko* rests on a low stand placed on the stage, and the drummer, less fortunate than the *kotsuzumi* or *ōtsuzumi* player who sits on a folding stool, must kneel on the stage, sometimes striking the drum from high above his shoulder, sometimes bending to cut off reverberations. The *taiko* is about eight and a half inches in diameter, but the only place struck is a round patch of deerskin about two inches wide pasted at the center.

The sounds of the instruments are accompanied by cries from the players. In general, a player utters a cry *(kakegoe)* before the half-beat. The variety of the cry and the strength of his beat give character to the sound. There are four basic varieties of cries: *ya*, delivered before the first and fifth beats, indicating that it divides the eight beats of a measure in two; *ha*, delivered before the second, third, sixth and seventh (and sometimes the eighth) beats; *iya* and *yoi*, delivered with odd-numbered beats, to demarcate the rhythmic patterns or serve as signals to points of tension.

The music for Kyōgen is far simpler. Most lines are delivered to a rhythmical, though not specifically musical, intonation. The standard opening line of a Kyōgen, "I am a person who lives in this vicinity," is delivered by actors of the Ōkura school as:

kore wa/ kono atari ni/ sumai/ itasu mono de/ gozaru.

This passage is in prose, but as the contemporary Kyōgen actor Shigeyama Sennojō explains, a rhythmical quality is imparted by giving each group of syllables, whether three or six, about the same length of time and a single accent, without ever slurring the pronunciation of unaccented syllables. Most important to the effect is the ringing Kyōgen voice, which Sennojō's great-grandfather Sengorō Masatora (1810–1886) once compared in vigor and clarity to the sensation of slicing vertically through a piece of green bamboo.

Occasional songs, called *kouta*, are interpolated in the plays. These popular songs of the Muromachi period are far lighter both in content and delivery than the music for Nō; they are, moreover, always identified as songs by the characters and not utterances which are sung. Usually, too, the *kouta* are not accompanied, but in some plays, especially those of a festive nature, drums accompany the dance of a god. In other plays Nō is parodied by having the foolish hero make his entrance to the conventional accompaniment of a flute and drums only to intone such unpoetical lines as, "I am glad to be returning home and I am eager to see my wife and children again." But musical accompaniments of whatever variety are exceptions: the Kyōgen plays are prose, spoken dramas with only occasional outbursts of song.

DANCE

Dance is no less close to the heart of Nō than music. By "dance," however, one should not imagine anything resembling even the stateliest of Western ballets. Some movements called "dance" in Nō seem hardly more than a solemn circling of the stage; others are so slow and so devoid of choreographic ornamentation that it is hard to tell when the dance begins or ends. With the exception of a handful of special dances, like the *rambyōshi* ("wild rhythm") of *Dōjōji*, the dances consist of familiar elements, repeated from play to play, on the surface little related to the actions or the characters. Instruction in performing the *shimai*, regularly published in the magazines directed at students of Nō, is likely to consist of a few diagrams depicting simple triangular or semi-circular patterns of movement and statements such as: "Stand when the chorus sings *the lightning flashing in the trees;* stamp the left foot at the syllable *re* at the end of the phrase *hi ka to koso mire;* at the words *truly the world is like a lightning flash glittering on the morning dew* take four steps forward, beginning with the left foot," and so on. The exact moment to open the fan or to sing a phrase, taking over from the chorus, is clearly stated, but if the dance were no more complex than these injunctions imply, it could not rank as an important part of Nō.

Our experience is quite otherwise. The dances in Nō dominate remembrances of the plays to such a degree that some critics have insisted that the plays themselves are little more than preparations or justifications for the dances. These dances never startle by their pyrotechnics; they are so rarely athletic that, like the singing, they are best performed by aged actors even in the roles of young women or warriors in their prime. An unearthly beauty pervades the dances. Oswald Sickert, writing in 1916 his impressions of the final dance in *Hagoromo*, declared, "The divine lady returned on her steps at great length and fully six times after I thought I could not bear it another moment. She went on for twenty minutes, perhaps, or an hour or a night; I lost count of time; but I shall not recover from the longing she left when at last she floated backwards and under the fatal uplifted curtain."

The movements of the dance are unassertive but they express and epitomize the texts, not by crude miming (though in a few realistic plays the actor's gestures may suggest actions described by the chorus), but by evoking the ultimate meaning, the "dignity" of the work. Kita Roppeita's performance as the angel in *Hagoromo*, even when he was a man in his sixties, enchanted audiences by an atmosphere of remarkable charm. Even at eighty his performance as the *shite*, a white heron, in *Sagi* was filled with a haunting, other-worldly beauty, though he appeared without a mask. By tradition this role is danced only by a boy under twelve or a man over sixty, someone untouched by worldly passions, and as Roppeita danced he communicated a magic power surely partaking of *yūgen*, a quality that could exist only in Nō.

The higher the "dignity" of a play, the fewer and simpler tne movements of the dances; unable to distract by mere virtuosity, the actor must transmute each gesture into symbolic utterance. Some roles, it is true, require great agility. The Kongō school in particular maintains a tradition of acrobatic display in a few plays. But though people still reminisce admiringly about the late Kongō Iwao turning somersaults as the demon in *Tsuchigumo*, even when in his fifties, the Kongō school itself prizes this skill less than the ability to execute with authority the unassertive movements of a *Matsukaze*. The audiences too attend Nō not for brilliance of footwork but for absolute assurance in every gesture of the head, arms, body and legs, an inevitability that expresses the nature of a role better than the most literal display.

We are often told about the glories of the actors of former days, which are contrasted unfavorably with contemporary performances. Normally it is impossible to prove or disprove these assertions, but the film of *Aoi no Ue* made in 1936 by Sakurama Kintarō (1889–1957) reveals an almost unbelievably accomplished performer whose every motion glows with controlled fire. In his later years Kintarō once advised amateurs how they should go about learning the *shimai*: "You should stand erect, your head perfectly straight, pulling your chin back as far as possible. If you pull back your chin your whole body—not only the line of your neck—will naturally be straight. The shoulders should be relaxed, but the arms kept at the sides and held in a gentle arc so that the elbows will not sag. This is worth noticing; most people, when told to stand erect, at once throw back their shoulders and their body freezes. You should let your strength flow into your abdomen without making any conscious effort to do so. As long as you maintain a steady posture your strength will naturally flow there . . . The small of the back, like the chin, should be pulled back somewhat, but you must avoid protruding the buttocks. The exact posture to be held can only be demonstrated on the stage.

"The first thing the actor must remember while onstage is to walk on his heels. Ordinarily one begins a step with the toes, but in Nō the actor puts his strength into his heels and walks from the heels. If he puts his strength into his heels his toes will naturally curve upwards somewhat. If he were deliberately to attempt to curve the toes it would look unnatural, but if he concentrates on his heels the toes seem to curve upwards of themselves. It is ugly if the actor permits his knees to bend excessively when walking.

"Movements of the eyes are also important. There is nothing less attractive than an actor with unsteady eyes. It sometimes happens that a single glance reveals the emotions of a character."

Dance in Nō has been defined as any action made by the actors on the stage, for not one motion is unpremeditated. In a narrower sense, dance can be defined as movements by the actor to the accompaniment of a flute at a time that the chorus is not singing. Dancelike movements executed while the chorus is singing and which may or may not be related to the words of the song are known as *kata*, or forms. These highly stylized gestures are best considered in terms of photographs. They provide much of the element of *monomane* ("imitation of things") in a performance, though far removed from literal representation. The *kata* provide intermittent clues to the texts, but the dances of Nō, usually abstract patterns, are almost synonymous with the art itself.

The varieties within each of the five categories of Nō dramas are distinguished as much by the dances as by the subject matter; indeed, the dances and subject matter are inseparable and affect the entire structure of each play. Two main divisions are made: *mai* and *hataraki*. *Mai* are recognizable as dance by their length, solemn atmosphere and complexity of movements, but *hataraki* may be so simple as hardly to seem dances. Often the *hataraki* consist of vigorous, even wild, steps, and are used especially for fierce gods or demons. The *hataraki*, unlike the *mai*, are generally not performed to the same rhythm as the accompanying flute. The *mai* contain no elements of representation, but the *hataraki* may embody *kata* which refer to the texts.

Seven varieties of dance can be found in plays of the first category, the god plays, alone: *kamimai* ("god dances"), *hataraki*, *gaku* (dances derived from *bugaku*), *shinnojonomai* (especially slow and stately dances), *chūnomai* (dances performed by female deities), plus *kagura* and *shishimai* ("lion dance") used in one play each. A play with a *kamimai*, for example, contains such features as: (1) two scenes, the first consisting of the *jo* and *ha* sections of the play, the second of the *kyū*; (2) a dance occurring in the second scene; (3) the *shite* in the first scene appears as an old man of lowly occupation, normally accompanied by another man who does not wear a mask; (4) the *shite* in the second scene appears as a youthful god and performs a vigorous dance to express his appreciation of the worshipers' sincerity, a token of his desire for the protection of the imperial family and the nation; (5) the *waki* as a rule is a courtier, accompanied by two to four attendants.

Obviously the nature of the dance grows out of the plot, which in turn must be made to fit smoothly into the pattern of expression provided by the dance. If the story tells of an aged god rather than a youthful one, the dance performed in the second scene must be a *shinnojonomai*. In this case the *waki* will be a Shinto priest rather than a courtier. Again, if there are two dancers a *hataraki* will be used; the *shite* of the first part, whether a man or a woman, will wear a mask of less exalted "dignity" than for a *kaminomai* or *shinnojonomai* role; and the costume will be plebeian. A mixture of the elements proper to different dances does not occur.

The typical dance in the warrior plays is called *kakeri*, a relatively short and simple dance usually performed by the *shite* as he enacts his confession of the sins of violence which have brought him torture.

Plays of the third category are almost all about women, though in two the *shite* is the poet and great lover Narihira. The dances are slow and elegant; more than half are *jonomai*, a dance of the slowest tempo. In these plays the *shite* of the first scene is a village woman of humble birth, but normally the same mask is retained for the second scene where she appears as a noblewoman. The *waki* is an itinerant priest. In some works a *taiko* is added to the accompaniment. This creates a somewhat livelier atmosphere, and the "dignity" is therefore lower than that of plays without the *taiko*. Another group of third category plays is of a more realistic nature and in one scene, like *Yuya*. Here the dance is a *chūnomai* of a faster tempo.

The fourth category contains the greatest variety of plays and dances, including those like *Hanjo* with a graceful *chūnomai* for the *shite*, a woman; or like *Semimaru* with an agitated *kakeri*; or like *Sotoba Komachi* with a brief *iroe*, a gliding about the stage rather than a dance; or like *Kanawa* with a fierce *inori* ("prayer") dance by which a demon is subdued; or like *Shunkan* with no dance at all. These plays rely less on the beauty of the dance (which may be the core of a work like *Matsukaze* or *Hagoromo*) than on what it contributes to the dramatic tension. It might be said of certain plays of the first or third categories especially that they are excuses for dances, but in plays of this category if the action does not require a dance, none is performed.

Plays of the fifth category, belonging to the fastest section of the program, almost all have *hataraki* rather than *mai*, regardless of the plot. A typical work concludes with the furious prancing of a demon, but in the special case of *Funa Benkei*, the *shite* of the first part is given a *chūnomai*, performed in the semblance of Shizuka, the beautiful sweetheart of Yoshitsune, as well as a *hataraki* in the second part, performed as the fierce ghost of Tomomori.

In addition to the *mai* and *hataraki* mentioned above, which figure in almost every Nō play, a few dances are performed in one work only, including the three different dances of *Okina* and the *rambyōshi* in *Dōjōji*.

The effortless lines described by a master actor's body as he moves in a dance are the despair of the amateur. Though the movements are simple in themselves, they approach a perfection that can be sensed though not measured in terms of the height of a leap, the number of entrechats, or the other obvious exhibitions of virtuosity in Western ballet. The depth of communication—the ability of the actor to express with his whole body the torment, serene joy or bittersweet longing felt by a character—is the only touchstone of his powers. Every passage in the text is given overtones by the actor's movements, though none may directly represent the words. Criticism of the dances by experts in Nō sometimes suggests to the amateur the emperor's new clothes, a beauty more in the eye of the beholder than in the performance, but repeated experiences in this theatre breed a virtuoso audience no less than virtuoso actors. The Nō actors, with the barest economy of means, achieve in song and dance a grandeur of expression fully intelligible only to spectators who have made comparable efforts to understand this endlessly rewarding art.

VI. THE NŌ STAGE AND ITS PROPERTIES

THE STAGE

The interior of a Nō theatre is unlike any other in the world. It is dominated by the large, gleaming stage projecting into the auditorium, a stage which by its size and majesty seems to assert that even without actors it would have sufficient reason to exist. Its ornate curved roof confirms this impression of independence: the stage, as we have seen, was formerly a separate building, and at the very beginning of its history may have served as the scene of ritual observances before the gods. Today, when the theatre building housing the Nō stage may be fashionably modern, and the audience attired mainly in business suits and Paris-inspired dresses, the stage still imposes its authority, hushing the voices of those entering its presence, even before the performance begins. The absence of a curtain, the unvarying lighting before and during a performance, the great pine painted on the back wall, all suggest less a Western stage—shabby and bare until it takes on life from a play—than a church, itself an architectural masterpiece but ready for the drama of the mass.

Each event that takes place in a performance emphasizes the presence of the stage. In a Western theatre, whether an ornate opera house or an intimate theatre-in-the-round, the stage itself is no more than the platform on which the actors perform. It may be chalk-marked to show the actors where to stand, or grimy with the residue of a thousand nights, or pockmarked with holes. Nothing in the world is so forlorn as a Broadway theatre after a performance, the abandoned set lit by a single, naked lamp. The Nō stage, by contrast, is a superbly finished object of art whose surface is polished rather than scuffed by the actors, their feet shod in white cloth *tabi*. The boards are immaculate. A famous anecdote tells of an actor who was complimented by an expert in Japanese fencing for having maintained an *en garde* position throughout a performance—except for one fleeting moment of uncertainty. "Yes," answered the actor, "that was when I noticed a speck of dust on the stage."

The importance of the stage to the plays is underlined by the precise nomenclature for the different areas and the equally precise functions that have been assigned to each. The *hashigakari*, an extension of the stage, affords superb possibilities for entrances and exits, whether the uncertain steps of the blind Yoroboshi, guided by an inner light, or the precipitous departure of one Kyōgen actor in pursuit of another. Some scenes take place entirely on the *hashigakari*, the actors disposed at the first second and third pines to form a pleasing composition. The railing of the *hashigakari* may also serve a function in the play, as when a demon vaults from it onto the stage. Even the entrance of the musicians at the start of a play is given a solemn dignity by their passage along the *hashigakari* that no entrance from the wings of a conventional Western theatre could approximate.

Once on the stage from the *hashigakari*, the *waki* and the *shite* will each go to his appointed place, and though they move away from time to time, they will presently return. It is not merely that the actors are so strongly bound by traditions that they cannot make innovations; the stage no more permits the *shite* to stand in the *waki*'s place than the rituals of a church would permit the officiating priests to alter their stations in the interests of more powerful dramatic effects. The actor's appearance on the Nō stage presupposes that he will obey its demands.

The actor acknowledges the importance of the stage by his pounding on it during climactic moments of his dances. Unlike the ballet dancer who attempts to create an illusion of weightlessness, the Nō actor insists that he tread the stage. If he leaps in the violent movements of a dance, he deliberately lands with a reverberating thud. Even the ghosts in Nō proclaim their reality by their footfalls.

The stage imposes its aesthetics. The plays, with few exceptions, can be acted without props, but even when props are used, they are never permitted to clutter the clean expanse of the Nō stage or to usurp the audience's attention. The prop—whether a boat, a tree, a hut or a carriage—is hardly more than an outline of the object represented. The boat in *Funa Benkei* is so small that only the boatman, Yoshitsune and Benkei can board it; the other soldiers sit on the stage outside the white frame of the boat in an attitude of being aboard. Of course it would be possible to build a more commodious boat, but the larger the prop the less easily it could be brought on by the stage assistants and removed when no longer needed; moreover, it would break the beautiful lines of the stage.

The present form of the Nō stage dates from the mid-Tokugawa period, when Nō achieved what may have been its final evolution. The earliest stages consisted of pieces of level ground, perhaps beaten earth like the rings for *sumō* wrestlers. Even today the torchlight Nō performances at the Kasuga Shrine in Nara take place on a stage consisting merely of boards over the bare ground. Originally—as at the Kasuga Shrine today—there was no *hashigakari*. The actors made their way to the stage from the dressing room, a curtained-off enclosure some distance away, entering the stage from the rear-center. The pines now planted along the *hashigakari* may be a memento of the trees passed by the actors in former days as they walked through the precincts of a shrine to the stage; similarly, the curtain that shields the mirror room from the *hashigakari* may be the descendant of the curtains around the original makeshift dressing room.

The bridge to the stage gradually developed into a formal architectural feature. At the time of the performances given in 1464 under the patronage of the Shogun Yoshimasa a passageway similar to the *hashigakari* extended from the dressing room to the stage-rear, meeting it perpendicularly. A curtain hid the backstage area beyond the *hashigakari*. Seats were arranged in a large circle around the stage: the area directly in front of the stage was reserved for the gods, and the best seats (adjacent to the gods') were occupied by the shogun (to the left) and his consort (to the right). Less favored guests sat at the opposite side of the circle, near the *hashigakari*. The presence of an audience on all sides suggests a style of performance dissimilar to that of Nō today, but the actors probably concerned themselves with pleasing the spectators directly before them—the gods and the shogun.

In the early Muromachi period the *dengaku* stage had two *hashigakari*, one on either side, presumably in imitation of the practice of *bugaku* dancers of entering from both left and right. Not long after the 1464 performances the Nō actors began to experiment with attaching the *hashigakari* to a side of the stage rather than to the rear. At first the *hashigakari* extended to the stage at stage-left, by the flute pillar, but presently it was switched to stage-right, by the *shite* pillar, perhaps because the side closer to the shogun's seat was considered more important. When stages came to be built within the compound of a daimyo's palace, less spacious than a Shinto shrine, the angle made by the *hashigakari* and the stage, at first almost forty-five degrees, steadily decreased. Today the horizontal boards of the *atoza* merge almost imperceptibly with those of the *hashigakari*.

By good fortune two magnificent old Nō stages have been preserved. The first, at the Itsukushima Shrine on the Inland Sea, was built in 1568 as an offering to the shrine by Mōri Motonari (1497–1551), a powerful warlord who found time amidst his more than two hundred military campaigns to become expert in poetry and the arts. The stage at Itsukushima is built so close to the sea that high tide flows between the stage and the spectators, creating the illusion that the realm of the plays is separated from our own not only by time and space but by the sea. The stage stands about three and one-half feet above the water. Its pointed roof thatched with *hinoki* bark and its unpainted pillars (unlike the satiny gleam of the pillars at other Nō stages) have a weather-beaten look that makes the contrast with the brilliant costumes all the more striking. The *hashigakari* from the dressing room meets the stage at rather a steep angle and its boards, instead of joining those of the *atoza*, cut across to those of the stage proper. The *hashigakari*, thatch-roofed like the stage, stands on stone posts, the better to resist the erosion of the sea water.

The stage at the Nishi Honganji Temple in Kyoto was originally constructed for Toyotomi Hideyoshi about 1595 and moved to its present site in 1626. It is still in use, together with a smaller practice stage which is slightly older. Seated in the temple hall surrounded by magnificent gold screens along the walls, it is easy for the spectator as he watches the plays today to imagine himself a daimyo. Beneath the eye-level of those seated in splendor within the hall stand the ground-lings on the gravel of the area around the stage. The elaborately carved horizontal beams under the stage roof are a further reminder of the grandeur of Hideyoshi's palace and of his great devotion to Nō. The *hashigakari* joins the stage, a separate building, at an angle conspicuously less acute than that at Itsukushima. The Nishi Honganji Temple stage may have been the first provided with large jars underneath for resonance—seven under the stage proper, two under the *atoza*, and three under the *hashigakari*. These jars are suspended by copper wires over pits in the ground to provide the maximum effect.

The conservatism of the Nō theatre accounts for its retaining the roof for the stage, the gravel bed around it, the steps leading down—all meaningless today in terms of function. Even the number and shape of the metal rings used to hold up the curtain at the end of the *hashigakari* have been carefully prescribed. Yet there have also been many changes, some unconscious, others reflecting almost imperceptible shifts in taste. A modern Nō theatre is equipped with the latest comforts, including an up-to-date restaurant that has largely replaced the lacquered lunch-boxes of the past, and the pine of the backdrop may be distinctly of the twentieth century, an angular tree that startles us by its unconventionality.

Some innovations have been adopted only after a long struggle. When it was first proposed that electric lights be installed in the Nō theatres, the conservative Hōshō Kurō and Umewaka Minoru were flatly opposed. Kita Roppeita, a younger *iemoto*, was willing to experiment, but at first allowed only one small light bulb and insisted that the audience be warned in advance that electricity would be used. Umewaka Minoru's son (who took his father's name) later recalled, "My father, a man of the old school, was curiously obstinate in some respects. In 1905 Mr. Iwasaki Yanosuke had complained that the stage was too dark when lit by candles only, and proposed that electric lights be installed, but my father was absolutely opposed. At the time, the theatre had two candles on either side of the steps at stage front, two before the *waki*'s seat, three on the *hashigakari*, and two thick candles in square glass boxes at the *kōken*'s seat and by the flute pillar. Mr. Iwasaki kept urging that these candles be replaced by electricity, and finally won the day when he pointed out that the glass boxes we were already using were no less foreign than electric lights."

The stage itself has changed little in recent years, but if future members of the chorus are unable to sit for prolonged periods on the wooden boards it may become necessary for stools or chairs to be provided, undoubtedly entailing some modification of the entire stage.

THE PROPS

Many plays are performed without props, but when used they add much to the visual pleasure of Nō. Yuya's journey to the blossoming cherry trees at Kiyomizu is given special brilliance by the carriage in which she travels. This prop is no more than a rudimentary evocation of the wheels and hood of a real carriage, but when Yuya stands inside to the accompaniment of music of suddenly heightened intensity, we feel poignantly the contrast between the loveliness of the blossoms and the sad thoughts of Yuya, who fears her mother may be dying. The prop lends a charm and pathos to the scene all out of proportion to the simple means employed.

Props are usually brought in along the *hashigakari* by the stage assistants before the play begins. In some plays, however, the prop is used only in the second part. It is particularly effective if the *shite* is first revealed to us when the wrappings of the prop, which represents a hut or a palace, are removed by the stage assistants. In *Kagekiyo* the wrappings drop away to disclose the old warrior in his hut, blind and despondent. If the character made his entrance along the *hashigakari* in the normal manner, the overpowering impression of withdrawal from the world would be much diluted. The hut in which Kagekiyo sits is barely large enough to hold a seated man. Once the wrappings are removed all that is left is four bamboo poles holding up a tiny thatched roof. The actor's appearance at that moment should be a clear indication of his interpretation of the entire role, whether he will emphasize the pathetic fate of the defeated warrior or the dignity of a man proud even in adversity. When at last Kagekiyo, having rejected his daughter, emerges from the hut, the prop makes this moment intensely moving. Of course the adept of Nō could easily visualize the pathos of the moment, even without the prop, but the flimsy little structure is more affecting than the hut that might be conjured up by the imagination.

Some elaborate props are used, like the great bell in *Dōjōji* into which the snake princess leaps, the platform ornamented with huge peonies used for the demons' dance in *Shakkyō*, or the chrysanthemum garden evoked by the prop in *Makura Jidō*. A few plays require props representing mountains or grave mounds from which the *shite* makes his appearance; usually these props are wrapped round with cloth and covered at the top with leaves to suggest the mountain vegetation. Pines, cherry trees and plum trees are represented by a standing branch held up by a square or circular frame. In *Izutsu* a frame with a spray of pampas grass represents the well-curb, and in *Hachinoki* the prop represents dwarf trees in their pots.

In addition to the stage props the actors often carry swords, halberds, sickles, Shinto wands, flower baskets, and a large variety of other objects intended to heighten their appearance in particular roles. Unlike the stage props which are dismantled after a performance, the accessories are solid, if often smaller-than-life, objects. The actor sometimes carries an accessory in his hand from his entrance, but in many plays he goes to the *atoza* and accepts the sword or cloak he will use from a stage assistant, returning it in the same manner when no longer needed. The stage assistants also produce the lacquered cylindrical cask which serves as a seat for the *shite* during moments of repose. This cask is commonly used in Kyōgen too, where it may represent a great variety of objects.

By far the most important of the accessories is the fan. Hardly a role in Nō does not require a fan. The signal for a dance by the *shite* is his lifting of the fan he keeps at his waist and opening it. The fan is not only indispensable to the dances of the *shite* but may be used, especially in Kyōgen, to represent other objects—a flask of saké, a saké cup, or a deadly weapon.

The importance of the fan in Nō reflects its peculiar role in Japanese life. A fan formed a part of formal attire in the past, and even today it is customary at New Year for ordinary citizens to carry a fan when making their first calls. As early as the eleventh century a fan was carried by military men when in attendance at court, and there are numerous accounts of court ladies, priests and others giving and receiving fans as presents on special occasions. The pictures painted on the fans include some counted among the masterpieces of Japanese art.

Three types of fans are used in Nō. The first, called *uchiwa*, is round and does not fold. A Chinese invention, it is carried only by Chinese personages in the Nō plays. (A variant, the enormous feather *uchiwa*, is carried by *tengu*, the feathered demons, as part of their outlandish getup.) The fan most commonly used in Nō is the *chūkei*, a folding fan. The folding fan was a Japanese invention—it was in fact a principal article of export to China during the Muromachi period—and its association with Japanese dance goes back at least to the twelfth century, when the *shirabyōshi* dancers beat time for their dances with a folding fan. *Chūkei* means something like "spread out from the middle," referring to the flaring out of the upper part of the fan. The *chūkei* used in Nō has fifteen ribs, either black or white (actually, the natural yellowish color of the bamboo). Black-ribbed fans are used for all female roles and for many male roles; white-ribbed fans for the roles of old men and priests. Fans with white ribs have monochrome paintings on white paper, but the fans with black ribs are decorated with brilliant colored scenes, the subjects determined largely by the category of the play. Fans used in plays of the first category in which the *shite* is a god are likely to bear a painting of phoenixes sporting among paulownia leaves and flowers. If the *shite's* role is that of an old man, the painting on his fan may be a *sumie* representation of the Seven Sages of the Bamboo Grove. The design of fans used in plays of the second category, the warrior plays, depends on whether the *shite* is victorious or vanquished. The victorious warrior's fan has a design of the rising sun amidst pine branches; the defeated warrior's shows the sun rising amidst the waves, reminiscent of the Heike clan, which perished at sea. Plays of the third category, the woman plays, often use fans with brightly colored pictures of carriages filled with flowers or of court ladies carrying sprays of blossom in a "flower tournament." However, if the *shite's* role is of an old woman the design may be of autumnal flowers or camellias. The obsessed women depicted in plays of the fourth category carry fans with a double design of profusely blossoming clematis and pine branches, no doubt to suggest the warring emotions in the *shite's* mind. Fans carried by the demons in plays of the fifth category usually depict a peony in full blossom against a vermilion ground. The *waki* if a priest carries a fan with a design of the moon among the clouds, an allusion to the peripatetic life of the traveling monk. Certain roles require special designs, and variations exist from school to school. The *chūkei* used in Kyōgen are less rigidly prescribed in subject, but tend to be parodies of the beauties depicted on the Nō fans, showing for example a huge turnip on a golden ground.

Another variety of fan, called *shizumeori*, is more like the fan used in daily life. It is carried by actors in some roles performed without mask, and also when dancing the *shimai*, the climactic dances of the plays, in "concert versions," wearing an ordinary formal kimono instead of the costume for the role. Members of the chorus also carry these fans, placing them on the stage before them until about to recite, then raising them as in ceremonial utterance. The *shizumeori* fans bear different designs for each of the five schools of Nō: a pattern of swirling water for Kanze, five-fold clouds for Hōshō, five "dumplings" for Komparu, nine "dumplings" for Kongō, and three-fold clouds for Kita. The Kyōgen *shizumeori* also indicate the school: a design of young pines in the mist for Ōkura and usually a design of snowflakes in a circle for Izumi.

The handling of the fan is an essential part of the dancer's art, and each motion is as carefully prescribed as the steps of the feet. The fan accentuates the motions of the arm and lends grace to gestures, particularly the characteristic sweeping movements found in the Nō dances. Of all the stage props and accessories it is the most pervasive, and so indispensable that Nō has been spoken of as a kind of drama performed with fans.

Compared to theatres elsewhere in the world and even to other varieties of Japanese theatre, Nō and Kyōgen depend very little on props and accessories. The stage offers nothing to distract the audience, certainly nothing in the nature of the facile realism of representational theatres. Even such accessories as swords or spears are not intended to convince by any realistic glint of metal. The stage props help create the illusion of a particular place or atmosphere; the accessories help to distinguish the persons, rather as a wheel, tower or handkerchief may distinguish a medieval saint and tell us the nature of her suffering or triumph. But however effective the props may be in their functions, they are dispensable; representation in Nō depends far less on the props and accessories and even the costumes than on the basic elements, the stage and the masks.

PLATES

1 and 2. *Takasago*   Kongō School

A priest on his way to the capital visits the Bay of Takasago, known for its great pine tree. He finds an old couple sweeping fallen pine needles, and eventually learns that this man and woman are the spirits of the pines at Takasago and Sumiyoshi. He continues his journey to Sumiyoshi, where the god of the place appears and, after telling of his age-old protection of the Imperial House, dances and promises to bring joy to the people. (A god play)

(1) The old woman, the spirit of the Takasago Pine, enters carrying a broom, followed by the old man, the spirit of the Sumiyoshi Pine.

(2) The old man and woman, now on the stage, remain seated as the chorus sings of the glories of the Takasago Pine. The priest and his companions also listen.

3. *Yashima*   Kita School
A priest and his attendants arrive at
Yashima. They stay in the hut of a
fisherman, who describes the battle
of Yashima so vividly that the priest
asks his name. The fisherman hints
he is the ghost of the great general
Yoshitsune. In the second part of the
play, while the priest sleeps, the
ghost reappears in his true guise, as
a young warrior. (A warrior play)

4. *Hagoromo*   Kanze School
A fisherman finds a robe of feathers
hanging upon a pine tree at the beach
of Miho. He declares he intends to keep
it, but a beautiful woman appears and
begs him to return the robe, saying she
cannot return to heaven without it. The
fisherman agrees to give her the robe if
she will dance for him. She performs
several dances before disappearing into
the heavens. Here she is begging the
fisherman for her robe. (A woman play)

5. *Genji Kuyō*   Kongō School

Some priests visiting the Ishiyama Temple are asked by a woman to say a memorial service for Prince Genji. She says that her failure to include such a service in her novel has kept her from gaining salvation. When asked if she is not Lady Murasaki, the author of *The Tale of Genji*, she disappears without answering. In the second part she confesses she is Murasaki. The priest promises to pray for Genji. (The photograph shows Murasaki's gesture of gratitude.) (A woman play)

6. *Yuya*   Kita School

Yuya, the favorite of the nobelman Munemori, learns that her mother is seriously ill. She asks permission to return home to the country, but Munemori insists that she accompany him and see the cherry blossoms. Later she composes a poem expressing her feelings so poignantly that Munemori permits her to go. Here she reads the letter in which her mother describes her illness. (A woman play)

◁ 7. *Izutsu*   Kanze School
A priest visits the Ariwara Temple where, many years earlier, the famous lover Narihira had lived with the daughter of Ki no Aritsune. As he prays, a young woman appears. She speaks of the past, especially of how she and Narihira as children had compared heights while standing by a well-curb (*izutsu*). She disappears, only to return, this time wearing the hat and cloak Narihira gave her. Here she pushes aside the bush of flowering *susuki* to peer into the depths of the well. She sees Narihira's reflection, not her own. (A woman play)

8. *Sotoba Komachi*   Hōshō School
Some priests on their way to the capital encounter an old woman. Gradually she reveals she is Komachi, and tells of her former beauty, contrasting it with her present wretchedness. As she speaks, the spirit of the man she treated cruelly possesses her, and she speaks in his voice. At the end, as she describes his death, she hopes she may yet gain salvation. Here, dressed in her lover's cap and cloak, she dances as she recalls in his voice the ninety-nine fruitless visits he paid her before he died. (A fourth-category play)

◁ 9. *Kagekiyo*   Kanze School

Kagekiyo, a defeated Heike warrior, is living in exile. His daughter visits him, but he is too proud to let her see him in his present state. He turns her away, denying he is Kagekiyo, but a villager informs the daughter that the man she has met is her father. She returns, and this time he admits his identity. He describes his last battle, standing in his hut. (A fourth-category play)

10. *Semimaru*   Kanze School

Semimaru, the forth son of the Emperor Daigo, is blind. His father gives orders that he is to be abandoned on Ōsaka Mountain. His sister Sakagami discovers him in his lonely hut, but after a moment of recognition the two must part. Here, Semimaru, still wearing his princely robes, is guided by a courtier to his hut on the mountain. (A fourth-category play)

12. *Kagyū*   Izumi School

Tarōkaja is ordered by his master to go into the ▷
woods and find a snail. The master uses *kagyū*,
a difficult word for "snail," describing it in such
terms that Tarōkaja, bumping into a *yamabushi*
(mountain ascetic), supposes he is a "snail." The
yamabushi is much amused by the mistake. (Kyōgen)

11. *Tsuchigumo*   Kongō School

The warrior Raikō is afflicted by a mysterious illness. A priest informs him that the illness is caused by a great spider
(*tsuchigumo*). Raikō sees through the priest's disguise and recognizes that he is the spider. They fight, and the wounded
spider flees. In the second part a retainer of Raikō tracks the spider to its lair and kills it. Here, the spider attempts
to enmesh the retainer in its web. (A demon play)

13. *Kirokuda* ("Six Loads of Lumber")   Ōkura School

A certain gentleman sends his servant Tarōkaja with six ox-loads of lumber and a cask of saké for his uncle. It is bitter cold, and Tarōkaja, stopping at an inn, drinks some of the saké to warm himself. As he gets drunk he explains to the proprietor how he plans to catch in his arms a quail, to eat with the liquor. (Kyōgen)

14. *Votive Performance at the Itsukushima Shrine*
At high tide the waters of the Inland Sea flow around the stage, separating it from the audience. To the right the Great Torii is faintly visible in the water.

15. *Nō at Chūsonji*
At the annual festival of the temple, Nō plays are presented in the open air, amidst the majestic trees.

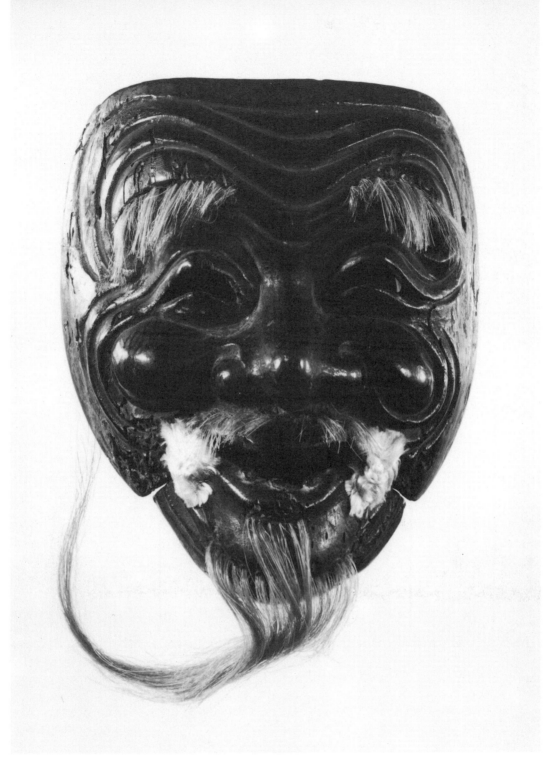

16. *Okina* by Nikkō. Umewaka Collection. 6¼″ × 5¾″.
This *okina* mask, used only for Sambasō in the play *Okina*, is of the oldest type. It is characterized by the *kiriago* ("split jaw"), meaning that the mask is in two pieces, tied together with string. The black variety is less aristocratic in features than the other two kinds of *okina* mask, and is well suited to the comic Sambasō role.

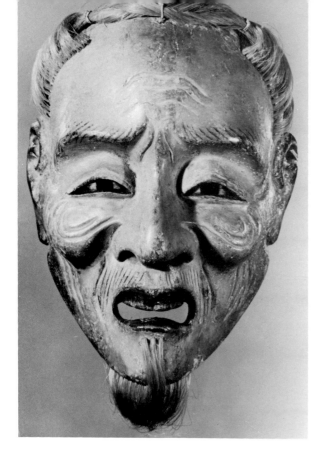

17. *Koujijō* by Kouji. Kongō Collection. $7\frac{7}{8}'' \times 6\frac{1}{4}''$.

The great dignity of this mask makes it appropriate for the roles of old men who prove to be earthly manifestations of gods, like the *shite* in the first part of *Takasago*.

18. *Ōakujō* by Shakuzuru. Kanze Collection. $9'' \times 7\frac{3}{4}''$.

This mask is used for powerful, frightening old men; its large size accounts for its name, meaning "large *akujō*."

19. *Yoroboshi* by Yamato. Kongō Collection. $8\frac{1}{8}'' \times 5\frac{1}{2}''$.

This mask of a blind boy is worn by the *shite* in *Yoroboshi*. The boy, falsely accused and disowned by his family, goes blind through grief and must beg for a living. The mask powerfully suggests his tragic fate.

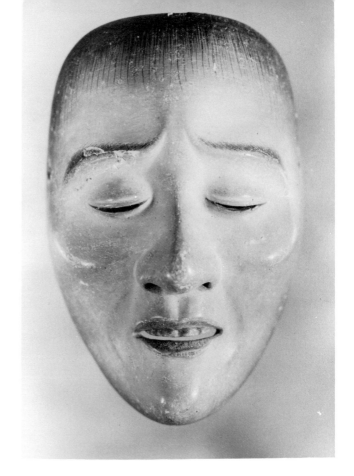

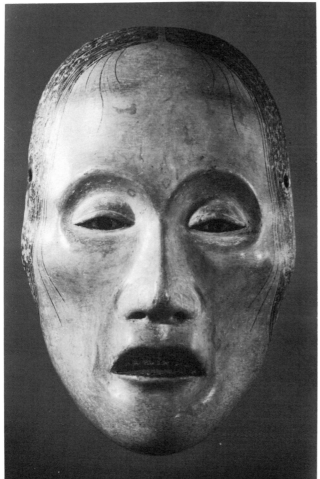

20. *Rōjo* by Himi. Umewaka Collection. $8'' \times 5\frac{3}{4}''$.

This is the mask of an old woman who once had been beautiful. It is especially suited for the role of Komachi, and is worn in *Sekidera Komachi* and *Sotoba Komachi*. The face reveals the character's age, but there are no wrinkles, a lingering reminder of her former loveliness.

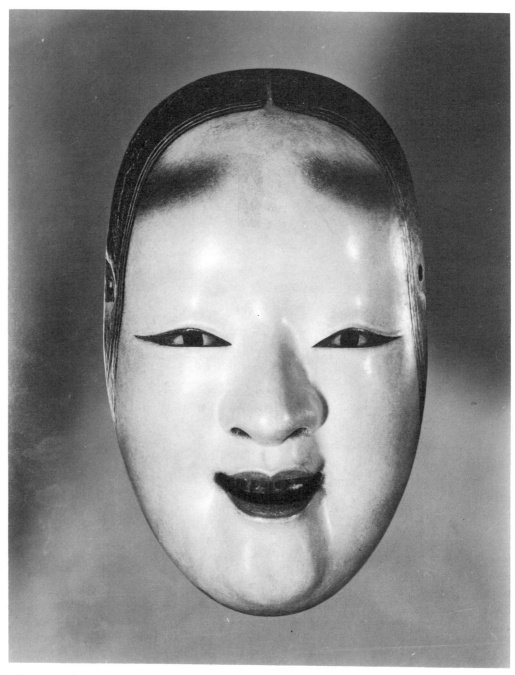

21. *Ko-omote* by Tatsuemon. Kongō Collection. 8¼″ × 5⅜″.
The cheeks of this mask are full, the forehead wide, and the face suffused with youthful beauty. This particular mask is known as the *yuki* ("snow") *ko-omote*; it was one of the three *ko-omote* masks by Tatsuemon prized by Toyotomi Hideyoshi.

LIST OF NŌ PLAYS CURRENTLY PERFORMED

Unless otherwise stated, plays are performed by all schools.

OKINA (翁) (first play)
Author unknown

ADACHIGAHARA (安達原) (demon play)
Author unknown
Referred to as *Kurozuka* by schools other than Kanze

AIZOMEGAWA (藍染川) (miscellaneous play)
Author unknown
Performed by Kanze and Komparu schools only

AKOGI (阿漕) (miscellaneous play)
Attributed to Zeami, but Zeami probably reworked text of an earlier play

AMA (海士) (demon play)
Author unknown, but work antedates Zeami

AOI NO UE (葵上) (miscellaneous play)
Adapted by Zeami from an Ōmi *sarugaku* play

ARASHIYAMA (嵐山) (god play)
by Komparu Zempō

ARIDŌSHI (蟻通) (miscellaneous play)
by Zeami

ASHIKARI (芦刈) (miscellaneous play)
Adapted by Zeami

ASUKAGAWA (飛鳥川) (miscellaneous play)
Attributed to Zeami
Performed by Kongō and Kita schools only

ATAGO KŪYA (愛宕空也) (demon play)
by Kanze Kojirō Nobumitsu
Performed by Kita school only

ATAKA (安宅) (miscellaneous play)
by Kanze Kojirō Nobumitsu

ATSUMORI (敦盛) (warrior play)
by Zeami

AWAJI (淡路) (god play)
by Kannami
Performed by Kanze, Komparu and Kita schools

AYA NO TSUZUMI (綾鼓) (miscellaneous play)
by Zeami
Performed by Hōshō, Kongō and Kita schools

BASHŌ (芭蕉) (woman play)
by Komparu Zenchiku

CHIKUBU SHIMA (竹生島) (god play)
Author unknown

CHŌBUKU SOGA (調伏曾我) (miscellaneous or demon play)

by Miyamasu
Performed by Hoshō, Kongō and Kita schools

CHŌRYŌ (張良) (demon play)
by Kanze Kojirō Nobumitsu

DAIBUTSU KUYŌ (大仏供養) (miscellaneous play)
Author unknown

DAIE (大会) (demon play)
Author unknown

DAIROKUTEN (第六天) (demon play)
Author unknown
Performed by Kanze school only

DAMPŪ (壇風) (miscellaneous or demon play)
Author unknown, but attributed to Zeami
Performed by Hōshō, Kongō and Kita schools

DŌJŌJI (道成寺) (miscellaneous play)
by Kanze Kojirō Nobumitsu

DŌMYŌJI (道明寺) (god play)
Attributed to Zeami
Performed by Kanze, Kongō and Kita schools

EBIRA (箙) (warrior play)
Attributed to Zeami

EBOSHI ORI (烏帽子折) (miscellaneous play)
by Miyamasu
Performed by all schools except Komparu

EGUCHI (江口) (woman play)
by Kannami

EMA (絵馬) (god play)
Author unknown
Performed by all schools except Komparu

ENOSHIMA (江島) (god play)
by Kanze Yajirō Nagatoshi
Performed by Kanze school only

FUE NO MAKI (笛之巻) (miscellaneous play)
Author unknown
Performed by Kanze school only

FUJI (藤) (woman play)
by Hiyoshi Saami (?)
Performed by Kanze, Hōshō and Kongō schools

FUJISAN (富士山) (god play)
Probably by Zeami
Performed by Kongō and Komparu schools

FUJI TAIKO (富士太鼓) (miscellaneous play)
Attributed to Zeami

FUJITO (藤戸) (miscellaneous play)

Author unknown, but generally attributed to Zeami

FUNABASHI (船橋) (miscellaneous play)
Adapted by Zeami from a *dengaku* Nō

FUNA BENKEI (船弁慶) (demon play)
by Kanze Kojirō Nobumitsu

FUTARI SHIZUKA (二人静) (woman play)
Author unknown
Performed by all schools except Hōshō

GEMBUKU SOGA (元服曾我) (warrior or miscellaneous play)
by Miyamasu
Performed by Kita school only

GENDAYŪ (源太夫) (god play)
Probably by Kiami
Performed by Komparu and Kita schools

GENJŌ (玄象) (demon play)
Author unknown

GENJI KUYŌ (源氏供養) (woman play)
Attributed to Zeami

GENZAI NUE (現在鵺) (miscellaneous or demon play)
Author unknown
Performed by Komparu and Kita schools

GENZAI SHICHIMEN (現在七面) (miscellaneous play)
Author unknown
Performed by Kanze and Kongō schools

GENZAI TADANORI (現在忠度) (warrior or miscellaneous play)
Author unknown
Performed by Kongō school only

GIŌ (祇王) (woman play)
Attributed to Zeami
Performed by Hōshō, Kongō and Kita schools

HACHINOKI (鉢木) (miscellaneous play)
Author unknown

HAGOROMO (羽衣) (woman play)
Author unknown

HAJITOMI (半蔀) (woman play)
by Naitō Tōzaemon

HAKURAKUTEN (白楽天) (god play)
Author unknown, but usually attributed to Zeami
Performed by all schools except Hōshō

HANAGATAMI (花筐) (miscellaneous play)
by Zeami

HANJO (班女) (miscellaneous play)
by Zeami

HASHI BENKEI (橋弁慶) (miscellaneous play)
Author unknown

HATSUYUKI (初雪) (woman play)
by Komparu Zempō
Performed by Komparu school only

HIBARIYAMA (雲雀山) (miscellaneous play)
Attributed to Zeami

HIGAKI (桧垣) (woman play)
by Zeami
Performed by all schools except Komparu

HIMURO (氷室) (god play)
by Miyamasu

HIUN (飛雲) (demon play)
Author unknown
Performed by all schools except Komparu

HŌJŌGAWA (放生川) (god play)
by Zeami

HŌKAZŌ (放下僧) (miscellaneous play)
Author unknown, but probably by Miyamasu

HŌSO (彭祖) (miscellaneous play)
Performed by Kongō school only
Author unknown

HOTOKENOHARA (仏原) (woman play)
Attributed to Zeami
Performed by Kanze, Kongō and Kita schools

HYAKUMAN (百万) (miscellaneous or demon play)
by Komparu Zempō
Performed by all schools except Hōshō

IKKAKU SENNIN (一角仙人) (miscellaneous or demon play)
by Komparu Zempō
Performed by all schools except Hōshō

IKARIZUKI (碇潜) (warrior or miscellaneous play)
Author unknown
Performed by Kanze and Kongō schools

IKUTA ATSUMORI (生田敦盛) (warrior play)
by Komparu Zempō
Performed by all schools except Kita

IWAFUNE (岩船) (demon play)
Author unknown

IZUTSU (井筒) (woman play)
by Zeami

JINEN KOJI (自然居士) (miscellaneous play)
by Kannami

KAGEKIYO (景清) (miscellaneous play)
Author unknown, but usually attributed to Zeami

KAGETSU (花月) (miscellaneous play)
Author unknown, but probably by Zeami

KAKITSUBATA (杜若) (woman play)
Probably by Zeami

KAMO (賀茂) (god play)
Author unknown, but attributed to Komparu Zenchiku

KAMO MONOGURUI (加茂物狂) (miscellaneous play)
by Komparu Zenchiku
Performed by Hōshō, Kongō and Kita schools

KANAWA (鉄輪) (miscellaneous play)
Author unknown

KANEHIRA (兼平) (warrior play)
Attributed to Zeami

KANTAN (邯鄲) (miscellaneous play)
Author uncertain, but probably by Zeami

KANYŌKYŪ (咸陽宮) (miscellaneous play)
Author unknown
Performed by all schools except Komparu

KAPPO (合浦) (demon play)
Author unknown
Performed by Kanze school only

KASHIWAZAKI (柏崎) (miscellaneous play)
by Enami Saemon Gorō
Adapted by Zeami
Performed by all schools except Kita

KASUGA RYŪJIN (春日竜神) (demon play)
Attributed to Zeami
Performed by all schools except Kita

KAYOI KOMACHI (通小町) (miscellaneous play)
by Kannami

KAZURAGI (葛城) (woman or miscellaneous play)
Author unknown, but attributed to Zeami

KAZURAGI TENGU (葛城天狗) (demon play)
by Kongō Nagatoshi
Performed by Kita school only

KIKUJIDŌ (菊慈童) (miscellaneous play)
Author unknown
Referred to as *Makurajidō* by schools other than

Kanze

KINSATSU (金札) (demon play)
  by Kannami
KINUTA (砧) (miscellaneous play)
  by Zeami
KISO (木曾) (miscellaneous play)
  Author unknown
  Performed by Kanze school only
KIYOTSUNE (清経) (warrior play)
  by Zeami
KOCHŌ (胡蝶) (woman play)
  by Kanze Kojirō Nobumitsu
  Performed by all schools except Kita
KOGŌ (小督) (miscellaneous play)
  Attributed to Zeami
KOI NO OMONI (恋重荷) (miscellaneous play)
  by Zeami
  Performed by Kanze and Komparu schools only
KOKAJI (小鍛冶) (demon play)
  Author unknown
KŌTEI (皇帝) (demon play)
  by Kanze Kojirō Nobumitsu
  Performed by all schools except Komparu
KOSODE SOGA (小袖曾我) (miscellaneous play)
  Author unknown, but attributed to Miyamasu
KŌU (項羽) (miscellaneous or demon play)
  Attributed to Zeami
KŌYA MONOGURUI (高野物狂) (miscellaneous play)
  Author unknown
  Performed by all schools except Komparu
KUMASAKA (熊坂) (demon play)
  Author unknown
KURAMA TENGU (鞍馬天拘) (demon play)
  by Miyamasu
KUREHA (呉服) (god play)
  Attributed to Zeami
KUROZUKA (黒塚) (demon play)
  Author unknown
KURUMAZO (車僧) (demon play)
  Attributed to Zeami
KUSANAGI (草薙) (miscellaneous or demon play)
  Author unknown
  Performed by Hōshō school only
KUSENOTO (九世戸) (god play)
  by Kanze Kojirō Nobumitsu
  Performed by Kanze school only
KUSU NO TSUYU (楠露) (miscellaneous play)
  Author unknown
  Performed by Kanze school only
KUZU (国栖) (demon play)
  Author unknown
MAKIGINU (巻絹) (miscellaneous play)
  Author unknown
  Performed by all schools except Komparu
MAKURAJIDŌ (枕慈童) (miscellaneous play)
  Author unknown
  Referred to as Kikujidō by schools other than
  Kanze
MANJŪ (満仲) (miscellaneous play)
  Author unknown
MATSUKAZE (松風) (woman play)
  by Kannami, adapted by Zeami
MATSUMUSHI (松虫) (miscellaneous play)
  Author unknown
MATSUNO-O (松尾) (god play)

Author unknown, but possibly by Zeami
  Performed by Hōshō school only
MATSUYAMA KAGAMI (松山鏡) (demon play)
  Author unknown, but possibly by Zeami
  Performed by Kanze, Kongō and Kita schools
MATSUYAMA TENGU (松山天拘) (demon play)
  Author unknown
  Performed by Kongō school only
MEKARI (和布刈) (god play)
  Author unknown
  Performed by all schools except Komparu
MICHIMORI (通盛) (warrior play)
  Text by Iami, revised by Zeami
MIIDERA (三井寺) (miscellaneous play)
  Author unknown
MIMOSUSO (御裳濯) (god play)
  Probably by Zeami
  Performed by Komparu and Kita schools
MINASE (水無瀬) (miscellaneous play)
  Author unknown
  Performed by Kita school only
MINAZUKIBARAI (水無月祓) (miscellaneous play)
  by Zeami
  Performed by Kanze school only
MINOBU (身延) (woman play)
  Author unknown
  Performed by Kanze school only
MITSUYAMA (三山) (miscellaneous play)
  Attributed to Zeami
  Performed by Hōshō and Kongō schools
MIWA (三輪) (woman or miscellaneous play)
  Author unknown
MOCHIZUKI (望月) (warrior or miscellaneous play)
  Author unknown
MOMIJIGARI (紅葉狩) (demon play)
  by Kanze Kojirō Nobumitsu
MORIHISA (盛久) (miscellaneous play)
  by Kanze Jūrō Motomasa
MOTOMEZUKA (求塚) (miscellaneous play)
  by Kannami
  Performed by all schools except Komparu
MUROGIMI (室君) (miscellaneous play)
  Author unknown
  Performed by Kanze and Komparu schools
MUTSURA (六浦) (woman play)
  Author unknown
NAKAMITSU (仲光) (miscellaneous play)
  Author unknown
  Performed by all schools except Komparu. Referred
  to as Manjū by schools other than Kanze
NANIWA (難波) (god play)
  by Zeami
NEZAME (寝覚) (god play)
  Author unknown
  Performed by Kanze school only
NISHIKIGI (錦木) (miscellaneous play)
  by Zeami
NISHIKIDO (錦戸) (miscellaneous play)
  by Miyamasu
  Performed by Kanze and Hōshō schools
NONOMIYA (野宮) (woman play)
  Author not certain, but generally ascribed to Zeami
NOMORI (野守) (demon play)
  by Zeami
NUE (鵺) (demon play)

by Zeami

OBASUTE (姨捨) (woman play)
by Zeami
Performed by all schools except Komparu

OCHIBA (落葉) (woman play)
Attributed to Zeami
Performed by Kongō and Kita schools

OJIO (小塩) (miscellaneous play)
by Komparu Zenchiku

OHARA GOKŌ (小原御幸) (woman play)
Author unknown, but sometimes attributed to
Zeami

OIMATSU (老松) (god play)
by Zeami

OMINAESHI (女郎花) (miscellaneous play)
Author unknown

ŌEYAMA (大江山) (demon play)
by Miyamasu

ŌMU KOMACHI (鸚鵡小町) (woman play)
Attributed to Zeami
Performed by all schools except Komparu

ŌYASHIRO (大社) (god play)
by Kanze Yajirō Nagatoshi
Performed by Kanze, Kongō and Kita schools

OROCHI (大蛇) (miscellaneous or demon play)
by Kanze Kojirō Nobumitsu
Performed by Hōshō, Kongō and Kita schools

RAIDEN (雷電) (demon play)
Author unknown
Performed by all schools except Komparu

RASHŌMON (羅生門) (miscellaneous or demon play)
by Kanze Kojirō Nobumitsu
Performed by all schools except Komparu

RINZŌ (輪蔵) (god or demon play)
by Kanze Yajirō Nagatoshi
Performed by Kanze and Kita schools

RŌDAIKO (籠太鼓)
Attributed to Zeami

RŌGIŌ (籠祇王) (miscellaneous play)
Author unknown
Performed by Kita school only

RYŌKO (竜虎) (demon play)
by Kanze Kojiro Nobumitsu
Performed by Kanze and Kita schools

SAGI (鷺) (woman or miscellaneous play)
Author unknown
Performed by all schools except Komparu

SAIGYŌZAKURA (西行桜) (woman and miscellaneous
play)
by Zeami

SAKAHOKO (逆矛) (god play)
Author unknown
Performed by Kanze school only

SAKURAGAWA (桜川) (miscellaneous play)
by Zeami

SANEMORI (実盛) (warrior play)
by Zeami

SANSHŌ (三笑) (miscellaneous play)
Author unknown
Performed by all schools except Komparu

SAOYAMA (佐保山) (god play)
Attributed to Zeami
Performed by Komparu school only

SEIGANJI (誓願寺) (woman play)
Attributed to Zeami

SEIŌBO (西王母) (god play)
Attributed to Zeami

SEKIDERA KOMACHI (関寺小町) (woman or miscellaneous
play)
Author uncertain, but probably by Zeami

SEKIHARA YOICHI (関原与一) (warrior or miscellaneous
play)
Author unknown
Performed by Kita school only

SEMIMARU (蟬丸) (miscellaneous play)
by Zeami

SENJU (千手) (woman play)
Often attributed to Komparu Zenchiku, but probably by Zeami

SESSHŌSEKI (殺生石) (miscellaneous or demon play)
Author unknown, but possibly by Saami

SETTAI (摂待) (miscellaneous play)
Author unknown
Performed by all schools except Komparu

SHAKKYŌ (石橋) (demon play)
Author unknown

SHARI (舎利) (demon play)
Attributed to Zeami

SHICHIKIOCHI (七騎落) (miscellaneous play)
Author unknown

SHIGA (志賀) (god play)
Attributed to Zeami
Performed by all schools except Komparu

SHIGEMORI (重盛) (miscellaneous play)
Author unknown
Performed by Kita school only

SHIRAHIGE (白髭) (god play)
Attributed to Kannami
Performed by Kanze, Komparu and Kita schools

SHIRONUSHI (代主) (god play)
Author unknown, but possibly by Zeami
Performed by Kanze school only

SHŌJŌ (猩々) (demon play)
Author unknown

SHŌKI (鍾馗) (demon play)
Author unknown

SHŌKUN (昭君) (demon play)
Author unknown, but text may antedate Zeami

SHŌZON (正尊) (miscellaneous play)
by Kanze Yajirō Nagatoshi

SHUNKAN (俊寛) (miscellaneous play)
Author unknown

SHUNNEI (春栄) (miscellaneous play)
by Zeami

SHUNZEI TADANORI (俊成忠度) (warrior play)
by Naitō Kawachi-no-kami
Performed by all schools except Komparu

SŌSHI ARAI KOMACHI (草子洗小町) (woman play)
Author unknown

SOTOBA KOMACHI (卒都婆小町) (miscellaneous play)
by Kannami

SUMA GENJI (須磨源氏) (demon play)
Adapted by Zeami
Performed by all schools except Komparu

SUMIDAGAWA (隅田川) (miscellaneous play)
by Kanze Jūrō Motomasa

SUMIYOSHI-MŌDE (住吉詣) (woman or miscellaneous
play)
Author unknown
Performed by Kanze, Kongō and Kita schools

SUMIZOME SAKURA (墨染桜) (woman play)
Author unknown
Performed by Kongō school only
TADANOBU (忠信) (miscellaneous play)
by Komparu Zenchiku
Performed by Kanze and Hōshō schools
TADANORI (忠度) (warrior play)
by Zeami
Performed by Kanze, Kongō and Kita schools
TAEMA (当麻) (demon play)
by Zeami
TAIHEI SHŌJŌ (大瓶猩々) (demon play)
Author unknown
Performed by Kanze school only
TAIZAN BUKUN (泰山府君) (miscellaneous and demon play)
by Zeami
Performed by Kongō school only
TAKASAGO (高砂) (god play)
by Zeami
TAKENOYUKI (竹雪) (miscellaneous play)
Attributed to Zeami
Performed by Hōshō and Kita schools
TAMAKAZURA (玉葛) (miscellaneous play)
by Komparu Zenchiku
TAMANOI (玉井) (god play)
by Kanze Kojirō Nobumitsu
Performed by Kanze, Kongō and Kita schools
TAMURA (田村) (warrior play)
Attributed to Zeami
TANIKŌ (谷行) (miscellaneous or demon play)
by Komparu Zenchiku
TATSUTA (竜田) (woman or miscellaneous play)
Author unknown, but probably by Zeami
Performed by Kanze school only
TEIKA (定家) (woman play)
Probably by Komparu Zenchiku
TENKO (天鼓) (miscellaneous play)
Author unknown
TŌBOKU (東北) (woman play)
Probably by Zeami
TŌBŌSAKU (東方朔) (god play)
by Komparu Zempō
Performed by Kanze, Komparu and Kita schools
TŌEI (藤栄) (warrior or miscellaneous play)
Author unknown
Performed by all schools except Kanze
TŌGAN KOJI (東岸居士) (miscellaneous play)
by Zeami
Performed by all schools except Komparu
TOKUSA (木賊) (woman and miscellaneous play)
Probably by Zeami
Performed by all schools except Komparu
TOMOAKIRA (知章) (warrior play)
Probably by Zeami
Performed by all schools except Hōshō
TOMOE (巴) (warrior play)
Author unknown
TOMONAGA (朝長) (warrior play)
Probably by Zeami
TORIOIBUNE (鳥追舟) (miscellaneous play)
Author unknown
TŌRU (融) (demon play)
by Zeami
TŌSEN (唐船) (miscellaneous play)

by Toyama Matagorō Yoshihiro
TSUCHIGUMO (土蜘蛛) (demon play)
Author unknown
TSUCHIGURUMA (土車) (miscellaneous play)
by Zeami
Performed by Kanze and Kita schools
TSUNEMASA (経政) (warrior play)
Author unknown
TSURUKAME (鶴亀) (god play)
Author unknown
UCHITO-MŌDE (内外詣) (god play)
by Kongō Matabei Nagayori
Performed by Kongō school only
UGETSU (雨月) (miscellaneous play)
by Komparu Zenchiku
UKAI (鵜飼) (demon play)
by Enami Saemon Gorō; adapted by Zeami
UKIFUNE (浮舟) (miscellaneous play)
Text by Yokoo Motohisa; music by Zeami
Performed by all schools except Hōshō
UKON (右近) (god play)
by Zeami (minor adaptation by Kanze Kojirō)
Performed by Kanze, Hōshō and Kongō schools
UME (梅) (woman play)
by Kamo no Mabuchi (?)
Performed by Kanze school only
UMEGAE (梅枝) (miscellaneous play)
Attributed to Zeami
UNEME (采女) (woman play)
by Zeami
UNOMATSURI (鵜祭) (god play)
Author unknown
Performed by Komparu school only
UNRININ (雲林院) (miscellaneous play)
Author unknown. Text in Zeami's hand survives
Performed by all schools except Komparu
UROKOGATA (鱗形) (god play)
Author unknown
Performed by Kongō and Kita schools
UTAURA (歌占) (miscellaneous play)
by Kanze Jūrō Motomasa
UTŌ (善知鳥) (miscellaneous play)
Author unknown
YAMAHIME (山姫) (woman play)
Author unknown
Performed by Kita school
YAMAUBA (山姥) (demon play)
Author uncertain, but probably by Zeami
YASHIMA (八島) (warrior play)
Author uncertain, but probably by Zeami
YORIMASA (頼政) (warrior play)
by Zeami
YOROBOSHI (弱法師) (miscellaneous play)
by Kanze Jūrō Motomasa
YŌRŌ (養老) (god play)
by Zeami
YOSHINO SHIZUKA (吉野静) (woman or miscellaneous play)
by Kannami
YOSHINO TENJIN (吉野天人) (woman play)
by Kanze Kojirō Nobumitsu
Performed by Kanze school only
YOUCHI SOGA (夜討曾我) (miscellaneous play)
by Miyamasu
YŌKIHI (楊貴妃) (woman play)

by Komparu Zenchiku

Yūgao (夕顔) (woman play)
by Zeami
Performed by Kanze, Kongō and Kita schools

Yugyō yanagi (遊行柳) (woman or miscellaneous play)
by Kanze Kojirō Nobumitsu

Yuki (雪) (woman play)
Author unknown
Performed by Kongō school only

Yumi yawata (弓八幡) (god play)
by Zeami

Yuya (熊野) (woman play)
Author unknown, but generally attributed to Zeami

Zegai (善界) (demon play)
by Takeda Hōin Munemori

Zenji soga (禅師曾我) (miscellaneous play)
Author unknown
Performed by Kanze, Hōshō and Kita schools

Note. The authorship of the plays has yet to be established firmly. The above attributions reflect current scholarship in Japan.

SOME RECENT BOOKS IN ENGLISH ON NŌ

Bethe, Monica and Karen Brazell. *Nō as Performance: an Analysis of the Kuse Scene from Yamamba*. Ithaca, N.Y.: Cornell University East Asian Papers, 1978.

Brazell, Karen (ed.) *Twelve Plays of the Noh and Kyōgen Theaters*. Ithaca, N.Y.: Cornell University East Asian Papers, 1988.

Flindt, Willi and Frank Hoff. *The Life Structure of Noh*. Tokyo: Hinoki Shoten, 1973.

Hare, Thomas Blenman. *Zeami's Style*. Stanford, Calif.: Stanford University Press, 1986.

Keene, Donald. *Twenty Plays of the Nō Theatre*. New York: Columbia University Press, 1970.

Komparu Kunio. *The Noh Theatre*. Tokyo: Weatherhill, 1983.

Raz, Jacob. *Audience and Actors: A Study of their Interactions in the Japanese Traditional Theatre*. Leiden: E. J. Brill, 1983.

Rimer, J. Thomas and Yamazaki Masakazu. *On the Art of the Nō Drama: The Major Treatises of Zeami*. Princeton, N.J.: Princeton University Press, 1984.

Shimazaki, Chifumi. *The Noh*, 3 vols. Tokyo: Hinoki Shoten, 1977–81.

Tamba Akira. *The Musical Structure of Nō*. Tokyo: Tokyo University Press, 1974.

Tyler, Royall. *Granny Mountains: A Second Cycle of Nō Plays*. Ithaca, N.Y.: Cornell University Papers, 1978.

Tyler, Royall. *Pining Wind: A Cycle of Nō Plays*. Ithaca, N.Y.: Cornell University East Asian Papers, 1978.

BIBLIOGRAPHY

Note: With two exceptions, the following list is confined to books.

Translations and Studies in Western Languages

Araki, James T. *The Ballad-Drama of Medieval Japan*. Berkeley, 1964.

Fenollosa, Ernest, and Pound, Ezra. *The Classic Noh Theatre of Japan*., New York, 1959.

Keene, Donald (ed.) *Twenty Plays of the Nō Theatre.* New York, 1970.

Komiya, Toyotaka. *Japanese Music and Drama in the Meiji Era*, Tokyo, 1956.

Nippon Gakujutsu Shinkōkai. *Japanese Noh Drama. 3* vols. Tokyo, 1955–60.

O'Neill, P.G. *Early Nō Drama*, London, 1958.

Peri, Noël. *Le Nô*. Tokio, 1944.

Renondeau, Gaston. *Nô*, Tokio, 1954.

Sakanishi, Shio. *Kyōgen: Comic Interludes of Japan*, Boston, 1938. (Reprinted as *The Ink-Smeared Lady and Other Kyōgen*, Tokyo, 1960).

Sieffert, René. *La Tradition Secrète du Nô*, Paris, 1960. (A translation of critical writings by Zeami, and of a program of Nō and Kyōgen plays.)

Ueda, Makoto. *The Old Pine Tree and Other Noh Plays*, Lincoln, 1962.

Waley, Arthur. *The Nō Plays of Japan*. London, 1921.

Texts of Nō and Kyōgen

Koyama, Hiroshi 小山弘志. *Kyōgen Shū* 狂言集. *Nihon Koten Bungaku Taikei* series. 2 vols. 1960–61. Texts of the Ōkura school in modern orthography. The notes consist mainly of quotations from the 1603 Japanese-Portuguese dictionary.

Nonomura, Kaizō 野々村戒三 and Furukawa Hisashi 古川久. *Kyōgen Shū. Nihon Koten Zensho* series. 3 vols. 1953–56. An excellent edition of texts of the now defunct Sagi school of Kyōgen.

Nonomura, Kaizō. *Yōkyoku Sambyakugojūban Shū. Nihon Meicho Zenshū* series. 1928. Valuable for the texts of plays no longer in the repertory.

Ōwada, Tateki 大和田建樹 *Yōkyoku Hyōshaku*. 1907. Outdated in most respects, this volume is still useful for texts not easily found elsewhere.

Sanari, Kentarō 佐成謙太郎. *Yōkyoku Taikan* 謡曲大観. 7 vols. 2nd ed. 1954. An indispensable work. Gives texts with modern language translations.

Sasano, Ken 笹野堅. *Nō Kyōgen*. 3 vols. *Iwanami Bunko* series. 2nd ed., 1956. Texts of the Ōkura school. A lengthy introduction but no notes.

Tanaka, Mitsuru 田中充. *Bangai Yōkyoku. Koten Bunko* series. 1950. Texts of plays not in current repertory. No notes.

Tanaka, Mitsuru. *Yōkyoku Shū. Nihon Koten Zensho* series. 3 vols. 1949–57. Notes, exceedingly scarce in the first volume, are generous by the third. Gives Kurumaya texts, the basic ones of Komparu school.

Yokomichi, Mario 横道萬里雄 and Omote, Akira 表章. *Yōkyoku Shū. Nihon Koten Bungaku Taikei* series. 1963. Excellent annotated texts, but a rigid criterion of authorship results in some masterpieces by unidentified writers being omitted or given far less attention than poor works by identified writers.

General Works

Engeki Hyakka Daijiten 演劇百科大辞典. 6 vols. 1961. An invaluable encyclopedia of the theatre.

Furukawa, Hisashi. *Nō no Sekai*. 1960. An unpretentious but excellent introduction.

Hayashiya, Tatsusaburō 林屋辰三郎. *Kabuki Izen*. 1954. A study of Japanese theatre and its social background before the rise of Kabuki.

Kobayashi, Shizuo 小林静雄. *Nōgakushi Kenkyū*. 1945. A scholarly and well-documented study of the history of Nō, especially during the Muromachi period.

Kongō, Iwao 金剛巌. *Nō*. 1948. Much of the material is elementary, but the book is dotted with observations worthy of a master actor.

Maruoka, Akira 丸岡明. *Nihon no Nō*. 1957. Interesting descriptions of performances since the war.

Miyake, Noboru 三宅襄. *Nō*. 1948. Excellent general study.

Nishio, Minoru 西尾実 and others. *Yōkyoku Kyōgen*. 1961. Extremely valuable for its surveys of studies in different aspects of Nō and Kyōgen, and for its reproduction of various important historical and critical texts.

Nogami, Toyoichirō 野上豊一郎. *Nō: Kenkyū to Hakken*. 1930. A pioneer work of scholarship, containing stimulating essays.

Nogami, Toyoichirō (ed.) *Nōgaku Zensho.* 6 vols. 1942–44. Indispensable collection of essays on all aspects of Nō and Kyōgen. The 1952–58 revision in five volumes is inferior.

Nose, Asaji 能勢朝次. *Nōgaku Genryū Kō.* 1938. The basic study of the development of Nō. A masterpiece.

Nose, Asaji. *Nōgaku Kenkyū.* 1940. Excellent essays on various topics.

Yokoi, Haruno 横井春野. *Nōgaku Zenshi.* 1917. Extremely detailed for Tokugawa period. Not to be consulted lightly.

Yokomichi, Mario and Masuda, Shōzō 増田正造. *Nō to Kyōgen.* 1959. Basic information on Nō and Kyōgen.

Ikeuchi, Nobuyoshi 池内信嘉. *Nōgaku Seisuiki.* 2 vols. 1925–6. A massive compilation of materials on Nō during the Tokugawa and Meiji eras.

Biographical

Kobayashi, Shizuo. *Zeami* 世阿弥. 1958. A brilliant study of Zeami's life, art, plays, and critical works.

Kobayashi, Shizuo. *Yōkyoku Sakusha no Kenkyū.* 1941. Biographies of the principal Nō dramatists. A careful study.

Kōzai, Tsutomu 香西精. *Zeami Shinkō.* 1962. Important essays on Zeami's life, religious beliefs, and style.

Nogami, Toyoichirō. *Kannami Kiyotsugu* 観阿弥清次. 1949. Stretches out to 155 pages a meagre number of facts.

Nogami, Toyoichirō. *Zeami Motokiyo.* 1938. A useful study of Zeami and his art.

Usui, Nobuyoshi 臼井信義. *Ashikaga Yoshimitsu* 足利義満. *Jimbutsu Sōsho* series. 1960. A useful biography of Zeami's great patron.

Nō Criticism

Kawase, Kazuma 川瀬一馬. *Gendaigoyaku Kadensho.* 1962. A translation into modern Japanese of Zeami's most famous work.

Konishi, Jinichi 小西甚一. *Nōgakuron Kenkyū.* 1961. Brilliant essays on the theories of Zeami and later dramatists.

Konishi, Jinichi. *Zeami Jūrokubu Shū.* 1954. A translation into modern Japanese of important treatises by Zeami.

Nishio, Minoru (ed.). *Karon Shū; Nōgakuron Shū.* *Nihon Koten Bungaku Taikei* series. 1961. Excellent edition with ample notes of Zeami's writings.

Nose, Asaji. *Zeami Jūrokubu Shū Hyōshaku.* 2 vols. 1944. Indispensable translation of and commentary on Zeami's writings.

Omote, Akira (ed.) *Bushō Goma* 舞正語磨. 1958. Text of the seventeenth-century attack on the Kita school, with an introduction.

Masks

Gotō, Hajime 後藤淑. *Nōmenshi Kenkyū Josetsu.* 1964. An important study of masks preserved at various remote shrines and temples. Provides a means of understanding the later masks.

Kaneko, Ryōun 金子良運. *Kamen no Bi.* 1961. A well-illustrated introduction to all varieties of masks in Japan, with helpful pointers for identifying them.

Kongō, Iwao. *Nō to Nōmen.* 1951. A great actor's personal view of the beauty of the masks.

Nogami, Toyoichirō. *Nōmen Ronkō.* 1944. A comprehensive treatment of the masks.

Noma, Seiroku 野間清六. *Nihon Kamen Shi.* 1943. Good especially for pre-Nō masks.

Shirasu, Masako 白洲正子. *Nōmen.* 1964. Fine photographs and a sensitive appreciation of the masks.

Costumes

Fujishiro, Tsugio 藤城継夫. *Shashin de Miru Nō no Funsō.* 1962. A most useful guide to Nō costumes.

Noma, Seiroku. *Kosode to Nō Ishō.* 1965. Lovely reproductions of Nō and Kyōgen robes, but the text is insufficiently informative.

The Actors

Nogami, Toyoichirō. (ed.) *Yōkyoku Geijutsu.* 1936. In addition to the general discussion by the editor, the book contains accounts by outstanding actors of their interpretations of different genres of Nō.

Sakurama, Kyūsen 桜間弓川. *Sakurama Geiwa.* 1948. A small volume of recollections and observations by a great actor.

Shigeyama, Sensaku 茂山千作. *Kyōgen Hachijūnen.* 1951. Reminiscences of the famous Kyōgen actor.

Shirasu, Masako. *Umewaka Minoru Kikigaki* 梅若実聞書. 1951. The story, in a transcription of his own words, of the son of the great Meiji actor, a self-effacing artist who never achieved the highest fame.

Yanagizawa, Hideki 柳沢英樹. *Hōshō Kurō Den* 宝生九郎傳. 1944. Ostensibly a biography of the great actor of the Meiji era, it hardly attempts to penetrate surface facts; valuable instead for its account of Nō during a critical period.

Regional Entertainments

Honda, Yasuji 本田安次. *Minzoku Geinō* 民族芸能. 1962. Brief descriptions with photographs of many regional entertainments.

Honda, Yasuji. *Nō oyobi Kyōgen Kō.* 1943. Miscellaneous essays in which the author attempts to discover early forms of Nō and Kyōgen in surviving rural theatricals.

Honda, Yasuji. *Okina sono hoka.* 1958. Intended as a continuation of the preceding title, it describes in addition to *Okina* various old forms of Nō and Kyōgen surviving today, including Mibu Kyōgen.

Ikeda, Yasaburō 池田弥三郎. *Nihon Geinō Denshō Ron.* 1962. Essays on the folkloristic and social background of the Japanese arts and their transmission. Popularly written.

Takeuchi, Katsutarō 竹内勝太郎. *Geijutsu Minzokugaku Kenkyū.* 1949. Includes essays on the beginnings of Nō and on Mibu Kyōgen.

Toita, Michizō 戸井田道三. *Nō: Kami to Kojiki no Geijutsu.* 1964. An interesting approach to Nō from a folkloristic and anthropological viewpoint.

Performance of Nō and Kyōgen

Araki, Yoshio 荒木良雄 and Shigeyama Sennojō 茂山千之丞. *Kyōgen*. 1956. The historical appreciation of Kyōgen by Araki is followed by Shigeyama's elucidation of the techniques of performance.

Kobayashi, Shizuo. *Yōkyoku no Kanshō*. 1939. Though intended primarily for high-school students, the book is important because of its discussion of how the plays considered are performed.

Miyake, Noboru. *Nō Enshutsu no Kenkyū*. 1948. The most detailed explanations of the *kogaki* and other aspects of performance.

Suda, Atsuo 須田敦夫. *Nihon Gekijō Shi no Kenkyū*. 1957. Devoted in part to a study of the Nō stage.

Music

Kikkawa, Eiji 吉川英史. *Nihon Ongaku no Rekishi*. 1965. An impressive study of all aspects of Japanese music.

Minagawa, Tatsuo 皆川達夫. "Japanese Noh Music" in *Journal of the American Musicological Society*, Vol. X, No. 3, 1957.

Yokomichi, Mario. "Nō no Ongaku" in booklet accompanying records of Nō produced in 1963 for the six hundredth anniversary of Zeami's birth.

INDEX

actors and acting, 15, 16, 17, 23–26, 27, 32–33, 34, 39–40, 42, 43, 57–59; training of actors, 57–59
Adachigahara, 59; see also *Kurozuka*
ado (Kyōgen role), 56
aesthetic appeal of Nō, 17
ageuta (Nō song), 49
ai (interlude), 21, 49, 55
ai-kyōgen (interval recitations), 21, 54, 55
ai-kyōgen actor, 21, 55
Akechi-uchi, 38
amateurs and amateur performances, 16, 37, 38, 45, 67; *see also* regional performances of Nō and Kyōgen
Aoi no Ue, 38, 51, 53, 63, 71
Aoyama Palace, Nō stage at, 43
Ariwara no Narihira, 52, 73, 87
Ashikaga Yoshihisa, 37
Ashikaga Yoshimasa, 37, 65, 66, 75
Ashikaga Yoshimitsu, 23, 31, 32, 33–34, 36, 37, 42, 43
Ashikaga Yoshimochi, 33, 34
Ashikaga Yoshinori, 31, 34, 35, 36
Ataka, 22, 53, 62
atoza (rear section of stage), 19, 75, 77
Atsumori (*Atsumori*), 50–51
Atsumori, 20, 26, 46, 50
audience, character of, 14, 16–17, 42, 73; seating of, 19, 75
audience appeal of Nō, 14–15, 16; of Kyōgen, 27, 56

ballet, Nō dance contrasted with, 71, 73
Bashō ("The Plantain Tree"), 65
bass drum, see *taiko*
benefit performances (*kanjin* Nō), 34, 35, 39, 40–41, 42
Benkei: in *Ataka*, 62; in *Funa Benkei*, 54, 75; in *Kanjinchō*, 53; in *Shōzon*, 54
"Benkei in the Boat," see *Funa Benkei*
Bernhardt, Sarah, 24
beshimi mask, 64
Biblical themes in Nō, 39
Bishamon, 64
Bishamon mask, 64

"Blind Man Looks at the Moon, The," see *Tsukimi Zatō*
"Book of Nō Composition, The," see *Nōsakusho*
"Book of the Transmission of the Flower, The," see *Kadensho*
"Book of the Way of the Highest Flower, The," see *Shikadōsho*
Buddhist elements in Nō, 17, 28–29, 36, 48
bugaku, 29, 39, 63, 75
bugaku masks, 63
Bunraku, 39, 41
Bushō Goma, 25

categories of Kyōgen, 26
categories of Nō, 21–22
categories of roles, 20–21
Central Asia, dance of, 29
character types in Nō, 23; in Kyōgen, 26
Chikatō, 54
child actors, 21, 32, 56, 57
child roles, see *kokata*
"chill," see *hie*
China, 14, 29, 31, 38, 78; Japanese relations with, 31, 38; theatre of, 14, 29
Chinese immigrants in Japan, 26
Chinese influences on Japanese dance, 29
Chinese personages in Nō, 38, 54, 77
chōken robe, 66
choreography, *see* dance as element of Nō
chorus, 19, 20, 21, 39, 67, 68
Chōryō, 37
chūjō mask, 61
chūkei fan, 78
chūnomai (Nō dance), 72, 73
chū-nori rhythm, 68
Chūsonji, Nō performances at, 92
climax, see *kyū*
color in costumes, 65–66
comedy, *see* Kyōgen
comic origins of Nō, 13–14
commedia dell'arte, 26
"companion," see *tsure*
Confucian ethics of Tokugawa shogunate, 39

Hōshō school of Nō, 30, 37, 39, 42, 44, 59, 60, 69, 78; scene from performances by, 87
Hōshō Yagorō, 42

Ichijō Kanera, 36
Ichinotani, battle of, 50
iemoto system, 58–59
Ieyasu, *see* Tokugawa Ieyasu
Ikkyū, 36
Imakumano Shrine, Nō performances at, 31, 32
"imitation of things," see *monomane*
"Imperial Warship," see *Miikusabune*
India, dances of, 25; music of, 29
Inland Sea, 19, 31, 75
innovations in modern Nō theatre, 76
inori (Nō dance), 73
interlude, see *ai*
interpretation of roles, 15, 16
introduction of Nō play, see *jo*
Inuō, *see* Dōami
"Iris, The," see *Kakitsubata*
iro, *see* color in costumes
iroe (Nō dance), 73
Ise Monogatari, 18
Ise Shrine, *see* Great Shrine of Ise
Ishigami, 56
Ishikawa Tatsuemon (mask-maker), 64, 96
issei (entrance song), 48, 68
Itsukushima Shrine, Nō performances at, 92; Nō stage at, 19, 75–76
Iwakura Tomomi, 43, 44, 58
Iwasaki Yanosuke, 76
Izumi school of Kyōgen, 41, 55, 60, 78; scene from performances by, 90
Izutsu, 23, 52, 77, 87

jars under Nō stage, 19, 76
Jinen Koji (*Jinen Koji*), 53
Jinen Koji, 32, 53
jo (introduction of Nō play), 21, 29, 48, 72
Jones, Stanleigh H., Jr., 51
jonomai (Nō dance), 73

Kabuki, 22, 37, 39, 43, 44, 53, 59
Kadensho ("The Book of the Transmission of the Flower"), 33
kagami-ita ("mirror boards"), 13
Kagekiyo (*Kagekiyo*), 69, 77, 89
Kagekiyo, 54, 69, 77, 89
Kagura (Shinto dances), 14
kagura (Nō dance), 72
Kagyū, 90
kakegoe (cry), 70
kakekotoba (pivot word), 46–47
kakeri (Nō dance), 73
Kakitsubata ("The Iris"), 16

kamigakari (style of Kyoto), 37
kamimai (Nō dance), 72, 73
kammuri (head ornament), 65
Kanawa, 73
Kanehira, 51
Kanjinchō, 22, 53
kanjin Nō, *see* benefit performances
Kannami, 25, 30, 31–32, 33, 36, 39; plays of, 32
Kantan, 54
Kanze Motomasa, 69
Kanze Sakon, 68–69
Kanze school of Nō, 30, 37, 39, 42, 44, 59, 60, 61, 78; scenes from performances by, 83, 87, 89
kashira wig, 65
Kasuga Festival, 37
Kasuga Shrine, Nō performances at, 13, 28, 75
Kasui, 54
kata (gestures), 16, 17, 72
Kayoi Komachi, 32
Kazumō, 64
kazuramono, *see* woman plays
Kintōshō, 35
Kinuta, 47–48, 53, 65
kiriago ("split jaw") mask, 93
kirido (door for chorus), 19, 20
kiri Nō, *see* demon plays
Kirokuda ("Six Loads of Lumber"), 91
Kita Roppeita, 23, 44, 59, 71, 76
Kita school of Nō, 39–40, 44, 59, 60, 78; scenes from performances by, 83, 85, 92
Kita Shichidayū, 46
Kiyohime (*Dōjōji*), 63–64
Kiyotsune, 26, 61
kobeshimi mask, 64
Kōfukuji Temple, Nō and *ennen* performances at, 28–29
kogaki variations, 60
Koi no Omoni, 45
Kojirō Nobumitsu, plays of, 36–37
kokata (child roles), 20, 21, 57, 66
kōken (understudy), 20
Kokinshū, 46
kokushikijō mask, 62, 93
Komachi: in *Kayoi Komachi*, 32; in *Sekidera Komachi*, 95; in *Sotoba Komachi*, 32, 87, 95
Kombu Uri ("The Seaweed Peddler"), 41
Kōmei, Emperor, 43
Komparu school of Nō, 13, 21, 37, 39, 44, 59, 60, 61, 78
Komparu Shirōjirō, 27
Komparu Zempō, plays of, 37, 54
Komparu Zenchiku, 33, 35, 36, 37, 65; plays and critical writings of, 36
Kongō Iwao (former), 44, 60, 62, 71; (present), 66
Kongō Magojirō (mask-maker and actor), 64

Nōgakusha, *see* Nō Society
Nonomiya ("The Shrine in the Fields"), 15, 38, 51–52, 54, 62
Nōsakusho ("The Book of Nō Composition"), 34
Nō Society (Nōgakusha), 44
Nō theatre, 19, 44, 74, 76; *see also* stage
"Nurturing the Aged," see *Yōrō*

ōakujō mask, 94
Oba ga Sake, 56
Obasute, 47
Ochiba ("Fallen Leaves"), 66
Okina (*Okina*), 62
Okina, 13, 21, 28, 29, 31, 32, 38, 42, 55, 58, 61, 62, 73, 93
okina mask, 13, 62, 93
Ōkura school of Kyōgen, 41, 55, 60, 70, 78; scene from performances by, 91
Ōmi, *sarugaku* style of, 33, 34
Ōmi onna mask, 64
omo (Kyōgen role), 55
Ōmura Yūko, plays of, 38
one-scene plays, 20
Ōnin Rebellion, 36
Onnami, *see* Motoshige
Ono no Komachi, *see* Komachi
ō-nori rhythm, 68
opera, Nō contrasted with, 19, 43
Orfeo ed Euridice, 20
oto mask, 64
ōtsuzumi, 15, 20, 70

patriotic plays, 44
Perry, Matthew C., 43
"person at the side," see *waki*
pine tree backdrop, 13, 17, 76; *see also* Yōgō Pine
pine trees on *hashigakari*, 19
pivot word, see *kakekotoba*
"Plantain Tree, The," see *Bashō*
Po Chü-i, 35, 46
poetry as element of Nō, 16, 17, 46–49, 51–52
Pound, Ezra, 17
"profundity" as element in acting, 23, 24
props, 17, 53, 75, 76–78
protagonist, see *shite*
public performances of Nō and Kyōgen, 14, 37–38, 40–41, 42–43, 44; *see also* benefit performances

Racine, 47
Raikō (*Tsuchigumo*), 90
rambyōshi (Nō dance), 44, 71, 72
"rank," *see* "dignity"
Rashōmon, 37
realism and non-realism in Nō, 15, 16, 25

regional performances of Nō and Kyōgen, 14, 92
"related words," see *engo*
religious elements in Nō, 13, 14, 28, 36; *see also* ritual nature and uses of Nō
Renshō (*Atsumori*), 50, 51
repertory of Nō, 16, 18, 41, 59–60
ritual nature and uses of Nō, 14, 39–40, 41
rōjo mask, 95
Rokujō, Lady: in *Aoi no Ue*, 63; in *Nonomiya*, 15, 16, 51
roles, categories of, 20–21
rongi (dialogue of *shite* and chorus), 49, 50

Sado, Zeami exiled to, 35
sageuta (Nō song), 49
Sagi ("The White Heron"), 23, 71
Sagi school of Kyōgen, 41, 55
Sakagami (*Semimaru*), 89
Sakato *sarugaku* troupe, 30
Sakuragawa, 61, 64
Sakurama Bamba, 44
Sakurama Kintarō, 71–72
Sakurama Kintō, 44
samai form of *bugaku*, 29
Sambasō (*Okina*), 62, 93
samurai as patrons and performers of Nō, 40
sangaku, 29–30
Sannimpu ("The Three Farmers"), 55
sannoku (passage of entrance song), 48
sarugaku, 29, 30–31, 32, 33, 34, 40, 58
Sarugaku Dangi ("Conversations on *Sarugaku*"), 34
sashi (passage of Nō play), 48–49
schools of Kyōgen, 41, 55, 60; *see also* Izumi, Ōkura, Sagi schools
schools of Nō, 37, 44, 59–60; *see also* Hōshō, Kanze, Kita, Komparu, Kongō schools
Schumann, Elizabeth, 24
"Seaweed Peddler, The," see *Kombu Uri*
second-category plays, *see* warrior plays
Sekidera Komachi, 18–19, 38, 40, 62, 95
Semi, 64
Semimaru (*Semimaru*), 89
Semimaru, 73, 89
Sengorō Masatora, 70
Senzai (*Okina*), 31, 32
Seven Sages of the Bamboo Grove, 78
Shakespeare, 47
Shakkyō, 77
shakumi mask, 61, 62, 64, 65
Shakuzuru (mask-maker), 64, 94
shamanism, 28
Shiba Park, Nō stage in, 44
Shibata, 38
Shibata Katsuie, 38
shidai (entrance song of *waki*), 48, 68
Shiga, 46
Shigeyama Sennojō, 70

The Art of the Japanese Puppet Theatre

INTRODUCTION

PUPPET and marionette shows have intrigued me since I was a child and saw my first *Aladdin and his Wonderful Lamp*. Something uncanny, and at the same time enormously endearing, gave these shows an allure which in later years I was mistakenly to attribute to the guilelessness of extreme youth. The association of puppet shows with the schoolroom proved so strong, indeed, that once I considered myself beyond the stage of childish pleasures I felt rather ashamed of my lingering fondness for the make-believe world of little wooden people. Only much later was I to discover, after beginning the study of Japanese, that in one country at least the puppet theatre had developed not only as an adult entertainment, but as the vehicle of a magnificent dramatic art. I came to realize that Bunraku (the common name for the Japanese puppet theatre) occupies a most important place in Japanese literary and theatrical history alike, and by no means belongs to the frivolous class of entertainments associated with puppets and marionettes in other parts of the world. I learned too that Japan's greatest tragic dramatist, Chikamatsu Monzaemon, wrote not for actors but for the Bunraku puppets, and when I later had the chance to attend the Bunraku Theatre, I found that the audience today as in the past is there to enjoy a true dramatic performance rather than an amusing display of the dexterity of the operators. I noted how much more frequently one saw an old lady brush away the tears induced by some pathetic scene than one heard the sounds of laughter we might expect in the West at Punch and Judy shows.

My active interest in Bunraku began long before I was able to visit Japan and witness a performance. In 1949 I completed a doctoral thesis about one of Chikamatsu's plays, depending on descriptions, photographs, and my imagination when attempting to describe its effectiveness as a work for the theatre. Much as I tried to persuade myself that a dramatic illusion could be sustained, despite the presence of three men operating each of the puppets in full view of the audience, the photographs did little to reassure me. The first thing to strike my eyes, whichever photograph I examined, was the face of the principal operator, then his costume, and only thirdly the doll in his hands. How, I wondered privately, could one forget the operators when they seemed so much more alive than the puppets?

Nevertheless, when finally I had the opportunity to see Bunraku in Japan, I discovered that the claims of enthusiasts had not been mistaken; after the first few minutes of uncertainty I found myself being drawn into the world of the puppets, and if I looked at the operators' faces afterwards it was by deliberate choice, and not because they drew attention to themselves. I remember particularly from my first experience of Bunraku the energetic exit of one puppet, dragging the three operators after him. The photographs, I could only conclude, had lied; their record of Bunraku performances did not correspond to reality.

What was my amazement, then, when last year I saw Kaneko Hiroshi's Bunraku photographs! For the first time, I felt, the magical life of the puppets onstage had been captured, and I understood why. The audience requires time once a Bunraku play begins to forget the presence of the operators, but photographs provide no interval for the process of moving from the human beings to the world of the puppets. Mr. Kaneko, perceiving this, and noticing also that at times in each performance the operators are concealed from the audience's sight by the movements of the puppets, waited for these moments to take his pictures. The puppets, freed of human ties, reveal in his photographs the peculiarly tragic beauty we sense in witnessing an actual performance.

The present book originated in a sensitive artist's recreation in photographs of the evanescent illusions of a Bunraku performance. For my part, I have added historical and interpretative material, in the hopes of increasing the reader's appreciation of this extraordinary art. Here too, the illustrative photographs of Mr. Kaneko have been essential. I have devoted my attention chiefly to Bunraku as a theatrical, rather than as a literary, art. Readers interested in the texts are respectfully referred to my book of translations *Major Plays of Chikamatsu* and to other works listed in the bibliography.

One further word, on the subject of the name Bunraku. Strictly speaking, it designates exclusively the puppet theatre in Osaka descended from the one founded by Uemura Bunrakken (or, Bunraku-ken) some 150 years ago. I have used it, however, to describe many varieties of puppet entertainments in Japan, including independent regional traditions and even the early puppet theatre, before the advent of Bunrakken, who gave his name to the art. Purists may object, I know, but the alternative would have been to call what is essentially the same art by a number of different names. Bunraku, incidentally, is not pronounced in normal English fashion, but as if written something like *boon-rah-koo*. Although derived, as I have said, from a man's name, the characters for Bunraku 文楽 have a meaning too, "the pleasure of literature," not an inappropriate designation for a theatre where the texts have always been treated with extraordinary deference.

DONALD KEENE

[NOTE: Throughout this book, Japanese names appear in the Japanese order, with family name first and given or adopted name last.—EDITOR]

BUNRAKU

I. THE PLEASURES OF BUNRAKU

MAN HAS been making images of himself for so many millennia and in so many parts of the world that this habit has come to seem an instinctive part of human behavior. Whether the compulsion expresses itself in the form of cave paintings or manuscript illustrations, monumental sculptures or miniature dolls, it has proved irresistible, and has led to the creation of many supreme triumphs of art. But, not content with fashioning semblances of himself, man has sought also to impart to them life and movement like his own. The clockwork man which strikes the hours, the doll which cries "Mama!" when tilted forward, the puppet which obeys the will of an unseen hand, all testify to man's delight in creating imitations of himself. In every instance the creator hopes that his imitation will convince by fidelity to its model, and that it will be accorded the highest compliment a mechanical doll, a puppet or a marionette can evoke—the exclamation, "It seems to be alive!"

The oldest known puppets, those of ancient Egypt, were probably used in religious ceremonies to represent the actions of the gods, perhaps out of some belief that human imitation of the gods would be sacrilegious. Eventually, however, puppet shows ceased to be ritual performances and became instead popular entertainments, especially farces, as we know from the familiar spectacle of Punch and Judy banging logs over each other's head with the exaggerated vigor possible in a theatre which need not take human weaknesses into consideration. Indeed, the possibility of representing non-human actions—whether flying through the air or splitting in two—remains an indispensable part of the charms of puppets, and although an operator, depending on his skill, may convince us that the puppet performing at his instigation is really alive, it is essential that we realize with a part of our mind that the puppet is not human, but moves in a world of its own. The pleasure we take in puppets is similar to that of watching the antics of monkeys. We see in them our own familiar gestures, exaggerated in their "human" quality by our awareness that non-humans are performing them. Monkeys have not sufficient intelligence to sustain our interest in their actions, much less to cast them into an artistic pattern, but the puppet, though lacking life of its own, can borrow life from its operator, and become whatever he desires. It can be a god or a stammering idiot, but never itself, for it has no identity. It is equally suitable for sacred rituals or the crudest of farces.

Obviously, the more skilled an operator and the more advanced the mechanism of his puppet or marionette, the more convincing will be the illusion that a living creature is performing. If the operator is a master, his puppet can seem the very embodiment of the words of the play; the puppet is unlike an actor, who always retains something of his own personality, regardless of the role. But the puppet forfeits its claim on our attention if it is not imbued with the mystery of the non-human being magically possessed of human attributes. It is conceivable that a marvelously talented operator could manipulate a doll of human proportions so adroitly that an audience would be incapable of distinguishing the doll from a human being. Such excessive realism, as Chikamatsu Monzaemon noted, far from pleasing the audience, would probably disgust instead; Chikamatsu insisted that stylization in art and not literal fidelity is what the audience craves. A puppet which was indistinguishable from a human being would certainly not be his equal, for it would lack intelligence and individuality. The danger of over-realism is present today in exceptionally skillful varieties of marionette shows, where, after our initial astonishment at the realism of the movements, we are likely to grow bored with the expressionless little creatures so uninspiringly performing as Faust, Tamino, or the Queen of Denmark.

Stylization must be present not only in the manipulation of the puppets but in the texts they perform. It is possible, of course, to put puppets through the motions of *Faust*, *The Magic Flute*, or even *Hamlet*, but in these parts they are at a grave disadvantage, for they cannot achieve the individual coloring of an actor, nor do the texts permit them to display their superhuman capabilities. It is better to see a puppet performance of *Aladdin* than of *Hamlet*, for *Aladdin* at least has room for fantasy. Miracles, prodigies of speed, sudden transformations, and defiance of the law of gravity or the weight of numbers are all easily within the puppets' abilities, but they cannot sit still for long. In the West this has meant that plays written specifically for puppets have generally been intended as fast-moving entertainment for children, but in Japan stylization has been achieved without loss of literary excellence.

Bunraku is the one theatre of dolls for which literary masterpieces have been especially composed. Its techniques have been much improved since its inception in the sixteenth century, but unlike similar shows in the West, it was never, even at the crudest, considered a theatre primarily for the young and foolish. Its progress, resulting from a steadily increased awareness of dramatic possibilities, may be measured in terms of the additional demands made on its audiences, as well as by the more usual standards of improvement in the texts, the puppets, and the music. Each step in the direction of further realism has generally been accompanied by a simultaneous step in the direction of non-realism, as if those responsible for the fate of Bunraku knew of the dangers of surfeiting the public appetite for verisimilitude. Originally (as in some regional theatres today) the puppet operators supplied necessary bits of dialogue, but when more literary texts were adopted it became essential to employ a chanter to declaim the lines. At first he remained hidden behind the scenery, but precisely when the texts became more realistic and closer to the circumstances of ordinary life, the chanter was moved from backstage to a place before the audience, as if to deny the illusion that the puppets were speaking for themselves, and to insist on the primacy of the written word. The texts in turn were written in an often non-realistic idiom in order to provide maximum opportunities for the puppets to reveal their unique capacities. The audience today divides its attention variously between the chanter and the samisen player, the puppets and the operators, and yet somehow it is able to surmount these seeming distractions and impediments to a unified impression, the results of a non-realistic style, and to experience instead the satisfaction of complete entertainment.

The demands of realism and non-realism might be expressed instead as demands of drama and aesthetics. To achieve more powerful dramatic effects the Japanese invented puppet heads with movable eyes, mouths, eyebrows and, in some special instances, noses and ears, but to satisfy the aesthetic conviction that a small head was more attractive than a large one, the puppet heads, no matter how advanced in construction, continued to be disproportionately small. The audience accepted this convention in the interests of beauty. Similarly, the female puppets, though provided with hands of great flexibility and delicacy, normally have no feet because it was felt that the lines of the kimono (which reaches to the ground) are more beautiful when uninterrupted by feet. On the other hand, the left arm of the puppets is very much longer than the right one, not because of aesthetic principles, but because the three-man puppet (an invention intended to afford greater realism and dramatic expression) requires the operator of the left arm to stand farther away from the puppet's body than the operator of the right arm. The audience accepts this convention too, or may not even notice the difference in the lengths of the arms, for it never expects literal accuracy of details. Bunraku, at any rate, is immune to the temptation known in certain theatres of the West of trying to persuade the audience it is watching reality and not a play.

The stylization of Bunraku extends to the language of the texts. Most of the plays in the current repertory date from the eighteenth century, and it is not surprising that the language should be hard to understand today. (Japanese has changed vastly more than English during the same period.) However, even when first composed, passages in the text, particularly the descriptions of the journeys of the suicidally bent lovers or the reflective comments which often open an act, must have been beyond the comprehension of most in the audience. Far from objecting to this elaborate, artificial language, however, the audience accepted it as part of the aesthetic setting of the play. Even the dialogue, which on occasion could be bitingly harsh, is written throughout in a stage language probably never encountered outside the theatre. Attempts in recent years to employ the modern colloquial usually seem ludicrous, because the excessive realism violates the sense of distance necessary in a theatre as delicately poised between reality and non-reality as Bunraku.

Part of our pleasure in watching Bunraku today comes from an awareness, however imprecise, that every gesture by the puppets, every shift in inflection of the chanter's voice, every intensification of accent in the samisen accompaniment is the product of conscious efforts over many years to achieve a perfect balance between realism and non-realism. It is said to take a chanter eight years to master the art of weeping, whether as a girl disappointed in love or as a fierce warrior moved to tears by overpowering grief; but the chanter's protracted sobs and incoherent gasps are scarcely imitative of human expressions of sorrow. They are instead an extraction and exaggeration of the essential qualities of the weeping characteristic of different kinds of people. Hearing the terrible, sustained anguish of the brave man who finally yields to desolation at the loss of his son, we understand more about him than realistic representation would permit. Indeed, as Chikamatsu stated, if a woman in a play were closely modeled on real women, she might conceal her emotions completely, but such accuracy of portrayal would destroy the dramatic appeal of the play. Art, he insisted, lay in the narrow area between realism and fiction.

The stylization of gestures and our continual awareness that we are witnessing a play make it possible for us to accept in Bunraku scenes which would be unspeakably horrible if realistically represented. When Matsuōmaru in "The Village School" examines the severed head of his son, the scene (approached in Shakespeare only by the cruder parts of *Titus Andronicus*) would either fill the audience with terror or stir uneasy laughter if it were not acted with ritual formality. The puppeteers not only make it possible for us to witness this scene without acute discomfort, but by daring to present such extremes of human feeling they may touch levels of emotion deeper than those of more realistic dramas. Performances of the same play by Kabuki actors achieve similar results because the actors continue to observe the puppet traditions. On a more elementary plane, scenes of mayhem or brutality can be funny (in the manner of Punch and Judy) or gruesome (as in the Bunraku play "Summer Festival") without offending our sensibilities.

To visit the Bunraku Theatre today is to witness the re-enactment of many traditions. In comparison, our performances of Shakespeare tend to insist on the contemporary validity of the texts and to deny the centuries separating Shakespeare and ourselves; the actors often deliberately speak the lines of great poetry as if they were prose, and the greatest ingenuity is devoted to inventing new stage business which will not violate the letter of the text. These methods certainly reap more successful financial rewards than the conservatism of Bunraku, but they threaten constantly to falsify, if not destroy, the play as originally conceived. Bunraku has thus far escaped this danger, probably because the conservative (in the literal sense) traditions are so strong in Japan. To cite one example: Customers entering the Bunraku Theatre are likely to buy programs; if not, they can always learn which plays are to be offered and the names of the performers by consulting prominently displayed billboards. Nevertheless, at the beginning of each scene, even as the chanter and his accompanist make their appearance to the right on a revolving platform which swings them into view of the audience, a man dressed in black with a black hood over his head proclaims the start of the play by beating wooden clappers and reciting in sing-song intonation the names of the artists. His presence, strictly speaking, is no more necessary than at a performance of ballet or of Kabuki, where changes of performers from scene to scene are noted in the programs but not reported aloud, yet without this man's announcement Bunraku would seem deprived of an important ingredient. He tells us that we are about to enter a special domain of make-believe, of theatre, and his fading voice as he turns to leave with a final *"Tōzai!"* (*"Hear ye!"*) is the proper signal for the first notes of the samisen.

The chanter generally begins his recitation with a melancholy series of virtually inarticulate sounds. If one examines the text, one will discover that the opening words are often something like "Thus it happened," and are, in fact, the conclusion of the previous scene, which is not performed. A Bunraku program today normally comprises selected scenes from four or five different plays, rather than one entire work, but for musical reasons a performance may thus begin with the dying notes of an earlier act.

Soon after the chanter enters his description of the new scene, the curtain is drawn aside to reveal the set, a naturalistic rendering of a landscape or interior. If the backdrop represents an outdoor scene, it is painted on a series of vertical panels which may be moved laterally to suggest that the characters (who remain in one place) are traveling. If an interior, the gate, framework of the house, and generally one room are depicted, with the suggestion of other rooms beyond. A garden and nearby buildings may also be represented. A doorway at the rear-center of the stage is usual, for it permits the female characters to make spectacular exits, displaying their figures from behind. Very few props are used; unless necessary to the action, the furnishings are generally painted on the backdrop, to allow the operators maximum freedom of movement.

The Bunraku stage, traditionally 36 feet wide, 25 feet deep, and 15 feet high, is divided into various playing areas. The main stage occupies about half the total area, and often serves as the interior of a house. Three raised partitions of different heights run across the width of the stage, standing before the trench-like passages in which the operators work. The partitions conceal the lower half of the principal operator's body, more of the operator of the left hand (who does not wear high-platformed clogs), and almost all of the operator of the feet; at the same time, they provide the apparent floor or ground level on which the puppets walk or sit. To the audience's right is a dais projecting into the auditorium from the stage. There the chanter perches on bulky cushions before an elaborately fashioned reading-stand; to his left, the samisen player sits on a single cushion, dwarfed by the chanter.

By the time the audience has taken in the scene, the first puppet will have made his entrance from the left, often with spectacularly vigorous strides, arms and legs thrust forward as if in excess of energy. Such exaggeration may withhold attention from the three men operating each of the puppets, but soon we will notice and perhaps be distracted by the principal operator, who usually wears a brightly colored, stiffly starched jacket over his kimono, and by his two assistants, less conspicuously attired in black. It takes time to forget their presence, but it regularly happens, as many visitors to Bunraku have discovered, including Arnold Toynbee, who wrote:

In looking on at a Japanese puppet show at Osaka one afternoon in November, 1929, I duly found, as I had been assured beforehand I should find, it possible to entertain the illusion that the puppets were animated by an autonomous life of their own, although the human artists manipulating them were in full view of the spectators. An artistic effect which, in the West, would have been produced by the artifice of keeping the manipulators out of sight, was produced in Japan by their artistry in keeping themselves out of mind notwithstanding their visibility. The Japanese manipulators achieved this *tour de force* of managing to deflect the spectators' attention away from themselves and on to their puppets by making their own movements appear lifeless and their own countenances impassive. They succeeded, in fact, in subjectively effacing their objectively visible living human forms...*

Once we have accustomed ourselves to the operators and even forgotten them, we are able to admire the wonderful expressiveness of the puppets and to understand why Japanese audiences accept the awkwardness of three grown men manipulating a doll two-thirds human size. Students of Bunraku invariably insist on the importance of the three men "breathing together"; it can readily be imagined what a blow would be dealt dramatic illusion if the puppet's left hand failed to meet the right hand when a gesture of clapping was intended. The performers at the Bunraku Theatre are of course far beyond the level of such elementary disasters, but clearly they are not all equally accomplished. It is exciting even to watch the least skilled among them, but when a master like Kiritake Monjūrō or the late Yoshida Bungorō manipulates a puppet we sense immediately the presence of life. The flutter of agitation in a woman's breast, the emotion she reveals only in the unconscious movement of a hand, the exquisite moment when, about to make her departure, she hesitates and casts a final glance at the room—all reveal a skill possessed by few real women of communicating to an audience the mysteries of the feminine heart.

If the three operators of a puppet must "breathe" as a single entity, it is no less essential that the three component parts of Bunraku, the narration, the music, and the puppets, "breathe" as one. The music of Bunraku on the whole is not especially tuneful (it is hard to imagine anyone whistling a favorite passage), nor, considering how frequently music from one play was borrowed in composing another, can it be said to be very distinctive. Yet the music is indispensable, both to the chanter, whose voice follows the musical line, and to the operators, who take their signals from the notes of the samisen. The samisen players, though the least feted of the Bunraku artists, bear the chief responsibility for guiding the performance. In a company of the excellence of the Bunraku Theatre the perfect fusion of the three elements seems so effortless as to be almost automatic, but, as a visit to any amateur performance would quickly demonstrate, the apparent effortlessness is the product of many years of individual training as well as of constant rehearsals to improve the coordination of the parts. The samisen player has been called the "wife" of the chanter; his function is not to call attention to his own dexterity but to heighten the effect of the chanter's delivery. It takes about five years, one samisen player estimated, before the partnership of chanter and player "breathes together." The relationship between puppet operators and the samisen is not as close, for they do not function as partners, but an unexpected tempo from the samisen unnerves an operator as easily as a chanter.

The pleasure of seeing these three forms of art combined together is that of a "universal work of art" (or *gesamtkunstwerk*, to use Wagner's term), a performance which satisfies simultaneously by the literary interest of the text, the musical appeal of the samisen, and the visual brilliance of the puppets. In opera, where these three elements take different forms, the music clearly is supreme, and a failure to become deeply absorbed in the story of *Lohengrin* or to be impressed by the stage appearance of the tenor is only a minor disappointment if the music is splendidly sung. In Kabuki, a theatre of virtuoso actors, even a foolish story like *Shibaraku*, which can boast no remarkable musical embellishment, maintains its popularity on the stage because it provides an actor with a magnificent opportunity to display his authority. In Bunraku, the three elements are nearly of equal importance, and a performance by masters of each art provides a thoroughly satisfying theatrical experience.

Of course, as might be said of any complex, traditional art, the connoisseur's enjoyment of Bunraku requires preparation. Unless one understands the text, it is impossible to appreciate fully

* Arnold Toynbee, *A Study of History* (London: Oxford University Press, under the auspices of the Royal Institute of International Affairs)

the skill of the narrator in rendering the emotions behind each phrase, however much one admires the extraordinary vividity of his expression. Familiarity with the text is no less essential in understanding the puppets' gestures, or what has occasioned the sudden sharpness of the samisen's tone. An acquaintance with past interpretations of the parts by the same or different artists also adds much to an appreciation of a new performance. Apart from such general considerations, the special characteristics of Bunraku require study too: the choice of head used for each character, the costuming, the patterns of gesture, the manner in which the Bunraku and Kabuki versions of the same play differ. A knowledge of the history of the art and techniques of Bunraku, though not indispensable to the enjoyment of a performance, also increases one's pleasure and understanding. It is hoped that the following chapters and the photographs will help to suggest the pleasures of Bunraku, though of course like all dramatic arts it can be fully appreciated only in the theatre.

II. THE HISTORY OF BUNRAKU

THE PUPPETS

Bunraku, the familiar name of the Japanese puppet theatre today, is a term dating back no further than the early nineteenth century. The art of puppetry, however, has been known in Japan for over a thousand years, though accounts in the old records are so cryptic that little can be said with confidence about its ancient history. Scholars have mulled over each word in the available evidence, and depending on their interpretations of the linguistic, folkloristic and literary materials, have reached quite different conclusions about the beginnings of puppetry in Japan. Some are convinced that the Japanese puppets were indigenous; others insist that they were introduced from abroad; and still others have attempted to find place for both native and foreign traditions.

The earliest Japanese name for "puppet" was *kugutsu*, a word found in an eighth-century gloss on a Chinese Buddhist text. This mysterious name has intrigued scholars for centuries; it has variously been traced to a Chinese word for puppet, pronounced approximately *kuai-luai-tzu* in the same period, or to *kuki* or *kukli*, gypsy words which some claim were probably the origin of both Chinese and Japanese terms. The Turkish *kukla*, and the late Greek *koukla* have also been cited as proof of the transmission of the art of puppetry from Asia Minor across the vast Central Asian regions to China, Korea, and eventually to Japan.

The possibility of foreign origins is intriguing, but the evidence is by no means conclusive. Japanese folklorists tend to reject such theories, pointing out that the sounds *kugu* or *kugutsu* are found in native shrine and deity names, a clue perhaps to some connection between the earliest puppets and religious worship at particular Shinto shrines. Puppets preserved today at shrines in scattered areas of Japan clearly suggest ancient traditions behind them. In the north, the worship of the god Oshira involves a medium who recites spells and stories accompanied by the two simple stick puppets she operates, one in each hand, raising, lowering, or confronting the puppets as she speaks. At two shrines in Kyushu, puppets, perhaps the oldest in Japan, perform dances and wrestling matches as part of the annual festival. These Shinto puppets are not representations of divinities (in the manner of Buddhist or Christian images) but, rather, wooden creatures temporarily "possessed" by the gods whose actions they recreate, much as the medium herself is believed to repeat, when "possessed," words uttered by the god himself. Puppet performances at a shrine are intended to depict deeds of the ancient past in order that men of later ages may know the glory of the divinity worshipped there. It is easy to imagine a purely indigenous art of puppetry developing from the sacred dolls used by mediums, but until the mystery of the name *kugutsu* is solved we cannot deny the possibility that puppet performances, introduced from abroad, were adopted in ancient times to Shinto worship.

What may have begun as fragmentary, incoherent utterances of a medium, accompanied by the rudimentary gestures of puppets, in time acquired a ritual and even dramatic form. Puppet plays (like sacred dances at Shinto shrines today) were probably offered to the gods by rich patrons in the hope of inducing them to grant additional prosperity. Because these performances were presented for the gods, human witnesses were unnecessary, but as the puppets came to attract spectators, an embryonic puppet theatre was created, and eventually, we may suppose, the pleasure of these spectators, as well as of the gods, was taken into consideration by the puppeteers. The simple movements of a stick puppet operated by a medium intoning ancient legends are, of course, a far cry from the sophisticated art of Bunraku, but even in its most primitive form we can detect one peculiar feature of the Japanese puppet theatre: the medium makes no attempt to conceal the fact that she is manipulating the puppets. Unlike puppet or marionette performances in other countries, then, the Japanese art normally did not require the illusion that the puppets were moving and speaking of their own accord.

The early history of Japanese puppetry might be interpreted entirely in terms of a spontaneous, native development, but probably continental influence was present even in the earliest stages. Certainly other entertainments, notably the comic *gigaku* and more stately *bugaku* dances, had been introduced to Japan from Korea and China by the seventh and eighth centuries. As in later times, one variety of theatrical performance could easily influence another: *gigaku* and *bugaku* masks and costumes may have contributed to the appearance of the primitive Japanese puppets. But this is no more than conjecture; it is more important to remember that dances ultimately originating in such distant regions as India and Central Asia were well known to the Japanese of the eighth century. It is likely too that along with these dances, humbler forms of entertainment, including puppetry, were introduced from abroad.

The oldest description of the Japanese puppeteers was written by the court scholar Ōe Masafusa (1041–1111). Though only 320 characters long, it has been scrutinized with desperate care by scholars of the Japanese theatre as the best source of information on the activities of these early puppeteers. It begins, "The puppeteers have no permanent place of residence nor fixed abodes, but live in tents. They move about freely, wherever there is water or grass; their customs much resemble those of the northern barbarians." Ōe's statement suggests that the puppeteers were not merely traveling entertainers but led a nomadic life, moving their beasts from place to place, depending on the supply of water and pasture. No other record indicates the existence of such nomads in Japan, and some scholars have therefore asserted that Ōe Masafusa merely used stock phraseology borrowed from Chinese accounts of foreign tribes to decorate his brief account of the puppeteers. Undoubtedly the choice of words was influenced by Chinese examples, but we cannot disregard Ōe's general implication that the puppeteers led lives so unlike those of the sedentary Japanese that they were taken for foreigners.

Ōe's account continues, "The men all use bows and horses, and make their living at hunting. Sometimes they fight with two swords or juggle balls; sometimes they make wooden puppets dance or peachwood puppets fight. These puppets faithfully depict the actions of living people. The puppeteers are almost as adept as the Chinese practitioners of magical transformations, and can change sand and stones into gold coins, or grass and wood into birds and beasts, cleverly deceiving the spectators' eyes." The main occupation of the puppeteers would seem thus to have been hunting, and their artistic talent only a secondary source of income, but this talent set them apart from other hunters and even other Japanese.

Ōe Masafusa turned his attention next to the womenfolk of the puppeteers. He tells us that they painted their faces, performed songs and dances, and enticed travelers to spend the night with them. The account concludes with the statement that the puppeteers, not being cultivators of the land, owed no allegiance to the local officials and showed no respect for the governors of the provinces where they lived. Immunity from taxation was the supreme joy of their lives; by way of thanks they worshipped their gods at night with much noisemaking.

Ōe Masafusa, in the interests of literary embellishment, may have exaggerated the rootlessness of the puppeteers. Documentary evidence indicates that as early as the twelfth century, puppeteers were in fact more or less permanently domiciled in different parts of the country, and owed some form of allegiance to the local rulers. It is nevertheless difficult to imagine that Ōe would have taken such pains to suggest that the puppeteers were aliens if, as some scholars claim, they were merely runaways from their normal ties to a particular domain. Their identity, like the origin of the word *kugutsu*, remains a mystery, but there is the strong inference that they migrated to Japan from the continent, bringing with them their art. Chinese records mention no such tribe of wandering puppeteers, but strikingly similar accounts are found in the Korean histories, which trace the *yangsuch'ŏk* as far back as the tenth century. Korean traditions, though no less vague than the Japanese, indicate that these entertainers, an outcaste group, were originally from Central Asia; the men, it would appear, on occasion operated puppets, and the women were witches and fortune-tellers. A Middle Korean word for puppet, *kuktu*, is tantalizingly close to *kugutsu*, but it has not yet been possible to prove the connection. The curiously gypsy-like attributes of both Japanese and Korean entertainers lend an intriguing note to the early history of puppetry in the Far East.

Accounts of performances by *kugutsu* say little about either their content or techniques. Clearly, however, the puppets were hand-operated, and not mechanical dolls of the kind so highly developed in China by the tenth century. The latter, described in Chinese records as early as the third century A.D., were originally introduced "from the West," and may indeed have been descended from the toys of ancient Egypt and Greece. Even if the Chinese first learned of such toys from the West, they quickly developed mechanical apparatuses far more sophisticated than those of their prototypes. An account from the early fourth century tells of a master doll-maker who fashioned a wooden room with a tiny housewife inside. When someone knocked on the door, the housewife would open it, come outside, bow, return to her room and shut the door. Another, even more complicated set of dolls was set in motion by four or five mice jumping on a kind of treadmill. The fondness of the Chinese court for these dolls led to increasingly realistic creations, including a doll which could pour wine with appropriate decorum at state banquets. It became a common cliché in describing these dolls to say that they were "exactly like human beings."

Evidence suggests that Chinese mechanical dolls were carried to Japan, perhaps as early as the tenth century, but the Japanese apparently lacked the technical skill either to create new devices or to repair old ones, and these expensive toys were presumably discarded once their mechanism failed. A description of a mechanical doll may be found in the *Konjaku Monogatari*, a late twelfth-century collection of stories. We are told how Prince Kaya in the ninth century, as part of a scheme to relieve a severe drought in Kyoto, built a mechanical doll over four feet high, which held buckets in both hands, and erected it in a field. When a bucket was filled with water, the doll would dash it over his face, so delighting spectators that they brought water from distant places in order to watch the doll perform. The fields were in no time amply watered and the drought relieved. The story, unfortunately for historians of Japanese puppetry, is of Chinese origin, and no other source indicates that the Japanese were capable of making such dolls before the fourteenth or fifteenth century.

The puppets used by the *kugutsu* were certainly more primitive than the Chinese mechanical dolls, but they were better suited to dramatic performances. No matter how complicated a series of movements a doll may perform, it cannot improvise beyond that series, and it is incapable of sustained actions. The *kugutsu* performances probably consisted originally of sword-play (as Ōe Masafusa mentioned) or wrestling (still performed today at the Kohyō Shrine in Kyushu), but eventually short dramas with more or less improvised dialogue spoken by the operators made up the *kugutsu* entertainments. An eleventh-century account describes a puppet play performed at a Shinto shrine during the course of which an aged man, after exchanging amorous words with his young wife, engages her in sexual intercourse. The spectators, men and women alike, were so amused that they "could not help cracking their jaws and splitting their sides with laughter." The salacious nature of this skit accords poorly with the holy precincts of a shrine but, as the account concludes, "Attending these performances brings two benefits: first, the spectator may worship the divine authority of the gods; second, he enjoys a pleasant relaxation."

Kugutsu performances undoubtedly were considered primarily as part of religious ceremonies held at a shrine; their amusement value was only incidental. Most puppet plays probably described in serious terms the history of a shrine or the miracles attributed to the deity worshiped there, perhaps in the manner of the Nō plays on similar subjects. Nothing suggests that, as in the later puppet theatre, plays were enacted to a text recited by a narrator. Puppets were preferred to actors as performers of the divine legends because they lacked the "smell" of human beings and could therefore impart mystery and authority to their gestures. The puppeteering techniques, as judged by later standards, must have been extremely crude, but probably characteristic human gestures were reproduced with sufficient fidelity to cause the spectators to say, in the traditional phrase, that the puppets seemed to be alive.

Despite the promise of a theatre worthy of the otherwise extremely literary and sophisticated world of eleventh-century Japan, the puppet entertainments offered by the *kugutsu*, far from developing with the years, suddenly cease to figure in the surviving documents. The name *kugutsu* occurs occasionally in legal records and elsewhere, but without any indication that persons known by that name were concerned with puppets. The *kugutsu* men, though generally domiciled on some manor, where they cultivated the land, were exempt from the usual taxes; they also sometimes engaged in hunting, as in the old days, or hired their services as laborers. The women were out-and-out prostitutes—the name *kugutsu* came to mean only "prostitute"—who worked in brothels situated along the principal thoroughfares. Some *kugutsu* with a lingering fondness for their art may have privately continued to operate puppets, or may have performed in regions not covered by existing records, but this remains conjectural.

A revival of puppetry occurred in the fourteenth century, apparently as a result of the importation of string-operated marionettes from China. A poem by the Buddhist monk Ryōsai (died 1365) is entitled "Puppets" (*Kairai*):

> They turn like toys in automatic movements,
> But their actions, filled with marvelous life, do not cease.
> A single string brings us a bodhisattva's face;
> An inch of thread tugs away a yaksha's head.

Mention of toys in the first line indicates that mechanical dolls, at least of a crude sort, existed in Japan at the time. The marionettes moved like these dolls, but unlike toys, their performance did not stop when the mechanism ran down. Mention of a single string operating a marionette dressed as a bodhisattva is probably not to be taken literally; at least three or four strings attached to the head, arms, and torso would be required to achieve any artistic effect. "An inch of thread" suggests that only a short distance separated the marionette's head from the platform above which the operator manipulated the strings. These meager clues have been interpreted as meaning that the marionettes were no more than a foot tall and that they moved on a stage about three feet wide and a foot and a half high. Probably only one or two marionettes appeared on the stage at a time, and the plays, like similar ones in China, dealt with Buddhist descriptions of heaven and hell.

Marionettes never attracted the Japanese as much as stick puppets. Although they enjoyed periods of popularity in the following centuries and survive today in a few rural temples as regional entertainments, they failed to achieve any great artistic development. The introduction of marionettes from China, however, apparently led to a reawakening of interest in the native forms of puppetry, which may have survived (as almost every form of Japanese theatrical entertainment known to us by name has survived to the present day) in remote areas, practiced by amateurs rather than by professional *kugutsu*.

In the fifteenth century, especially, the importation of Chinese mechanical dolls (as part of the Shogun Yoshimitsu's mania for things Chinese) stirred Japanese craftsmen into imitations and refinements. Some devices were operated by strings, others by using water power, and they became increasingly complex. By 1579, to cite one example, a mechanical toy was invented which set in motion 2000 soldiers in a battle for control of a castle six feet square. The manufacturer and operation of such mechanical toys came to be considered the speciality of the outcaste *(eta)* class, which otherwise figures most importantly in the history of the Japanese theatre. In 1461, we are told, the Shogun Yoshimasa visited an outcaste village to the west of Kyoto especially to see some mechanical dolls perform. The use of such dolls on festival floats began about this time and continues to this day.

In the middle of sixteenth century, with the arrival of Christian missionaries from Europe, new varieties of mechanical toys were introduced. A letter from a Portuguese missionary in the province of Bungo, written in 1562 to his superior in the Society of Jesus at home, describes a performance at Easter: "We showed them such scenes from the Bible as the children of Israel leaving Egypt. We constructed a Red Sea and made it open to permit the passage of the Israelites, and close when Pharaoh crossed with his troops. We also showed the prophet Jonah emerging from the whale's belly and other scenes."

Neither the Chinese nor the European mechanical dolls had any major influence on the subsequent development of the puppet theatre in Japan, but in one respect at least these toys may have been important: the use of strings inside the puppet to manipulate its eyes, mouth, and fingers (as opposed to external strings used with marionettes) may have been suggested by the strings which set in motion the mechanical dolls. A poem by the celebrated monk Ikkyū (1398-1481) gives a philosophical interpretation of the puppets:

> The puller of strings is himself the chief actor,
> As earth and water unite at the will of fire and air.
> When the play on the stage has ended,
> The setting suddenly is empty again.

The poem apparently means that a puppet, though it seems to move independently, is but the external manifestation of the operator's will, just as the visible phenomena of the world obey the invisible influences of fire and air. When the play has ended, and the guiding spirit no longer exerts its will, the stage—and the world—suddenly reverts to emptiness. In another poem on the puppets, Ikkyū relates that they perform so successfully as nobles or commoners that the spectator forgets they are merely wooden figures, and wonders if they are not actually human.

Ikkyū's poems are obscurely worded, and we cannot be sure that the strings he mentions operated puppets from inside, rather than marionettes from above, but the term he employs for stage suggests a puppet theatre. His mention of nobles and commoners is also too vague for us to guess the plots or even the general nature of the plays, but we know from other sources that by the middle of the fifteenth century puppets were used to perform Nō dramas and Kyōgen farces. It is hard to imagine the effect of the stately, symbolic Nō dramas when performed by crude little puppets, but the Nō and Kyōgen plays constituted the only available repertory, and the puppeteers accordingly continued to perform them for centuries. In 1614, for example, a program combining one play written especially for the puppets and several Nō plays was presented at the palace. In the middle of the seventeenth century, programs of Nō plays alternating with puppet plays were offered, but the audiences so much preferred the latter that before long the Nō plays were relegated to the intermissions. The development of an adequate repertory of puppet plays was, however, a slow process, and for many years the works performed either belonged to another theatre or were merely crude exhibitions of the puppeteers' skill.

Developments immediately before the emergence in the late sixteenth century of a puppet theatre worthy of the name are closely connected with the activities of the *ebisu-kaki*. These operators apparently originally served as menials at the Ebisu Shrine at Nishinomiya but learned the art of puppetry from outcastes in order to present legends concerning the god Ebisu. In 1555, as contemporary accounts relate, four *ebisu-kaki* staged a performance of Nō, attracting such attention that from this time on puppet performers, despite their base origins, were frequently invited to the palace. When peace was restored in 1600 after centuries of warfare, the services of *ebisu-kaki* were widely in demand at shrines and temples throughout the country. Eventually they broke their connections with the Ebisu Shrine in Nishinomiya, and were absorbed into the newly created puppet theatre, but the word *ebisu* continued to possess the meaning of "puppet," as we know from the *ebisu-mai* (or "*ebisu* dances"), the miniature puppet shows of the late seventeenth century. Pictures of the *ebisu-mai* show the operators with a box which served as a stage slung from their necks. One woodcut shows two operators, each carrying a box fashioned like a tiny Nō stage complete with a roof, who stand side by side, about a foot apart. The stages, about sixteen inches square, have no floor; instead, the puppets are held up at stage level from beneath by the operators, their hands concealed by the base of the stage. The effect of a single play performed on two separated stages is hard to imagine, but perhaps only Nō dances were attempted. Later examples of *ebisu-mai* stages were less elaborate, but strings were employed to advantage in manipulating the arms and legs of the puppets, by this time about eight inches high.

One further variety of late sixteenth-century puppet entertainment was the *hotoke-mawashi* or "Buddha turning," which (judging from illustrations) resembled the *ebisu-kaki*, but used hand-puppets a foot and a half tall. Unlike the *ebisu-kaki*, however, *hotoke-mawashi* was associated primarily with Buddhist temples instead of Shinto shrines, and it is supposed that the operators acted out Buddhist texts and sermons. The nearest surviving examples of such puppets are those manipulated by mediums of the Oshira cult (described above) in reciting the legend of the gallant horse Kurige and his love, the Princess Tamayo, who eventually became the gods of silkworm cultivation. The Oshira puppets, first mentioned in 1598, are moved in a stiff, ritualistic manner well suited to the monotonous recitation. Their actions possess only slight representational or dramatic interest, for the performance is considered a sacred rite, not a play designed to please an audience. This may also have been the purpose of the early *hotoke-mawashi*, but gradually the sermons developed into plays. If, like the Oshira puppets, the *hotoke-mawashi* plays combined puppets with a narrated text, they represented an important development in the direction of the future art of Bunraku. The puppet theatre was subsequently to present not plays in a Western sense (with texts divided into parts assigned to the different characters), but narratives which included in addition to the dialogue many descriptive passages assigned to no character, but recited by a chanter-commentator. In the earlier theatre the operator may have supplied dialogue for his puppet, as in some regional theatres today, but with the adoption of narrated texts all parts came to be taken by a chanter who modulated his voice suitably in assuming different roles or in describing a scene. The union between Buddhism and the puppets effected by the *hotoke-mawashi* is important otherwise because it prefigures the *sekkyō-bushi*, a kind of morality play acted by puppets which became popular in the seventeenth century. The religious and ritual significance of the early puppet theatre, whether Shintoist or Buddhist in coloring, remained of dominant importance until late in its development.

THE TALE IN TWELVE EPISODES OF JŌRURI

Puppet shows, as we have seen, had a history of perhaps eight hundred years behind them by the times of these events in the sixteenth century, but only with the creation of texts written especially for the puppets (and not merely adopted for puppet performance from some other medium) is it possible to speak of a puppet theatre, in the sense of the modern Bunraku. The puppets, of course, gave Bunraku its most distinctive feature, but the texts were to develop this theatre into a truly artistic medium, and to distinguish Bunraku from puppet and marionette entertainments elsewhere in the world. Even today, at the beginning of a Bunraku performance, the chanters lift the text to their foreheads to indicate respect; it would be unthinkable that, like actors, they would feel at liberty to add or delete phrases to suit their own tastes. Of the three elements in Bunraku —text, puppets, and musical accompaniment—the text is clearly the most important, and Bunraku thus fundamentally differs from Kabuki, where, even when a Bunraku text is performed, the actor is the center of interest and the text hardly more than a vehicle. As the person closest to the text, the chanter *(tayū)* ranks above the samisen players and puppet operators, and though there have been musicians and operators whose exceptional talents have dominated a company, the chanter, the servant of the text, more frequently gives the performance his personal cachet.

Bunraku, though a form of puppet show, and in this sense comparable to similar entertainments in other countries, whether the marionettes of Europe or the shadow plays of China and Java, is basically a narrative art. The chanter declaims the story, altering his voice in the dialogue to suggest the tones of a warrior, a woman, or a child, and at times, in poetical passages, rising from speech to song.. But he is neither an actor nor a singer, but a storyteller. Ideally perhaps, he should not be visible at all, but Japanese audiences prefer to see the narrator, though his presence destroys the illusion that the puppets, for all the movements of their mouths, are speaking for themselves. The celebrated chanters have enjoyed great popularity; audiences delight in the extraordinary range of expression which crosses their faces, and in the tears which fall from their eyes in tragic scenes. Indeed, in some parts of Japan performances are preferred of the chanters alone without the puppets, as if the latter were an unnecessary or even undesirable addition to a master chanter's rendering of the text. The Bunraku plays, it need hardly be said, are written specifically for a narrator rather than for actors, as one can tell immediately from the almost invariable addition of such concluding phrases as "thus he spoke" or "he said with a smile." These comments are natural in a narrative, but would be unnecessary in a theatre of actors. Bunraku, then, is a form of storytelling, recited to a musical accompaniment, and embodied by puppets on a stage.

The history of Bunraku may be traced back in different directions, depending on the focus of one's interests. Up to this point I have considered it mainly as a form of puppet theatre, and have therefore discussed early puppeteers rather than the chanters or samisen players. But if we turn our attention to the antecedents for the texts, a different series of events must be reported, and the same is true of the samisen. The confluence of three different performing traditions in the middle of the sixteenth century created the art of Bunraku.

Bunraku, as has been mentioned, is a modern term. The older designation for the art was *jōruri*, the name of the heroine of a fifteenth-century romance usually called "The Tale in Twelve Episodes of Jōruri" *(Jōruri-Jūnidan Sōshi)*. Although rewritten more artistically in later times, the text was essentially a narrative meant to be recited by professional storytellers. Like "The Tale of the Heike" *(Heike Monogatari)*, its thirteenth-century predecessor, "The Tale in Twelve Episodes" was altered and expanded by successive storytellers, who recited the text to the accompaniment of the musical instrument (rather resembling the mandolin) called the *biwa*. At a time when other entertainments were scarce, villagers delighted in hearing even for the hundredth time the storyteller's narration of the great deeds which occurred during the warfare between the Taira and the Minamoto, especially the more pathetic and lyrical episodes. The *biwa*, a melodious instrument, provided a kind of musical comment on the narrated passages (rather like the harpsichord during the recitatives of a Mozart opera), and was not an accompaniment to the narrator's voice in the manner of the samisen of later years. The narrator's delivery was rhythmical, and sometimes rose to musical expression; in order to emphasize the rhythm, he beat time with a fan. We may suppose that each storyteller had favorite sections of this long work which displayed his particular talents to best advantage. He might eventually augment such episodes from "The Tale of the Heike" with additional material from other traditional sources or of his own invention. His audiences, like those in India today for recitations of the Sanskrit epics, enjoyed the poetic language even though it is difficult at times to understand, and apparently never tired of hearing about its heroes. By the middle of the fifteenth century, however, recitations of the original "Tale of the Heike" waned in popularity, and other stories about the same heroes, particularly the gallant Yoshitsune, became the staples of the storytellers' repertory. "The Tale in Twelve Episodes" belongs to this category.

The story is a jumble of fantastic and believable events, which neither in style nor in incidents remotely approaches the grandeur of "The Tale of the Heike." Listeners, however, undoubtedly welcomed the romantic treatment of the hero. Yoshitsune, accompanied by a retainer, leaves the capital for the Eastern Provinces. While journeying through the province of Mikawa he catches a glimpse of a peerlessly beautiful lady and falls in love at first sight. Later, when this lady is making music with her companions, Yoshitsune, outside her gate, joins in with his flute, playing so beautifully that Jōruri invites him into the house. Yoshitsune goes that night to Jōruri's room, and after much persuasion induces her to yield her favors. As they are sorrowfully parting the next morning, Jōruri's mother surprises them together, and the disconcerted Yoshitsune flees. When he reaches the strand of Fukiage he is stricken with a mysterious, wasting sickness, and seems at the point of death when Shō-Hachiman, the protective deity of his family, appears in the guise of an old priest and offers to bring help from the capital. Yoshitsune requests that Jōruri be summoned instead, and the god, complying with his wish, appears the next instant before Jōruri's maid and informs her of Yoshitsune's illness. Jōruri and the maid rush to Fukiage, and after much difficulty they find the cottage where Yoshitsune lies dying. At first it seems they have arrived too late, but after Jōruri has purified herself in the sea and prayed to all the gods and Buddhas of Japan for Yoshitsune's recovery, tears falling from her eyes into his mouth revive the dying man. At this point sixteen mountain priests mysteriously appear, and by dint of their prayers and spells Yoshitsune recovers. Once restored to health he must leave again on the journey, in order that he may fulfill his destiny of one day destroying the Heike. The lovers part in grief, with vows of meeting again.

Though "The Tale in Twelve Episodes" includes such charming scenes as the description of Yoshitsune falling in love at first sight with Jōruri, it is puzzling why this particular, essentially inartistic story should have continued to please successive audiences for almost a century or why, for that matter, a work with so few dramatic incidents should have furnished the puppet theatre with its first text. We must not forget, however, the extraordinary popularity of the legends about Yoshitsune, the closest Japanese approximation to an epic hero. Even the Catholic missionaries at the end of the sixteenth century chose "The Tale of the Heike" as the most suitable text for teaching Japanese to beginners and prepared an edition in roman letters. Sections from "The Tale of the Heike" had been employed almost unaltered in the Nō theatre, where the prevailingly gloomy tone, stressing the tragic brevity and uncertainty of life, was entirely appropriate and could be appreciated by the aristocratic audience. The puppet theatre, however, aimed at plebeian spectators, and therefore naturally preferred the more romantic Yoshitsune of "The Tale in Twelve Episodes." Successive texts of the Jōruri story show moreover a tendency to emphasize episodes especially suited to performance, and to omit less dramatic parts. As early as 1531, as we know from the diary kept by the poet Sōchō, blind storytellers were "singing" the story of Jōruri, and by the end of the sixteenth century the name Jōruri had come to designate not merely the character in the romance, but a particular variety of entertainment provided by the storytellers. By the latter part of the sixteenth century, *jōruri* recitations had attained extraordinary popularity in Kyoto; a list of popular entertainments offered in 1592 is headed by *jōruri*.

THE FUSION OF THE THREE ELEMENTS OF BUNRAKU

There are many legends but little documentary evidence concerning the manner in which puppets and the samisen were joined to the narration of the *jōruri*. Our earliest records go back to about 1600, when, as part of a special entertainment offered in Kyoto, *ebisu-kaki* puppeteers were invited to perform in conjunction with *jōruri* recitations. The combination proved such a success that similar programs were later arranged. An entry in a nobleman's diary for 1614 tells us: "Rain. Went to the palace. After dinner they performed a play called "The Chest-Splitting of Amida" (*Amida no Munewari*). Players of the *ebisu-kaki* variety attended, and put on a performance after first setting up a curtain in the palace garden. It was most extraordinary. They also performed *Kamo, Daibutsu Kuyō, Takasago*, and other Nō plays." The performance was staged by command of the Retired Emperor Goyōzei, whose interest in the art was so great that some sources credit him with having first suggested that puppets be employed to perform the story of Jōruri. His son, the Emperor Gomizunō, is believed to have begun the practice of bestowing honorary court ranks on the outstanding performers. Such evidence of imperial interest in the fledgling puppet theatre is tantalizingly incomplete, but it is clear at least from the nobleman's diary that by 1614 not only were puppets commonly joined to the narration, but new works had been composed to take the place of the overly familiar story of Princess Jōruri.

The samisen was apparently introduced to Japan from the Ryukyu Islands before 1570. An account for 1575 relates how natives of the Ryukyus appeared before the daimyo of Satsuma, and sang to the accompaniment of a "*jabisen.*" The name was written with characters which mean "snakeskin strings," though snakeskin was in fact used not for the strings but for covering the body of the instrument. A similar three-stringed instrument is still played in South China, undoubtedly the source of the Ryukyu *jabisen*. The name was quickly modified in Japan to shamisen or samisen, and came to be written usually with characters meaning "three-flavor strings." Before long the snakeskin covering gave way to catskin, both because snakeskins of the appropriate size were rare in Japan, and because the Japanese played the samisen so vigorously, in the traditions of the *biwa*, that the plectrum was likely to damage snakeskin. Catskin was not only more durable but produced a clearer, harder tone which made it an ideal instrument for accompanying the recitations.

At first the Japanese, ever eager for curiosities from abroad, prized the samisen mainly as a novelty, and it was played by female entertainers especially. Its popularity is attested by mentions in lists of entertainments from the late sixteenth century, but nothing suggests the samisen had already been combined with the *jōruri* recitations which figured in the same programs. Probably "modern" *biwa* accompanists experimented for a time with the samisen, as in the late nineteenth century violins were tried out as background music for Kabuki plays, without any decision being made for or against adopting the new instrument. Later, as the expressive capacities of the samisen were improved, accompanists found that its sharp, almost percussive notes were ideally suited to guiding the narrator in his delivery and the operators in maneuvering the puppets. The difference in effect between the *biwa* and the samisen when used as an accompaniment is comparable to the difference between accompanying a singer with a violin or a piano.

Once the three elements of Bunraku had at last been joined, the combination began to seem inevitable. A performance then as now was guided first of all by the text, which chanters, samisen players and puppeteers studied alike in the hopes of bringing out its full meaning in their various domains. The mutual dependence of the three elements is so great that we can hardly imagine Bunraku in any other terms, but our knowledge of the puppet theatre in the early seventeenth century, imperfect as it is, suggests that what now seems so inevitable probably was largely accidental in the first instance, and only with time and the gradual perfection of each of the three branches of the art did the ideal interdependence, so often mentioned by admirers of Bunraku, acquire its present meaning.

Paintings from the early seventeenth century give us valuable indications about the nature of the performances. A screen painted about 1622 shows two tiny puppet theatres in operation. The theatres themselves seem hardly able to hold twenty-five people each—men and women, clearly of the plebeian class, who watch with gaping mouths a stage at one side of the rectangular enclosure. The puppets are held up over a cloth-covered partition by the operators, who are invisible below. The puppets are small, apparently only about a foot tall, and have no arms, though in some cases the kimono sleeves are held at angles to suggest arms (as in modern Bunraku the feet for female puppets are delineated by the hems of her kimono). One of the two puppet theatres depicted on the screen belongs to the normal *jōruri* tradition. Neither chanter nor musical accompanist is visible, in keeping with practice at the time. The other theatre probably is performing *sekkyō-bushi*, a didactic, Buddhist-inspired puppet play which originated almost contemporaneously with *jōruri* in the early seventeenth century, and for a century was its rival in popular favor. Two men seated to the left of the stage in the *sekkyō-bushi* theatre, though partly concealed by a wall, seem to be the chanter and his accompanist, an indication that their appearance before the audience antedated this practice in *jōruri*. But, of course, a screen painting is not necessarily to be trusted as an accurate representation of theatres at the time.

Our earliest extended description of a *jōruri* performance comes from the pen of Hayashi Razan (1573–1657), a Confucian philosopher who attended a performance in 1648. He described a variety of wooden puppets—men, women, monks, laity, immortals, soldiers, and so on—which danced, propelled boats, skirmished in battle (with heads flying), and executed various prodigies of transformation. He praised the chief operator, Koheita, then considered to be the most accomplished puppeteer in Edo, and concluded his description in the time-honored manner by declaring that the puppets seemed to be alive. We may doubt that the crude puppets which Koheita held up over his head and manipulated in the movements of dancing or fighting could really have induced anyone to believe they were alive, but compared to earlier, even cruder performances, Koheita's probably seemed remarkably vivid.

It appears likely that when puppets first accompanied the narration of the story of Jōruri their motions were intended not to embody the meaning of the texts (as in later times) but rather to create pleasing visual effects complementary to the narration. Thus, a passage in "The Tale in Twelve Episodes" utterly devoid of action might, particularly if the language lent itself to lyrical declamation, provide a suitable background for a dance, much as the recitations of the Nō chorus often provide the setting for a dance whose movements may be virtually unrelated to the circumstances described in the texts. Early *jōruri* performances were certainly heavily dependent on examples from the Nō, if only because the puppeteers customarily also performed Nō plays, as has been mentioned. The development of *jōruri* as a theatre whose texts were directly and even literally reflected in the actions of the stage was to mark a notable shift of direction in Japanese dramatic techniques. Perhaps Hayashi Razan, remembering the stylized, remote movements of the Nō plays, was more struck by the realism of the puppet theatre than a modern audience would be.

The art of *jōruri* showed a steady development during the course of the seventeenth century, mainly in the use of increasingly artistic texts and a correspondingly artistic manner of delivery by the chanters. Most of the early *jōruri* plays depended heavily on supernatural and miraculous elements, as we might have expected in works derived largely from Buddhist and Shinto sources. ("The Tale in Twelve Episodes," though the earliest *jōruri*, included comparatively few supernatural elements because of its secular origins.) The activities of ghosts, dragons, and foxes, so much admired by Razan, illustrate one advantage the puppets held over actors, whose physical limitations made convincing miracles difficult to achieve onstage. The puppeteers naturally exploited this advantage, either by using mechanical dolls *(karakuri)*, some of which could be operated by remote control with the use of long strings, or else by allowing their puppets a freedom from gravity and the other earthly controls that prevent actors from achieving feats of superhuman quality. The poorly educated audiences had an enormous appetite for such stunts, and even a master dramatist like Chikamatsu, who had no need to rely on tricks in his plays, was obliged at times to yield to this craving for the miraculous.

The names of the major chanters of the seventeenth century are important because each man contributed a distinctive style of narration, usually known by his name. The chanters were responsible for reducing the original twelve episodes of the *jōruri* story to the six acts of the early *jōruri* play, and for later further reducing this number to five, probably influenced by the number of Nō plays presented in a single program. An equation was made between the five acts of the *jōruri* and the five Nō plays of a program, and the same progression of tempo was demanded, going from the expository solemnity *(jo)* of the first two plays (or acts of *jōruri*) to the intenser, more broken emotions *(ha)* of the next two plays, and finally to a climax in the furious tempo *(kyū)* of the concluding work. Expressed in terms of plot, the first act was usually devoted to a description of the villainy which gives rise to the play. The second act shows virtue beginning to assert itself even amidst the triumph of evil. In the third act, the advantage shifts to the side of virtue, thanks to some deed of self-sacrifice. The fourth act depicts the struggle between virtue and vice, culminating in the triumph of virtue, and in the fifth act, usually the shortest, the annihilation of the original villainy is celebrated. Undoubtedly the *jōruri* equivalent of the programs of five Nō plays represents a debasement or at least a popularization of the lofty aesthetic ideals of Nō, but the presence, even in this form, of influence from the aristocratic Nō drama not only fostered the development of *jōruri* considerably as a literary art, but caused the texts to be embellished with quotations from both the Nō and the poetry of an even more distant past. It served also to distinguish the puppet theatre from Kabuki, an art which sprang into being at almost exactly the same time as *jōruri*, and remained its close rival for two hundred years. Bunraku, despite its humble origins and its continued dependence on a virtually illiterate public in the countryside as well as the cities, acquired, by borrowing from Nō, a literary importance which Kabuki, always more dependent on the skill and personality of the great actors than on the text, would never possess.

Bunraku, like Kabuki, had its inception in Kyoto, but developed during the early seventeenth century most conspicuously in Edo. The people of this new city, populated largely by samurai and other persons unfamiliar with the traditional Kyoto culture, welcomed the vigorous rhythms of the new *jōruri* works, particularly those dealing with the adventures of the incomparable martial hero Kimpira. The chanter of these plays, Satsuma Jōun (1595–1672), whose renditions of the Kimpira stories enjoyed immense popularity in Edo, is reported to have beat time with an iron bar, the better to maintain the fierce atmosphere of the plots. Satsuma Jōun is otherwise credited with having been the first to reduce the twelve episodes of the original Jōruri story to six acts of *jōruri*. The popularity of the Kimpira plays spread to other parts of the country, even to Kyoto, where the gloomily moral *sekkyō-bushi* was firmly entrenched. Bunraku might, however, have remained predominantly an Edo theatrical art had it not been for the disastrous Great Fire of Edo of 1657, which killed more than 100,000 people and destroyed most of the city. As a result of the fire, the leading chanters, despairing of making a living in the ruined city, moved to the Osaka and Kyoto area; from this time onwards Bunraku ceased to be of great importance to Edo, where Kabuki instead was to reign supreme.

Ever since the late seventeenth century Bunraku has been associated especially with the city of Osaka. Scholars have often asserted that this fact reflects the commercial temper of Osaka, as opposed to the bravado of Edo or the refinement of Kyoto, but they fail to indicate what precisely in puppet performances would appeal especially to merchants. It is probably safer to explain the persistent popularity of Bunraku in Osaka, even when it had lost ground elsewhere, as a historical accident—a fortunate one, for any art firmly entrenched in the commercial metropolis of Japan enjoyed financial security. Under the patronage of the Osaka audiences, Bunraku developed rapidly in the mid-seventeenth century.

THE GOLDEN AGE OF BUNRAKU

The celebrated chanter Takemoto Gidayū (1651–1714) established the Takemoto Theatre in 1684 on the Dōtombori, a street of theatres, restaurants, and other places of entertainment in Osaka. The first work that he presented was the historical play "The Soga Heir" (*Yotsugi Soga*) by Chikamatsu Monzaemon (1653–1725), the greatest of the *jōruri* playwrights. The auspicious combination of two geniuses was to impart true drama to what had frequently been moralistic or else coarse forms of entertainment. The production of "Kagekiyo Victorious" (*Shusse Kagekiyo*), a *jōruri* by Chikamatsu in 1686, is considered to mark the beginning of the "new" *jōruri*; from this triumph the two men went on to effect startling improvements in the medium. Their key success was probably "The Love Suicides at Sonezaki" (*Sonezaki Shinjū*) in 1703. Its importance may be measured in financial terms, for it assured the fortunes of the Takemoto Theatre after some shaky years of poor attendance. It also determined Chikamatsu, who had been dividing his energies between Bunraku and Kabuki, to devote himself exclusively to the writing of *jōruri* texts for Gidayū. This decision was followed by his removal from Kyoto, still an important Kabuki center, to Osaka. Most importantly, the success of "The Love Suicides at Sonezaki," which describes in realistic fashion a young merchant of soy sauce who commits suicide with the prostitute he loves, led to the series of tragedies on which Chikamatsu's reputation as a dramatist is largely based. These plays, inspired by actual happenings known to the audience, differed enormously from the traditional *jōruri*, which delighted in describing the fantastic deeds of the ancient heroes. Instead of attempting to intrigue the spectators with the grotesque posturings of superhuman heroes or the miraculous interventions of the gods and Buddha, Chikamatsu sought in his domestic plays to depict on the stage (in fictionalized form, of course) the tragedies which occur in ordinary daily life, giving them stature by means of the beauty of his language and the stylization possible in a theatre of puppets. The earlier *jōruri* plays had exploited the capability of the puppets to represent feats beyond human powers, but in these intensely human works the function of the puppets is instead to lend artistic distinction to what otherwise might seem merely painful or even sordid occurrences.

Nevertheless, a constant progression in the direction of realism may be traced through the history of *jōruri*. Not only did the texts, particularly Chikamatsu's domestic plays, depict the lives of actual people more faithfully than earlier works, but the puppets and the techniques employed in manipulating them were constantly being improved with the aim of achieving greater resemblance to human behavior. The puppets in the older *jōruri* plays, like those found in certain regions of Japan today, had neither arms nor legs, but the operator might, for example, brandish a sword or fan by concealing his own right hand in the sleeve of the puppet's kimono (as in the screen painting of 1622). The puppets were not provided with functional arms until the 1690's, when a citizen of Osaka, declaring that the existing puppets were no better than childish toys—they consisted merely of heads stuck on frames draped with kimonos—contrived to add movable arms to the puppets. By 1727, the same year that it became possible to open or shut the eyes and mouths of the puppets, the puppets' fingers could be manipulated, and in 1733 the fingers were further improved to permit the first joints to move independently. These improvements in the puppets owed much to the rivalry persisting between the Takemoto Theatre (Gidayū's) and the Toyotake Theatre; each tried to attract customers by displaying some novelty the other as yet did not possess. The series of developments also represented a response to public demand for more convincing puppets.

We must not, however, ignore the balancing emphasis on non-realism. During the first performance of "The Love Suicides at Sonezaki," the scene of the lovers' journey to their suicide was performed with a translucent curtain instead of the usual wooden partition concealing the area underneath the stage; this permitted the audience to watch the operators manipulating the puppets. Two years later, in 1705, the performance of another play by Chikamatsu, "The Mirror of

Craftsmen of the Emperor Yōmei," marked the beginning of the tradition that Bunraku operators be fully visible. On this occasion too the chanters (who had hitherto remained concealed in the wings) appeared before the audience on a platform at the side of the stage. The personal popularity of the operator Tatsumatsu Hachirobei is sometimes cited to explain this change, which was presumably compounded by the jealousy of the chanters. Certainly Tatsumatsu's popularity was a contributing factor but, as I have mentioned, each step in the direction of realism tended to be accompanied by a step in the direction of non-realism; whether or not the audiences or performers were aware of this general truth, they may have sensed that an excessive emphasis on realism would force the theatre out of the slender margin between the real and unreal. In the earlier *jōruri* there had been no question of the theatrical, unreal natures of the performances, and it was appropriate therefore that the sources of the movements and voices of the puppet—the chanters and operators—remained concealed, lest all dramatic illusion be destroyed. But with the introduction of plays in which quite ordinary people spoke the familiar language of the gay quarters, the audiences welcomed the visible presence of operators and chanters, the better to distinguish between real life and the theatre. The adoption in 1734 of puppets operated by three men enabled Bunraku to attain subtleties of performance unrivaled by any similar company in the world, but it involved the conspicuous presence of three men around each puppet, a challenge to dramatic illusion too great perhaps for non-Japanese audiences to accept. A multifold combination of opposites characterizes Bunraku and accounts for much of its greatness.

The success of "The Love Suicides at Sonezaki" and other domestic tragedies did not cause Chikamatsu to abandon the composition of historical plays filled with displays of heroics. The domestic plays, being too short to constitute a full day at the theatre, could be performed only as a part of a program, usually at the end of a long historical play. "The Love Suicides at Sonezaki," his first domestic tragedy, was not divided into acts, but Chikamatsu's later works in this form were usually in three acts, each divided into scenes. The high point of the plays was the *michiyuki* or "journey," in which the lovers travel together, often to the place where they will commit a double suicide. The lyrical beauty of these episodes, contrasting with the realism of the previous scenes, supplied a welcome diversion, and the magnificent poetry lavished by Chikamatsu in his descriptions imparted to the characters the stature necessary for them to command not only our pity but our admiration. Chikamatsu eventually came also to incorporate in his historical plays some scenes marked by the down-to-earth realism of the domestic tragedies. Most works of the heyday of *jōruri*, the mid-eighteenth century, belonged to a mixed genre which combined the excitement and extravagance of the historical plays with the pathos and humanity of the domestic tragedies. The couplings were not always smooth or entirely convincing, but they met the public demand for both realism and non-realism in the same work.

Chikamatsu's high reputation as a dramatist has saddled him with the unfortunate sobriquet "the Shakespeare of Japan." His plays, however, are seldom performed today by the Bunraku artists in their original form, a reflection in part of public preference for the kind of exaggerated expression more characteristic of later plays than those by Chikamatsu; by the standards of Chikamatsu's successors, his plays seem insufficiently engrossing or even pallid because of the scarcity of scenes featured by acts of self-immolation or by a retainer's sacrifice of his child to substitute for his master's. Sometimes these "deficiencies" in Chikamatsu's works have been remedied by extensive revision at the hands of later men, who have not hesitated to add melodramatic passages or surprise situations in an attempt to make Chikamatsu's works fit more smoothly into the pattern of later *jōruri*. The purist cannot but deplore such intrusions, which usually lower the dignity of a masterpiece, but in order to satisfy the public it was necessary for the Bunraku troupe to provide the puppets with more opportunity for display than Chikamatsu, in his concern for literary excellence, saw fit to supply.

A second difficulty in presenting Chikamatsu's text as originally composed is that he wrote for the kind of puppets used by Tatsumatsu Hachirobei—small, easily maneuvered creatures which were held up over the stage by the puppeteer working below. When the three-man puppet came into general use it was discovered that Chikamatsu's dialogue did not provide the slower, more cumbersome new puppets sufficient time to move through their parts. The lines had to be cut substantially if the plays were to be performed at all; but even this expedient was unsatisfactory, for the cut versions, unlike subsequent texts composed especially for the three-man puppets, offered no occasion for displaying the special realistic effects of which the new puppets were capable and which the public demanded.

A final difficulty arose from the tendency of the varieties of heads used in the puppet theatre to become increasingly rigid. The heads were divided not only into male and female, old and young, but also into good and evil. This meant inevitably that the nature of a character became apparent merely from his head as soon as he stepped on the stage—whether a good old man or a wicked middle-aged woman, and so on. There was little room for the individuality which Chikamatsu tried at times to impart to his portrayals. Surprising twists in the plot were not only possible but normal, as when Matsuōmaru in "The Village School" is revealed as having actually been loyal to his old master despite all appearances, or when we discover that Kumagai in "Kumagai's Camp" has killed his son to save his presumed enemy; but it was not possible to keep a character from being wholly good or wholly evil, or even to cause us to withhold judgment on his nature, as Chikamatsu sometimes attempted. In the revised versions of his texts the ambiguous characters become from the outset unmistakably good or evil.

The puppet theatre in the period from the death of Chikamatsu in 1725 to the 1780's enjoyed its greatest popularity, easily surpassing that of Kabuki, probably the only instance in theatrical history where puppets have been preferred to actors for such a long period. The supremacy of Bunraku was undisputed in Osaka, and in Edo, where Kabuki remained more popular, the actors felt obliged to borrow *jōruri* texts and even details of performance from the puppets. The later texts failed to equal Chikamatsu's in beauty of language or skill of construction (some of the most famous works, such as *Sugawara Denju Tenarai Kagami*, consist of a sprawling series of almost unrelated, though individually effective, scenes), but they showed an unparalleled mastery of the art of the puppet theatre. Just as a Kabuki play stands or falls in terms of the opportunities it affords the actors for displays of histrionics—moments when the actors can "really act"—so the *jōruri* came to depend on familiar but invariably effective display scenes for the puppets. In neither the Kabuki nor the later *jōruri* was literary excellence a principal objective, and although the language is often effective and even poetic, the plays usually lack the artistic finish which might enable them to survive as literature; these texts, in this respect, are more like opera libretti than like independent dramas. Most famous eighteenth-century works were written by three or more collaborators, each contributing an act or two in his special vein of excellence; sometimes, it would appear, little attempt was made by the different authors to reconcile the plots of their respective sections of the play. But although the literary value of these plays may be questionable, the authors knew exactly how to please the public, and their works have remained to this day the staples of the repertory.

A few of the post-Chikamatsu plays deserve to be treated as masterpieces, especially the celebrated *Chūshingura* (1748) by Takeda Izumo, Miyoshi Shōraku, and Namiki Sōsuke. This recounting of the vengeance executed by the forty-seven loyal retainers of the Lord of Akō, a fictionalized version of events which took place in Edo some forty-five years before, proved the most successful work ever written for puppets, and is still staged whenever a theatre desperately needs a sure-fire attraction. When performed in entirety *Chūshingura* lasts about eleven hours, but more commonly one or two acts are performed on a given occasion. Indeed, it is relatively rare for any of the famous eighteenth-century plays to be presented except in extracts ranging from a single scene to an act or two. Because these works were originally composed as a series of scenes, no great violence is done to the text if only one episode is presented, though the same would hardly be true of a more highly organized play; the sleepwalking scene from *Macbeth* would not make much sense to an audience unfamiliar with the rest of the play. The Bunraku audiences today usually prefer a set of scenes from five different plays to a single complete work, enjoying the highlights, marked usually by such non-literary devices as a chanter's prolonged hysterical laugh or violent weeping and sobbing, or a striking sequence of poses by the puppets.

The disproportionate importance of such non-literary elements did not lessen in any way the dependence of Bunraku on the texts. A prodigal outpouring of new puppet plays by many writers attracted audiences, eager for novelty, to Bunraku, and Kabuki could do no better than follow its lead. Eventually, however, the flood of talent subsided, and with the death of Chikamatsu Hanji (1725–1783), Bunraku lost its last great author. Once playwrights deserted Bunraku for Kabuki, its days of prosperity were ended. The last decades of the eighteenth century saw the closing of the Takemoto and Toyotake theatres, the two pillars of Bunraku whose competition had fostered so much progress. Only small theatres scattered in various parts of Osaka preserved the texts and traditions.

THE NINETEENTH CENTURY AND AFTERWARDS

At this dark moment in *jōruri* history, a puppeteer from the island of Awaji named Masai Kahei, but familiarly known by his stage name of Bunrakken (or Bunraku-ken), performed with his troupe and scored something of a success. He decided to start a club for amateurs of the art, and after a time had gathered enough talent around him to form a local company. A small theatre was established inside the precincts of the Inari Shrine in Osaka where, under the name of "Bunrakken's Company," it staged puppet plays. Despite many vicissitudes, some occasioned by the drastic governmental reform of the theatre in 1842, Bunrakken's Company not only established itself as the outstanding puppet troupe in Osaka, but eventually in 1872, with the opening of the Bunraku Theatre, the name Bunraku itself came to be used as the general name for the Osaka variety of orthodox puppet entertainments.

The Meiji period (1868–1912) marked a sharp revival of interest in Bunraku, and the names of the great chanters, puppet operators, and samisen players of that time are now almost legends. Most celebrated of all was the samisen player Toyozawa Dampei (1827–1898), a man fanatically devoted to his art, whose influence extended to every aspect of Bunraku. Not only did Dampei's phenomenal skill win for the samisen an esteem it had never before enjoyed in the puppet theatre, but under his merciless tutelage several chanters became masters, and puppet operators were inspired to new heights. Dampei himself composed new plays and scores, including "The Miracle at Tsubosaka Temple" (*Tsubosaka Reigen-ki*) (written with the collaboration of his wife), the most recent *jōruri* to gain a firm place in the repertory. In 1884, when a new Bunraku theatre was founded at the Goryō Shrine, Dampei left the company over a disagreement, and joined the newly founded Hikoroku Theatre. His participation in the new company initiated a period of strenuous rivalry between the two theatres reminiscent of that between the Takemoto and Toyotake Theatres over a hundred years before, and resulting eventually in the attainment of the highest standards of performance since that time. The outstanding puppeteer, Yoshida Tamazō (1829–1905), is today ranked with Tatsumatsu Hachirobei and Yoshida Bunzaburō, masters of Chikamatsu's day, as one of the three supreme puppet operators of Bunraku history, and the combination of Dampei, Tamazō, and the powerful chanter Nagatodayū approached perfection. Dampei died of a cerebral hemorrhage during the course of a performance while playing at the Inari Theatre, the successor to the Hikoroku Theatre.

Despite the general prosperity of the Bunraku Theatre during the Meiji period, its affairs were badly managed by Bunrakken's descendants, and in 1909 the theatre and its assets were sold to the Shōchiku Company. The troupe at the time the management changed included thirty-eight chanters, fifty-one samisen players, and twenty-four puppet operators. *Jōruri* recitations enjoyed a considerable vogue during the late Meiji era, thanks mainly to attractive women chanters who accompanied themselves as they sang and recited the plays, but the Bunraku Theatre itself seemed clearly on the downgrade.

A disastrous fire in 1926 destroyed the Bunraku Theatre together with most of the valuable old puppet heads, treasures which could never be replaced. Re-establishing Bunraku entailed serious financial problems for the owners, and not until the end of 1929 was a new theatre made available. In the meanwhile, the Bunraku company had traveled widely in Japan, notably to Tokyo, creating a new popularity in that city, where puppet plays had not enjoyed much favor since the seventeenth century. The company included splendid artists in all three branches, the most famous of whom were Toyotake Kōtsubodayū (born 1878, later known as Yamashiro-no-shōjō), Yoshida Bungorō (1869-1962, later known as Naniwa-no-jō) and Yoshida Eiza (1872-1945). Kōtsubodayū, a marvelously expressive chanter, was renowned especially for the psychological understanding he displayed of the major works, a quality which set him apart from the famous chanters of the previous generation, who owed their fame to their sweet voices or ringing tones or echoing laughs rather than to any depth of understanding. To watch Kōtsubodayū recite a part was in itself a theatrical experience which needed no puppets. The leading puppeteers (notably Bungorō and Eiza) were no less skillful in their art, both being known for their interpretations of the female roles. Such artists would in the past have drawn large audiences to see Bunraku, but hardly had the company settled in its new theatre than, in 1931, the Manchurian War began. Admissions had been disappointing during the previous year, and in the attempt to arouse public interest otherwise absorbed by the war, such patriotic works as "Three Heroes, Glorious Human Bullets" (1932) by Matsui Shōō, dramatizing an incident in the fighting at Shanghai less than two months before, were elaborately staged, with great attention devoted to mechanisms which permitted the puppets taking the parts of soldiers to smoke cigarettes convincingly. The new plays enjoyed some success, but did not alter the basically gloomy prospects for Bunraku. In 1933 the Japanese Diet passed a bill which had as its object the preservation of the Bunraku Theatre by governmental subsidy, underlining the inability of the puppet theatre to draw audiences of the size attending the films or Kabuki. In the same year, the Bunraku Theatre was turned into a newsreel theatre, and for almost a year the company was forced to perform outside Osaka. It was rumored even among the players that Bunraku's days were numbered. The company struggled through the thirties, the members supplementing their meager earnings with outside teaching. During the war years 1941-45 Bunraku enjoyed a temporary resurgence of activity thanks to the government encouragement of "pure" Japanese art, but this period came to a crashing close with the bombing of Osaka and the burning of the Bunraku Theatre in 1945, this time completing the destruction of such treasured old properties as had survived the fire of 1926.

Once the war ended, Bunraku started performance again in 1946 in the hastily rebuilt, dingy theatre at Yotsuhashi. The company was good as ever, but it drew small audiences, and again voices of doom were heard. The institution by the government of the designation "Human Cultural Properties" called the public's attention to the many superlative artists in the company, ushering in another brief period of prosperity. The company moved in 1956 to a new, luxurious theatre on the Dōtombori, its traditional site, and in 1963 was placed under the management of the newly formed Bunraku Association (Bunraku Kyōkai), an organization which superseded the Shōchiku Company in the management of Bunraku, and transferred direction of the theatre to a non-profit organization which included the performers and representatives of the government and the Japan Broadcasting Corporation. New plans were announced for raising the standards of programs, but again a brief flurry of general interest and excitement quickly subsided.

One reason for the loss of a wide public following is that the texts, written in the poetic, artificial language of two hundred years ago, have become difficult to understand. The texts are so intimately associated with the music and the movements of the puppets that it would not be feasible to simplify them; in any case, drastic changes in the familiar words would be resisted by lovers of Bunraku as much as a modernization of Shakespeare would be in England. Not only do the words fail to capture the full attention of most spectators, but Bunraku usually seems extremely slow to people accustomed to the helter-skelter pace of motion pictures. Fundamentally, however, the problem in appreciation of Bunraku today is that the plays belong to a Japan which either no longer exists or is buried so deeply as to be almost undiscoverable. Bunraku attracted large audiences in the eighteenth century because the theatre staged new plays of immediate appeal. It attracted audiences on an equally large scale in the Meiji period, though by that time it had become chiefly a repertory theatre, because Japan and the Japanese had not changed very greatly in the intervening century or so. The young man of 1890 knew from childhood the plots of the famous plays and even snatches of the dialogue. The language, though not his own speech, presented no great difficulties, if only because the popular novels of the day were filled with the same, traditional phrases. And the ideals implied in the plays, certainly not those of the new, enlightened Meiji era, were still perfectly familiar, and the appeal of the situations as strong as ever.

The greatest popular successes, on the whole, belonged to the romantic variety of theatre which depicts actions of which the public imagines itself capable, though unlikely ever to perform, rather than life as it is normally led. Chikamatsu tended to romanticize his characters—surely not *all* prostitutes of his day could have been so self-sacrificing and faithful to their true loves as those portrayed in his plays—but his domestic tragedies were reasonably faithful to the society in which he lived. Most of the plays of the later eighteenth century, on the other hand, even if given a historical setting, evoke a world of fantasy and dream fulfillment. The frequency of scenes of head inspections, of extraordinary self-sacrifice, or of peerless devotion of wives to their husbands reflects actual life less than it expresses how the townspeople, even men and women leading most sedentary, unexciting lives, liked to imagine themselves behaving, much as pharmacists or grocers in the American West today feel a sense of identification with the heroes of films about frontier days. The man who could not possibly suppose that he would ever have to behead his own son in order to save his master's child nevertheless liked to think himself potentially capable of the deed; he was convinced that though killing one's own child was an indescribably painful act, it was amply rewarded by the joy of securing the safety and happiness of one's master.

Modern critics of the "feudal mentality" expressed in these plays usually fail to distinguish between the anger which such subservience arouses in themselves and the sense of gratification which men of the past felt at the thought they had well served their masters. A masterless samurai (a *rōnin*) or a merchant with no master to serve felt less a sense of proud independence than of deprivation. Though no man in his right mind would wish to kill his own son or inspect his brother's severed head, the man who had no chance in his life to demonstrate the fund of loyalty dormant within him found satisfaction in the Bunraku dramas.

The plays still possess dramatic validity, as anyone who permits himself to surrender to their mood will testify, but it is not surprising that many young Japanese declare that they can understand neither the old-fashioned poetic language of the plays nor their outmoded philosophy. Their attitude is regrettable, but we cannot ignore the fact that Bunraku stopped developing at the end of the eighteenth century. Its existence since then, chiefly as a repertory theatre where beloved old classics are performed, has required an audience familiar in advance with the language and even the plots of works to be presented. It is possible to imagine another kind of audience, similar to that in the West (or Japan) for Italian or German opera, which not only tolerates but relishes unconvincing or even ludicrous texts and performances, because the medium itself offers so many compensating beauties. As yet, however, despite efforts to interest students in Bunraku by offering performances at greatly reduced prices, this new kind of audience has not materialized.

In other attempts to attract new customers Bunraku has staged various new works, ranging from adaptations of *Hamlet* and *Madame Butterfly* to modern Japanese tales about a faithful dog, or about a poor half-Negro child, left in the wake of the American occupation, who is mocked by his Japanese classmates for his dark skin, and who finally stands in the snow (until he freezes to death) so that his skin will at last turn white. With the exception of Bunraku adaptation of familiar Nō or Kabuki plays, however, no work composed in the twentieth century has established itself in the repertory.

The collapse of Bunraku has frequently been predicted, but this seems unlikely today in view of the extensive governmental support. A more serious danger is that younger performers, unwilling to put up with the rigorous training which novices accepted in the past as a matter of course, will lower the standards of performance, and that the new audiences, unable to distinguish between mediocre and great artists, will complacently accept the deterioration of standards. But this gloomy shape of things to come is by no means certain. A new generation, bored with the vulgar absurdities of the films and television, may discover that behind the seemingly outdated Bunraku plots, genuine human emotions are expressed in magical language, and that the presentation, unlike the hastily contrived popular entertainments of our day, is artistically conceived and executed to the last detail. If this discovery takes place in time, we may witness in the near future at least a silver age of this unique art.

III. THE TEXTS AND THE CHANTERS

LONG BEFORE the end of the sixteenth century, when the original tale of Princess Jōruri was first shaped into the text of a puppet drama, the Nō theatre had achieved a high degree of literary and dramatic distinction. Its history could be traced back many years, and though its origins had certainly been humble, it was granted the protection of the shoguns in the late fourteenth century, and was subsequently recognized as an important and even indispensable adjunct of court life. The texts of the Nō plays, dating mainly from the early fifteenth century, were carefully preserved in beautifully inscribed Books, and were studied by the nobles, some of whom appeared in private performances given for their own pleasure. Commoners had relatively few opportunities to witness performances of Nō by master actors, but the stories of the plays and the famous passages in the texts were widely known.

It is not surprising, in view of the respect that Nō commanded, that it should have influenced the nascent art of Bunraku, but fundamentally the two arts are so different that the great scholar Watsuji Tetsurō concluded *jōruri* is best understood as a negation of the aesthetic principles of Nō. He contrasted the poetic understatement and powers of suggestion of Nō with the bright coloring and sometimes overblown rhetoric of the *jōruri* texts, comparing the former to the monochrome washes of Muromachi painting and the latter to the polychrome brilliance of the late sixteenth-century screens. Nō, like the monochrome landscapes or the tea ceremony, was guided in its manner of expression by Zen Buddhism, and in the attempt to express ultimate reality tended to ignore or neglect literal truth. The gestures of the Nō actor in time became so stylized that an uninformed spectator could not guess their meaning, though the connoisseur recognized in them indications of an imprecisely but acutely sensed world beyond the visible actions on the stage. The Nō actor playing the part of the blind beggar Yoroboshi must suggest the world of darkness in which he wanders but also the inner light that guides him. The actor's movements are schematized as if in negation of natural walking or gesturing, but in this manner he can suggest in terms at once pure and profound the essential nature of his condition, as the painter of a monochrome landscape using swift, seemingly arbitrary black lines may convey more successfully than a master of color the essence of a landscape. The symbolic, unspoken beauty of the Nō plays was strengthened by the absence of scenery, except for the pine painted on the back wall, by the use of props which are no more than evocative outlines of real objects, and by the musical accompaniment, which serves to punctuate the silence and order it, rather than to please by its melodies.

In Bunraku, on the other hand, thoughts and emotions are not only outwardly expressed but pushed to the limits of exaggeration. The Nō actor indicates that he is weeping by touching his sleeve to his forehead, but the Bunraku chanter may deliver instead a five minute crescendo of sobs and gasps. Like a Momoyama screen painting which depicts cherry blossoms in relief, larger than life, Bunraku attempts to achieve truth in its portrayals by expanding ineffectual or inadequately expressed thoughts and emotions to their full natural implications. Chikamatsu once stated his belief that bluntly saying "How sad!" about an unfortunate happening killed all possibility of evocative expression. He felt that the *jōruri* playwright should be able to convince the audience of the pathos or joy in a situation without characterizing it with the most obvious adjective. His opinion was exceptionally astute, but when we examine his plays, even those ranked as masterpieces, we discover immediately numerous examples of the most unambiguous characterization of emotions. Chikamatsu's relative restraint becomes apparent only when we compare his texts with those of his predecessors. As he himself realized, a *jōruri* play must be filled with exaggerated movement and vitality if life is to be imparted to the wooden puppets. In case of conflict between dramatic and purely literary interest, *jōruri*, unlike Nō, invariably chose the former.

The puppet theatre imposed many demands on its playwrights. The Nō actor consciously attempts to remove human mannerisms from his movements; the puppet operator desires above all that the non-human figure in his hands will display unmistakably human gestures. The *jōruri* text must therefore assist the puppet operator by providing intensely "human" situations. In Nō, any suggestion of lovemaking on the stage, even the barest intimation of a caress, would be unthinkable. To avoid the possibility that the element of romance will introduce an undesirable human touch, the part of the martial hero Yoshitsune is taken by a small boy in plays which concern Yoshitsune and the beautiful Shizuka. In *jōruri* texts, on the other hand, romance is essential, along with such other typically human actions as gross violence, low clowning, and demonstrations of physical prowess, all rejected by the Nō theatre.

If the *jōruri* is correctly interpreted as a reaction to the aristocratic, ritualized symbolism of Nō, we should expect it to be popular, free in its expression, and direct. These qualities are all present, though if we compare *jōruri* to twentieth-century drama instead of to Nō, it may seem of almost aristocratic distinction. The closest parallel, though clearly not an exact one, between *jōruri* and the drama in the West is the Elizabethan theatre. Both stages catered alike to gentry and groundlings; *jōruri* pleased the former by the novelty of its plots and the flights of beautiful language, and the latter by the mixture of adventure, lachrymose scenes, and low comedy. The main basis of support for *jōruri* came from the commoners, including illiterate farmers who flocked to village performances when the troupes went on tour. The popularity of puppet plays lingers today in remote rural areas, especially on the islands of Sado and Awaji. Originally, the lower classes may have attended *jōruri* rather than Kabuki because the tickets were cheaper, but from the first, despite the imperial patronage it enjoyed, Bunraku was considered a humbler variety of entertainment than Kabuki, which maintained glamorous connections with the gay quarters. The Bunraku dramatists, rather like their counterparts in Elizabethan England, imposed their literary genius on audiences which might have been satisfied with less adorned entertainment, and thereby created a repertory which has survived to this day.

We can easily imagine why audiences, whether aristocratic or plebeian, responded so eagerly to the *jōruri*. However crude the early texts may have been, they were the first full-length dramas performed in Japan. A Nō program consisted of separate one-act plays divided by comical sketches, but a *jōruri* program was usually devoted to one play which related a single, continuous story. *Jōruri* presentations, unlike Nō, made increasing use of settings, props and stage machinery. The musical accompaniment, unlike the austere, staccato drums of Nō, was lively and sometimes erotic, and the combination of declaimed passages (in which the chanter realistically imitated the voices of the characters) and sung passages of greater lyrical beauty, provided an enjoyable variety, keeping the narration even of long monologues from becoming tedious.

Most importantly, the *jōruri* approached drama in the European sense, stressing the conflict between characters and the violent actions which Nō conspicuously avoided. It is true that even in Chikamatsu's works *jōruri* retains such elements of the storyteller's art as descriptions of the scene by the chanter, but his characters possess a dramatic autonomy which contrasts with the vaguely defined personages in Nō, who sometimes speak for themselves, sometimes describe their actions as if seen by an outsider, and at still other times have their own dialogue pronounced for them by the chorus. The ancient heroes depicted in the Nō plays are often deprived of the very attributes which occasioned the original legends about them except for the one trait deemed essential by the dramatist. *Jōruri*, on the other hand, can describe characters in novelistic detail without impairing the dramatic effect. The early *jōruri* and *sekkyō-bushi* (Buddhist morality plays) attempted to engross audiences with their stories rather than to suggest the symbolic world of Nō. The result was inevitably a diminution of the poetry, but it brought a truly theatrical quality to the Japanese drama.

The clearest way to illustrate the new elements found in the *jōruri* texts is to give an example of a typical work. One of the most famous early *jōruri* was *Amida no Munewari* ("The Chest-Splitting of Amida"), performed in 1614 before the Retired Emperor Goyōzei, apparently the first instance of a puppet play having been staged before a palace audience. The courtiers, accustomed to the language and content of the Nō plays, may initially have smiled at the crudity of "The Chest-Splitting of Amida," a work virtually devoid of aristocratic pretensions, but the very unfamiliarity undoubtedly pleased spectators bored with the oft-repeated Nō plays. As so often in Japanese literary or theatrical history, the nobles were ready to welcome a provincial or popular entertainment, whether Nō in its primitive stage or a new kind of verse-making, but generally they attempted before long to modify this novelty to better suit their own tastes. "The Chest-Splitting of Amida," by its very crudity, may have moved an otherwise sophisticated audience into a kind of religious ecstasy, as Watsuji has suggested.

"The Chest-Splitting of Amida," though ostensibly set in India, is Japanese in conception and in all details. The work is in six acts, in keeping with early *jōruri* usage.

The first act describes a rich man who owns seven treasures, including demon-quelling swords and a pine tree which restores youth. Most of all, however, he prizes his two children, a girl of seven and a boy of five. One day the man says to his wife, "Other people worry about the future life because they expect to meet the bodhisattva Miroku when he appears in this world. But we can always make ourselves young again, whenever we like, with our pine. There is no need for us to pray for the future life because we will never die. Why shouldn't we enjoy ourselves by doing wicked things instead of good deeds, for a change?" The wife is easily persuaded, and the couple thereupon devote themselves to doing the opposite of whatever people consider to be good; they burn Buddhist temples, refuse alms to the priests, envy other people's good fortune, and delight in evil. Shakyamuni Buddha, disturbed by the baleful influence of the rich couple on other people, decides to make them cease their wicked ways. He asks the devil kings' help, but when they visit the rich man's house he wards them off with a magic sword. Buddha then sends a multitude of gods of pestilence to afflict the couple but the sword repels them too. Buddha is now absolutely determined to make the rich man suffer. He assembles all his disciples and commands them to fetch the devils of hell. They eagerly comply and return immediately with some three hundred who undertake Buddha's orders. The devils succeed in outwitting the rich man by melting his magic sword with fire. In the end, the man's treasures are destroyed, his servants killed, and molten iron is poured down the throats of the once arrogant couple. Buddha, however, orders the devils not to harm the two children.

The second act relates the plight of the two orphans, who wander the streets as penniless beggars, rejected everywhere. The years pass, and it is now the seventh anniversary of their parents' death. The boy, distressed that he and his sister cannot make the customary offerings to their parents' memory, proposes that they sell their flesh "as food for eagles or hawks" and use the money they receive to pay for sutra-readings and the erection of a commemorative stone. The sister agrees, and the children travel to a nearby kingdom where they offer themselves for sale.

but in vain. In great dejection they go to the temple of Amida to pray for a buyer. Amida appears that night in their dreams, praises their devotion, and informs them where they will find a rich man willing to purchase their bodies.

In the third act we are told of a potentate with an only son of twelve who has been stricken by a mysterious malady. The father summons the most famous doctor of India, who declares that the boy's sickness can be cured only if the rich man finds a girl born in the same year, the same month, the same day and the same hour, rips the liver from her body, washes it seventy-five times in an elixir of long life, and feeds it to his ailing son. The rich man offers a huge reward for a girl of the right description, but although more than 350 candidates, all girls of twelve, present themselves, none fits the specifications exactly.

In the fourth act the rich man, learning of the brother and sister who have come to his house to offer themselves for sale, addresses the girl and discovers she was born at precisely the same hour as his son. He directs his wife to give the girl whatever she asks on condition that she allow the liver to be torn from her body. But the wife, struck by the girl's remarkable beauty, suspects that she must be the transformation of some god or Buddha, and fears that if the girl is sacrificed, the wrath of Heaven will descend on the family. She attempts (by describing her son's desperate illness) to persuade the girl to sacrifice herself voluntarily. The girl bursts into tears, not out of self-pity, but because she wonders who will look after her brother if she sacrifices herself. The rich man and his wife join in tears of sympathy.

In the fifth act, the climax of the work, the girl agrees to be sacrificed on condition that the rich man build a temple in memory of her parents, and enshrine in it an Amida triptych. The rich man gladly accepts, and in twenty-one days the work is completed. The girl begs the rich man's protection for her brother. He assures her he will consider the boy as his own son. The girl, satisfied, goes to pray before Amida. She declares, "I offer you this temple, built at the cost of my life. I pray that, however heavy my sins, you will save me because of the merit of this act and bring me rebirth on the same lotus with my parents." She reads aloud sections of the Lotus Sutra: the fifth chapter for her father, the sixth chapter for her mother, the seventh chapter for her brother and for those present, the eighth chapter for herself. The brother is bewildered by these events, but to comfort him the girl declares that she is to become the rich man's bride. She urges the boy to take orders as a monk so that he may pray for their parents' repose. He consents, and exhausted by emotion falls asleep, his head on his sister's lap. She recalls how inseparable they have been through the years and, as she combs his disheveled hair, she remembers that never has a day passed but that she has arranged his hair at least three times. "After tomorrow who will be a sister to him and bind his hair? How sad this is!"

The sixth and final act describes the girl's last day. The rich man's son has become desperately ill, and no further delay is possible. The desperate father sends five soldiers to the temple where the girl is staying, with orders to rip out her liver. They go, but cannot bring themselves to kill so beautiful a girl. She insists and even directs them as to what they must do. In the end they cut open her chest and remove the liver. The rich man has it washed seventy-five times in the elixir of long life, as the doctor prescribed, and feeds it to his son, who at once perceptibly improves. By that night, the boy having recovered completely, his overjoyed attendants go to examine the dead girl's body. They discover her and her brother sleeping peacefully, hand in hand. Beside them the statue of Amida Buddha is streaming with blood from a terrible rent in its chest, and it is apparent to all that Amida has offered his own liver to save the girl. The rich man decides on the spot that the girl will be his son's bride. The brother, as he previously agreed, will become a priest. People gather from everywhere to pay homage before the mutilated, blood-stained statue of Amida Buddha.

"The Chest-Splitting of Amida" has been described in detail because it differs so conspicuously from either the Nō dramas or the stories about Princess Jōruri, based as they were on familiar materials and couched in traditional language. The play is noteworthy also for the many themes which were to figure prominently in the later puppet theatre. Watsuji Tetsurō, noting that the first mentions of "The Chest-Splitting of Amida" date from about 1614, when major edicts by the government aimed at the prohibition of Christianity were promulgated, has suggested that Christian influence may account for certain curiously untraditional aspects of the plot. In the first act, for example, Shakyamuni Buddha, not at all resembling the all-compassionate deity described in other Buddhist works, is filled with divine wrath at the arrogance of the rich man who fears nothing from the world after death, and sends avenging devils to torment the man, who is finally stripped of his vaunted treasures. The story is reminiscent of Job's, and the Shakyamuni here is more like Jehovah than Buddha. The Amida Buddha of the final act, however, suggests Christ; nothing in previous Japanese depictions of Amida accounts for the scene of people worshiping a holy image streaming with blood, in the manner of European (and especially Iberian) representations of Christ on the cross. Amida's sacrifice of himself to save the girl also suggests Christ's offering himself to save mankind. It is impossible to prove the existence of direct influence, but one can surely recognize an enormous difference between the deity here described and the traditional portrayals of Amida in his remote Western Paradise. Christian art and even stories from the Bible were well enough known to some Japanese at the time to account for this unconventional Amida.

The theme of substitution, stated in "The Chest-Splitting of Amida" in such extreme terms, was to be a most familiar feature of *jōruri* texts. In Chikamatsu's first great success, "Kagekiyo Victorious" (*Shusse Kagekiyo*, 1685), the final scene is largely devoted to a description of the miracle by which Kannon, the special object of Kagekiyo's devotion, saves him from execution by substituting her head for his; the bloodstained, decapitated image of Kannon is discovered after Kagekiyo had presumably been beheaded, much as in the play about Amida. Substitutions of one person to save another may be found in earlier Japanese literature and need not have derived from Christian sources or even from "The Chest-Splitting of Amida," but its prominence as a theme probably owes much to this early *jōruri* success.

Other themes in this play which would frequently reappear include the sufferings of innocent children whose devotion to the memory of their parents is finally rewarded, and the use of some extraordinary medicine to work a seemingly impossible cure. One might mention especially "Gappō's Daughter Tsuji" (*Sesshū Gappō ga Tsuji*, 1773), in which the young Shuntoku, suffering from leprosy, is cured by drinking blood from the liver of a woman born in the hour of the tiger, the day of the tiger, the month of the tiger and the year of the tiger, obviously an echo of the Amida play written over 150 years before.

"The Chest-Splitting of Amida," it needs hardly be said, bears no resemblance to the condensed, intricate structure of a Nō play, either in plot or language. Its ancestry, apart from possible foreign influence, is to be found in the popular stories composed in the Muromachi period about the miracles of the gods and Buddhas. The diction is simple and rarely poetic, and there is no attempt to suggest any profounder truths than the story so straightforwardly told. It is superior to the Nō in purely dramatic terms, if only because it contains a variety of characters, and is not focused exclusively on one central figure. The play is interesting otherwise because, unlike the original "Tale in Twelve Episodes" it appears to have been composed from the start as a puppet play. The scene in which the soldiers tear the liver from the girl's body, for example, could be performed realistically, thanks to the use of puppets. At the same time, in more artistic terms, it was possible to assign the major roles to children; in a theatre of actors one may not be able to find a twelve-year-old who can read convincingly a series of passages from the Lotus Sutra, but in the puppet theatre where all parts are delivered by the chanters, a child puppet can be entrusted with the most difficult roles. Certainly one difference between the Japanese and European theatre of the seventeenth and eighteenth centuries is the prominence of children in the former.

The contrast with the Nō must have been welcomed by the blasé aristocrats, and some may not only have patronized the *jōruri* but written texts as well, sensing its as yet scarcely explored literary and dramatic possibilities. But most advances in the artistic techniques of *jōruri*, whatever contributions the nobility may have made, are closely connected with the successive famous chanters, each of whom strongly impressed his personality on the art.

The chanters have been at once the servants and creators of the texts. In the Kabuki theatre, where the actors always remained the center of attention, the playwright wrote his texts to fit the special talents of a particular actor, who felt free to alter the text in any way he chose. Even Chikamatsu had to yield to this convention, though unwillingly; it is often suggested that he turned from Kabuki to Bunraku because of his irritation at the liberties the Kabuki actors took with his texts. The Kabuki text tended to be no more than a vehicle for the histrionic talents of the actors. Chikamatsu himself on occasion left the climactic scene of a play a mere outline, knowing actors would prefer to improvise their lines. In Bunraku, on the other hand, the chanters are bound to the text, which they have before them throughout the performances though they know every word by heart. They could not make radical departures from the text even if they so chose without considerable advance preparation, for the movements of the puppets and the samisen accompaniment must correspond exactly to the text; if the chanters improvised like Kabuki actors the effect would be disastrous. Even the prolongation of a syllable becomes in Bunraku a major change, establishing a new tradition of reading a part; the second Tsunadayū, when chanting Hambei's confession from the "Saké Shop" scene in 1822, added a cough which has since become traditional among chanters who bear the name Tsunadayū.

Although the chanters are far more closely bound to the text than Kabuki actors, even in the same parts, they have inspired and even created the styles of the *jōruri* playwrights. When the chanter Uji Kaga-no-jō (1635-1711), known for his musical talents and his fondness for the Nō plays, expressed preference for more melodious and elegant works, the *jōruri* playwrights met his requirements, much as Kabuki playwrights provided the first Ichikawa Danjūrō with opportunities to dazzle the audiences with his "roughhouse" *(aragoto)* antics, or the romantic Sakata Tōjūrō with his tender love scenes *(wagoto)*. Chikamatsu wrote *Yotsugi Soga* ("The Soga Heir"), perhaps his maiden work, for Kaga-no-jō in 1683, and the chanter's influence is apparent in the work. Earlier plays about the Soga brothers had emphasized their bold deeds, but in this work attention is shifted from the heroic brothers to the courtesans Tora and Shōshō. Not only did this create a more sophisticated atmosphere, the demi-monde so familiar in Chikamatsu's later works, but it provided room for displaying Kaga-no-jō's voice to best advantage. The Kyoto audiences, which had never taken to the Edo-style heroics, were delighted, and the triumph was shared equally by Kaga-no-jō and Chikamatsu. Later, when Chikamatsu composed texts for Gidayū, he gave his historical plays a tragic depth such works had previously lacked. Gidayū's peculiar talents inspired Chikamatsu to compose the first domestic tragedies, the two men apparently collaborating closely. After Gidayū's death, Chikamatsu again changed his style, this time to accord with the less powerful delivery of Masadayū, the youthful successor of Gidayū. The proportion of domestic tragedies to Chikamatsu's entire output of plays dropped markedly, presumably again in response to the chanter's demands. The composition of the texts indeed was so closely related to the chanters that for the period of *jōruri* before Chikamatsu the texts are known by the names not of the playwrights but of the chanters, and even today the authors' names are often omitted from the playbills.

The chanters have always been considered the intellectuals and even the gentlemen of Bunraku. The outstanding chanter Takemoto Tsunadayū, to cite one instance, was an accomplished scholar of *jōruri* texts, though some puppet operators are virtually illiterate. By its very nature, of course, the chanter's work involves not only imitation of his predecessors, equally true of puppet operators and samisen players, but continual study of the texts. When neglected plays are revived the chanter is often obliged to interpret the parts afresh, for the notations in the old texts are generally too crude to be of much service. Of course, it is desirable in such cases to find someone with knowledge of the old traditions. In 1920, for example, Tsunadayū discovered that the wife of a Bunraku scholar had learned as a child from an elderly samisen player the traditional delivery of Chikamatsu's play *Kasane-izutsu*, a work which had not been performed since 1877. Tsunadayū studied the play with her, but not until 1952 did he have the opportunity of reciting the part at the Bunraku Theatre, where it was revived after a lapse of seventy-seven years. Tsunadayū, having once learned the traditions, was able to recall them thirty-two years later, a feat of memory not considered exceptional in a chanter.

A beautiful voice is of course a great asset to a chanter, but even if his voice is weak or (like Gidayū's) a metallic rasp, he may still reach the heights of his profession by the effectiveness of his interpretation and recitation of the texts. He need not possess an actor's looks, but he must be equipped with the stamina to throw himself completely into as long as a full hour's impassioned solo delivery. In the past, chanters normally were the sons (real or adopted) of other chanters, and men who attempted to enter the profession from the outside were looked upon with suspicion and even contempt. This attitude stems from the belief that only someone familiar with the sounds of *jōruri* and its traditions from earliest childhood could hope to master them. The great Toyotake Kōtsubodayū (born in 1878), honored by the court in 1947 with the title of Yamashiro-no-shōjō, suffered in his early career from the disadvantage of having been born in Tokyo and not in Osaka, the home of Bunraku. Even today this feeling has not entirely disappeared, though an artist like Kōtsubodayū eventually can overcome such prejudices by his undeniable skill.

Tsunadayū, Kōtsubodayū's successor, began his career in Bunraku very early. He was first taken to the theatre by his father, a Bunraku enthusiast, at the age of four or five, and began his study of chanting with a teacher in the neighborhood shortly afterwards. On August 15, 1911, at the age of seven, he was formally accepted as a pupil by Kōtsubodayū, who bestowed on the boy the name Toyotake Tsubamedayū, a name he himself had used early in his career. In Bunraku, as in Kabuki, the names of great performers are preserved by transmitting them from one generation to the next. These names all have rankings and special traditions. The name Tsunadayū, for example, was one within Kōtsubodayū's power to bestow. As early as 1941 he felt that Tsubamedayū was ready for the honor of assuming the name of the eighth Tsunadayū, but his pupil was reluctant to accept this honor, and took instead a lesser name, the sixth Orinodayū, an early name used by the sixth Tsunadayū. Not until 1947, when Kōtsubodayū received his court title, did his pupil finally succeed as the eighth Tsunadayū.

He had demonstrated his right to this honor by distinguishing himself at each of the prescribed stages in a chanter's career. His performing career began at the age of thirteen in 1917 with a minor part, barely half a page long, in the middle section of the opening act of *Chūshingura*. He moved next to chanting the beginning and middle sections of the conclusion of first acts, then to the beginning and middle sections of the second act, and finally to the beginning of the third act, a vital stage in a chanter's career. At this level the chanter may progress either to the conclusion of the first act, or to the middle of the third act, both considered extremely demanding. The concluding section of an act carries the most prestige for a chanter; in Kōtsubodayū's words, "The first time a chanter sees the notation 'conclusion' beside his name in the program, he feels like a university graduate looking at his diploma." However, the conclusion of the second act, technically ranked as a section of major importance, tends to be dull and is therefore generally assigned to unpopular though senior chanters. Tsunadayū relates that he enjoyed especially performing the beginning of the fourth act, not only because of the opportunities it offered to display his talents, but because it was usually performed just after lunch, and the audience was likely to be larger and more attentive than when hungry.

The third and fourth acts are the high points of the performance, and the chanter is allowed to deliver these sections only after he has fully demonstrated his proficiency. Normally an attempt is made to assign chanters congenial roles, but often the best roles have been pre-empted by a senior performer, and only when he falls ill or retires can the younger chanter, however proficient, hope to assume them. Substitution at the last moment for an ailing star is the dream of all Bunraku artists, for it offers the one opportunity of advancing more quickly than by mere seniority. Tsunadayū was called upon to substitute for his teacher Kōtsubodayū on several important occasions, and so distinguished himself each time that as a reward he was assigned roles normally taken by much senior men. Needless to say, such proficiency was the product of his intense study both of the performances of his teacher (and other great chanters) and of the texts. Tsunadayū amusingly related how, when he learned he was to substitute for his teacher in reciting "Gappo's Daughter Tsuji," one of the most difficult plays of the repertory, he gorged himself on steaks, eels, and every other variety of especially nourishing food in order to fortify himself for the ordeal.

Many stories describe how chanters struggled to improve their art. A famous anecdote tells of the chanter who perfected a heroic laugh by delivering it from successively higher floors of the seven-storied pagoda of the Tennōji, demanding each time of a friend on its ground if it could clearly be heard. Even if he does not resort to such expedients, the chanter's training is highly demanding. Apart from learning how to render the texts, the young chanter must be familiar with the traditional etiquette expected in his relations with his teacher and other seniors. It is a disciple's duty, for example, to offer his teacher tea at pauses in the narration; it has been claimed that a pupil who knows how to serve tea properly himself ranks as a full-fledged artist. This means that the pupil must be so sensitive to the master's voice that he will be aware instantly of any departures from its usual standards, and will know whether ground ginger or a raw egg in the tea would best alleviate the particular vocal defect. Moreover, he must not wait for the master's cup to be emptied before he fills it again, nor should he allow the tea to grow cold. In the dressing room the young Bunraku performer must show his awareness of his humble position by wearing only cotton kimonos. The pupil, whether in the dressing room or a private place, may not sit on a cushion in his teacher's presence; Tsunadayū recalled that only after Kōtsubodayū retired did he at last comply with the suggestion that he sit on a cushion, though even then with great hesitation and feelings of impropriety. Such deference was considered essential in the past, and remains the general practice today. Some artists have rebelled at the old system—Tsunadayū himself, in disgust at the rarity of opportunities given him to perform important roles, for five years (from 1936 to 1941) elected to perform *jōruri* without puppets as a member of a small company of similarly-minded younger artists. Again, after the end of the war, when a Bunraku union was formed, most of the senior performers, including the chanter Toyotake Kōtsubodayū, the puppet operator Yoshida Bungorō and the samisen player Tsurusawa Seiroku, refused to join, believing that it was improper for artists to bicker about money. "As long as you have the chance to show your talent, people won't forget you," Kōtsubodayū told his pupil. At first Tsunadayū, who belonged to a younger generation less governed by such traditional views, took the side of those who had formed the union, but the ties of master and disciple proved too strong, and before long he rejoined Kōtsubodayū. The company, however, remained divided, the break not being formally mended until 1963 with the formation of the Bunraku Association. In the meanwhile, the chanters had continued to perform their task of training their successors. On August 15, 1953, exactly forty-four years after his father, Tsunadayū's son was accepted as a pupil by Yamashiro-no-shōjō and given the name of Tsunakodayū. Despite the gloom of some prophets, the traditions of the chanter's art seem in no immediate danger of perishing.

IV. THE SAMISEN AND THE PLAYERS

THE SAMISEN (or shamisen) is by far the most popular Japanese musical instrument. In the smallest of its three common sizes it is an indispensable element in geisha entertainments, the old-fashioned boating party, or the folk festival. It serves also as the accompaniment for a large variety of ballads ranging from brief love-songs to long, painfully narrated monologues about the chivalrous gamblers of a century ago. In the Kabuki theatre it provides the basic melodic background for the *nagauta* and other types of narrative singing. The middle size of samisen is used in the style of narration called Tokiwazu and in *jiuta*, an instrumental ensemble which often accompanies dancing. The largest samisens, considerably heavier than the *nagauta* variety and played with a plectrum almost twice as big, are employed exclusively in *jōruri* performances, where strong and incisive notes, rather than melodious or poetic tones, are required. Paul Claudel once likened the sound of the *jōruri* samisen to that of a nerve being plucked.

Whatever the size of the samisen or the manner of playing, it is primarily an accompaniment to the voice, and not a solo instrument. It is tuned to no fixed basic pitch, but can be modulated at will to blend with the voice of the singer. The samisen consists of three main elements: the body, the neck, and the handle. The materials used to make each part have been tested and improved over the centuries, and are now carefully ranked in order of desirability. For the body of the instrument Chinese quince is preferred, followed by mulberry wood; cherry wood is considered a poor substitute. The neck and handle are preferably of *kōki* wood, followed by red sandalwood, then by oak or cherry wood. The tuning pegs in the handle are of black sandalwood or ivory. The kind of skin used to cover the box, the materials for the three strings, the bridge, the plectrum, and all the other parts of the samisen have been studied with infinite care, and the proportions and shape of the instrument have been subjected to many changes. Such attention to improving the samisen, an instrument associated with the world of pleasure rather than with the noble Confucian art of music, suggests its peculiar appeal to the Japanese, as well as the awareness of successive generations of musicians of precisely the kind of sounds they desired. The music of the samisen employed in *jōruri* is not nearly so ingratiating as the *nagauta* samisen, but this is no accident or fault of the musicians; in Bunraku the samisen's function is to enhance the chanter's recitation and to guide the puppet operators in their movements. Opportunities for exhibiting virtuoso musicianship exist, but they are of only secondary importance.

The exact methods of tuning and playing the samisen are rather beyond the scope of a general essay such as this. Even though the non-musician who attends a Bunraku play may be uninformed about these technical matters, he cannot escape becoming aware of the samisen's decisive role in a performance. When, at the beginning of a scene, the turntable on the dais to the right of the stage revolves and brings before the audience a chanter and a samisen player, it will almost certainly prove to be a combination so perfectly matched that it is hard to distinguish the part of each man in the total effect. Takemoto Tsunadayū, for example, was accompanied for more than twenty-five years by Takezawa Yashichi, and the two men formed so sensitive a partnership that Yashichi could tell intuitively, almost from Tsunadayū's first phrase, how his performance would go that day. If he sensed that Tsunadayū was in his best form, he would feel free to vary the tempos in order to afford Tsunadayū maximum opportunities for virtuoso display, but if, on the other hand, he judged that Tsunadayū's performance would be slow in reaching its normal level, or that he was having an off-day altogether, he would adjust his playing accordingly to cover the deficiencies. The inarticulate cries with which the samisen player punctuates his performance may help the chanter when he himself is in difficulty, but if he is in good voice he is likely to resent these interruptions which divert attention from himself. When a combination of chanter and samisen as well-matched as Tsunadayū perform, the samisen player may not utter a single *hah* or *oh* all evening, but usually the beginning of a new scene, particularly the *michiyuki*, or a change in atmosphere within a given scene, will elicit a sharp cry from the samisen player. Some players indulge ostentatiously in a whole repertory of cries, but this violates the proper functions of an accompaniment, and though welcomed by members of the audience, is essentially the mark of an inferior artist.

The interpretation of the text is usually determined by the chanter, then conveyed to the samisen player, who becomes the conductor of the performance. The chanter cannot sing until he hears the appropriate notes, nor can the puppet operators move out onto the stage. The temptation to be a tyrant exists, but the samisen player usually takes advantage of his position as conductor only so as to impart the flexibility necessary in a performance to keep it from growing stale. The familiar cliché that the samisen player must be a "wife" to the chanter sometimes has an ironic ring; the "wife" may turn out to be a shrew and compel the chanter to act the part of the docile husband. The samisen virtuoso Toyozawa Dampei was famous for having on one occasion repeated so many times a series of notes calling for a certain exclamation from the chanter that the latter collapsed with exhaustion over his stand. Dampei, it should be said, was not indulging in sadistic torment of a fellow artist. He had decided that this particular effect was necessary in terms of the performance as it had progressed that day, and he used his prerogative as leader of the ensemble to impose his artistic conception on the chanter. Dampei was a unique figure, and no samisen player today would repeat his stunt; nevertheless, however unassuming the player may be, his authority is like that of the opera conductor, whose beat must be followed even by the temperamental prima donna if the combination of voices and orchestra is not to be cacophonous. An indecisive or blurred samisen accompaniment can work equal devastation on the manipulation of the puppets if it causes the operators to miss their cues. The player's responsibility is heavy, and the training for his share of a Bunraku performance is accordingly strict.

Samisen players are usually born in the Bunraku milieu; if not, they are likely to have family connections with another school of playing. Lessons begin early for the child who shows an avocation for the samisen. By the time he is seven or eight he may have already demonstrated his proficiency sufficiently to be enrolled as the pupil of an established Bunraku player. Being the pupil of a great performer may in practice mean no more than having unlimited opportunities to hear him play. Actual instruction is given mainly by older pupils, and often this used to consist (if no longer true today) of blows and harsh words, rather than of helpful advice. The justification for such savage treatment was that it served to weed out young people not wholly devoted to their art. The scalp wounds dealt by the master's plectrum were the samisen player's equivalent of the Heidelberg dueling scar.

The young player, to a greater degree even than the fledgling chanter or puppet operator, was constantly kept practicing. One distinguished artist recalled how as a child he had begged for a fire in the bitter-cold rehearsal room. "Very well, I'll see that you get a fire," said his teacher to the overjoyed boy, only to add, "Just as soon as you learn how to play." Rehearsals in the summer were even more arduous. One teacher is reported to have insisted that each pupil keep practicing until a pint of sweat could be wrung from the sheet on which he sat. Such training inevitably drove some young men into other professions, but it also produced masters whose likes may never be heard again.

Today the samisen player at the chanter's left on the revolving dais sits erect in formal Japanese style, his legs tucked under him, but, as we know from old paintings, this was not the original posture for playing the instrument. In the seventeenth century the samisen player sat cross-legged, or on a little chair, or with one knee raised. The posture now considered essential to a good performance originated about 1700 in the licensed quarters of Kyoto and Osaka, and spread then to the theatre. The Bunraku player sits with the base of his samisen resting on his right leg, two to five inches from the kneecap. He holds the instrument at a forty-five degree angle, the handle pointing over his left shoulder. He props the neck of the instrument between the thumb and index finger of his left hand, gripping it with the remaining fingers. A plectrum held in his right hand is used to strike the strings stretched over the body of the samisen.

Forty-eight positions of the left hand on the strings have been distinguished, each designated by a letter of the Japanese syllabary. This system of notation was invented at the end of the eighteenth century by Tsurusawa Seishichi, reportedly a boy of twelve at the time. The player presses one of these forty-eight points with the index finger of his left hand and produces the desired note when the plectrum hits the string. The samisen has two bridges, one at the base of the instrument, and the other in the handle. The lowest of the three strings does not pass over the upper bridge, but reverberates over a cavity in the handle with a sound characteristic of the instrument. Other typical sounds occur when the plectrum strikes the string and the catskin at the same time with a sharp snap, or when the operator slides his left hand down the strings. The range of the first string extends from B below middle C to B above middle C; of the second string from E above middle C to the E one octave higher; and of the third string from B below high C to the B one octave higher.

The musical notation for the samisen indicates the note and its length (normal, double, four times). The length is relative, not measured by a metronome, giving the player a good deal more leeway than in Western music. Notations sometimes indicate the mood (sad, joyous, and so on) produced by the manner of touch and, in the case of the *jōruri* samisen only, describe the chanter's delivery, whether declamation or song, and the pitch and length of his notes. Certain fixed patterns signaling the end of a scene, the entrance and exits of the puppets, and other important moments are also noted in the score.

A performance, whether of a complete play or of only a single scene, invariably begins with a samisen passage which creates the desired mood. In addition to such fairly extended solos, brief motifs serve as shorthand indications of emotions being portrayed. Resignation, for example, is expressed by playing B below middle C on the first string, high C on the third string, and F on the second string; joy by high C followed by high E on the third string; love merely by high C on the third string. Imploration requires seven notes, and confusion twelve. A combination of such patterns runs through the musical accompaniment of the plays, indicative of the samisen's primary function of corroborating the words of the chanter and the gestures of the puppets.

The composition of the music for a puppet play has generally been left to the samisen players. The most demanding part of the task is the composition of the solo passages which give the player his brief moments of glory. In some works five or six samisens play simultaneously to create a colorful and usually cheerful effect, and in the *michiyuki* sections of the plays, popular ballads of the period are introduced, affording additional scope for the player's talents. There are a few traditional feats, reminiscent of the drum major with his baton, which allow the player a rare chance to perform a vaudeville turn. Apart from these infrequent opportunities, the samisen's role is auxiliary, and the music seldom more than the chords accompanying recitative in a European opera.

Certain other instruments besides the samisen are occasionally heard in Bunraku performances. The *koto*, a seven-stringed, zither-like instrument, is featured in several famous scenes, and the *kokyū*, a violin-like instrument played with a bow, sometimes accompanies tragic moments because of its peculiarly doleful sound. Offstage battles are indicated by drums and gongs; and bells, flutes, and other instruments make their appearance when required by the text. The war play "Three Heroes, Glorious Human Bullets," produced in 1932, is remembered today because it introduced the bugle to Bunraku.

V. THE PUPPETS AND THE OPERATORS

BUNRAKU owes to the puppets, its most distinctive feature, the high reputation it has won at home and abroad. The leading puppeteers enjoy a personal popularity at least as great as that of any chanter or samisen player, and a master like Kiritake Monjūrō could impose his interpretations on a whole performance. We should expect, then, that the operators would be considered no less than the equals of the chanters and samisen players, but the situation has clearly been otherwise. Puppetry and the operators themselves were long subject to denigration, not only on the part of society but as an official policy of the government, which imposed restrictions on the activities of puppet operators that did not apply to chanters or samisen players. Even today the operators tend to be looked down on socially, if only because many are badly educated or given to drink and gambling. Beneath such objections it is also possible to detect traces of the ancient belief, going back to the days of the *kugutsu-mawashi*, that puppet operators were foreigners, unlike other Japanese. In rural areas where primitive varieties of puppet plays are still preserved, the operators are sometimes subjected to open discrimination, and if such attitudes are no longer taken seriously by educated people, they account for an undercurrent of opinion that the chanter and the samisen player rank as artists, but the puppet operator is little better than a skilled workman.

Certainly it is true that the operators' approach to this task differs markedly from the chanters' or samisen players'. He is bound by traditions no less than they, but these traditions are completely unrecorded, and are remembered more by the body than by the mind. If one asks a chanter or samisen player to explain some detail in his performance, he will probably be able to answer convincingly, but the operator, because his memory is physical rather than verbal, may content himself with saying, "There's no particular meaning." Unlike the chanter who interprets the texts and brings out a significance which may not be apparent to the reader, or the samisen player who employs musical means to create the atmosphere he deems appropriate, the operator does not use the puppet to express his own conceptions; he enables it to express its own emotions by imparting the strength of his body. We can forget his presence more easily than a chanter's or a samisen player's because he is hardly more than an extension of the puppet. He should be as impersonal as the electric current which indifferently makes a train run on its tracks or brings us over the radio a performance of *Don Giovanni*.

Strictly speaking, of course, this statement is inaccurate: the operators are more than mere motivating forces. Each man not only moves his body like a tennis player in graceful, almost automatic reactions to a changing situation; he must endeavor to allow the puppet a free and natural expression of feelings. Nevertheless, it is fitting that he disappear and that he be unable to verbalize his actions; an intellectual puppet operator would surely be a grotesque failure. Whatever the original causes for the social inequality among the three branches of Bunraku, anonymity is most desirable in the operator. His seeming lack of artistry (the better the operator, the more the puppet appears to move of its own volition), though made light of by other performers, makes it possible for the inanimate puppets to come to life.

The puppets may be classified in various ways. First of all, a division is possible among the different species: marionettes operated from above by strings, mechanical dolls, puppets held above the operators' heads, small puppets worked on a portable stage, large puppets operated by one man and, finally, the three-man puppet of Bunraku. All these varieties still may be found in rural parts of Japan, sometimes preserved by only a few men. The most advanced puppets in every way are those of the Bunraku troupe in Osaka, together with the somewhat coarser variants used by troupes on the island of Awaji and in Tokushima Prefecture. Most Bunraku puppets are operated by three men, but minor characters (bystanders, soldiers, servants) or animals (foxes, horses, tigers) are operated by one man, rather in the manner of the one-man puppets used in *bunya-bushi*, *sekkyō-bushi* and Noroma, three old types of *jōruri* preserved today mainly on the island of Sado. In the seventeenth and eighteenth centuries marionettes and mechanical dolls sometimes supplemented the normal Bunraku puppets for purposes of special effects, but this practice has now disappeared.

Another traditional way of distinguishing the puppets, particularly the Bunraku varieties, is by the sex and age of the characters, both with respect to the frames used for the bodies and to the heads, the focal points of interest in a performance. The male puppets, much larger and heavier than the female, have frames consisting of a straight piece of wood for the shoulder line and a bamboo hoop for the hips. Between the two is pasted thick paper (or sometimes cloth) to form a back and front. Occasionally, in roles which require the puppet to bare his chest, the upper part of the torso is fashioned in the round of cotton cloth, more or less realistically. As a general principle, however, parts of the body covered by the kimono are not delineated. The puppet's head is inserted into the shoulder board, and the arms and legs suspended from the same board at the padded ends. The male puppets are equipped with a fixed bamboo rod at the right of the hoop which the operator uses as a prop to support the weight. The smaller and simpler female puppets lack the feet, the bamboo rod, and the highly articulated hands and facial features.

The three-man puppet is worked by a principal operator, an operator of the left hand, and an operator of the feet. The principal operator inserts his left hand into the puppet from the back under the *obi*, and his right hand through the opening in the upper part of the puppet's right sleeve. With his left hand he grips the armature which extends down from the puppet's neck, thereby moving the head and (if the head is so equipped) the eyes, eyebrows, and mouth, by strings fastened to flexible whalebone strips. With his right hand he operates the puppet's right hand, using a toggle halfway up the puppet's arm to move the whalebone "springs" in the hands. The operator's left hand also moves the puppet's body, whether in motion across the stage or in agitated breathing as it sits in one spot.

The second operator moves the left hand by means of a stick about fifteen inches long joined to the puppet's arm near the elbow. A stick of this length is necessary because this operator cannot come as close to the puppet as the principal operator, who holds the puppet in his arms. The second operator pulls with his right hand cords attached to a toggle on the manipulating stick. Normally he makes no use of his left hand in moving the puppet.

The third operator works the feet of male puppets, guiding himself by the principal operator's movements. He makes the puppet walk or run, stand or sit, as the text requires. This operator not only must convince the audience that the puppet is actually moving on solid ground, but supply appropriate noises of stamping or running by striking his own feet on the floorboards. Female puppets are not provided with feet unless a role specifically requires them. The operator simulates the motions of legs and feet within the kimono by bunching the hems as the character walks, or by rounding the kimono to suggest knees when the puppet sits. Sometimes use is made of a kind of weighted pillow suspended from the bamboo hoop of the puppet frame to give an additional roundness to the figures of female puppets when they sit. As in the case of male puppets, excited movements onstage are amplified by the operator's stamping his feet.

The operators of the left hand and of the feet are attired completely in black and wear gauzy black hoods over their heads. Originally the principal operators were so attired, in the interests of complete anonymity, but as time went on, they came to rival the Kabuki actors in the care with which they adorned themselves. Today, the principal operators normally perform without a hood and in brightly colored formal costumes, though in plays of a particularly tragic nature, they may wear black, and in new or recently revived works they may also wear a hood. Not only the vanity of the principal operators but public demand to see the faces of the famous operators accounts for their rather excessively conspicuous presence in most plays, a violation of the anonymity which should mark these devoted servants of the puppets.

Traditionally, an operator was expected to spend ten years operating the feet and ten years more operating the left arm before he assumed the principal role. In practice, however, there has been no fixed rule. As in other branches of the art, training begins from childhood. The late Kiritake Monjūrō became a pupil of the late Yoshida Bungorō at the age of eight, and made his first stage appearance at twelve. At fourteen he had already gained recognition as an exceptionally skilled operator of the feet, doubtlessly thanks to the guidance he received from Bungorō, long renowned as a master of this art. The young Monjūrō's greatest joy and satisfaction came when he was chosen at fourteen to operate the feet of the puppet Jihei in the *michiyuki* from "The Love Suicides at Amijima," assisting Bungorō, the principal operator. When Monjūrō first put on foot-high clogs, the mark of the principal operator, at the age of twenty-seven, Bungorō, noticing the young man's panic, himself took over the left hand in order to steady his pupil. On one occasion, as Monjūrō gratefully recalled, Bungorō even manipulated the feet to help his pupil, who had been suddenly deprived of his usual assistant.

Such kindness from his teacher undoubtedly contributed enormously to Monjūrō's remarkable development as a puppet operator. His case, it must be said, was unusual. For the most part the senior operators have not only been extremely loath to give away the secrets of their own excellence as performers, but have demonstrated a brutality towards their assistants far surpassing that of senior chanters or samisen players. Their reluctance to impart systematically to pupils the fruits of their own experience mainly reflects their ignorant fear and jealousy of young talent. The operation of puppets, unlike the recitation of texts or the playing of the samisen, depends not so much on maturity of interpretation as on the acquisition of certain knacks which could be taught fairly easily and which contribute enormously to the total effectiveness of a performance. It may readily be conceived that a man who has spent years painfully mastering these little skills without benefit of guidance would be reluctant to impart them to a pupil in the course of an hour's instruction.

Many of the best operators have been self-taught. The first Yoshida Eiza (1872–1945), considered by critics to have been the most accomplished puppeteer of this century, once explained how he came by the mild, uncomplaining nature for which he was famous:

I first began my career as a puppet operator at the age of eight, when I was encouraged to study under Yoshida Kinshi, who was appearing then at the Horie Theatre. An apprentice's training in those days was very strict in any case, but my teacher was especially severe. When I first became his pupil, it was my task to arrange his footwear at the door and to accompany him when he went out. When he returned home, I was expected to do everything from cleaning the house inside and out to helping in the kitchen. When I finished my other tasks, I used to make dust cloths from old rags. I was obliged to massage the shoulders not only of my teacher but of his wife and daughters as well, supposedly to strengthen my fingers. And my teacher never said to me, "Please massage me," but rather, "You may have the honor now of massaging me." Whenever I went out with him he kept up an uninterrupted stream of complaints, saying I was walking too close or too far away or I wasn't holding the lantern properly. At the theatre it was my job to hold up corpses or tobacco trays at the level of the railing, keeping my hands out of sight (we didn't use a stand in those days). If I moved even the least bit I was immediately scolded. Then, after a while, when I came to practice manipulating the feet, using a puppet suspended from the ceiling, I tried my best to learn, but my teacher would continually hit me with his metal tobacco pipe, saying I was operating the feet clumsily or that I wasn't steady.... At last when I was able to move the feet, I was permitted to appear in the theatre holding a one-man puppet. I spent three full years practicing in this way, but during all this time I didn't receive a penny.... When I got back home at night I never had more than three hours of sleep. I was so sleepy even when I was walking that I would bump into telegraph poles, or fall over mail boxes and doze off on the spot. Many times when I set off for the theatre I felt as if I were about to drop right down into hell. After that kind of training you can see why I became the kind of nincompoop I am today.

Whatever benefit Eiza may have obtained from Yoshida Kinshi's instruction, he never sought guidance from another teacher. He learned entirely by observation of the masters and by helping them with the feet or left hand of their puppets.

Eiza's first appearance at the puppet theatre came when he was twelve. He was assigned a part, considered suitable because of his small stature, which required him to pull a puppet's body and head over his own head, and to climb on the shoulders of another puppeteer. The stunt delighted the audience, especially when it first realized that the feet it could see belonged to a child and not a puppet. At the end of the scene, however, Eiza and the puppet were both dumped unceremoniously into a basket, so painful a jolt that the boy saw stars each time. Eiza assumed the principal operator's part for secondary characters at the age of fifteen, but he still continued to work the feet of the puppets for other operators. One role compelled him to hold a puppet absolutely motionless for twenty minutes. If he so much as budged he was immediately kicked by the principal operator with his high clogs, so viciously that the boy's shins were covered with welts.

Eiza's first important chance came in 1895, when he was twenty-three. A puppeteer who was to have appeared in Dampei's puppet version of the Kabuki play *Kanjinchō* suddenly fell ill, and Eiza was chosen as his substitute. Eiza, who had never before operated a large male puppet, was unprepared for the weight, which proved almost too much for him, but he successfully performed the part.

In the following year Eiza joined the Bunraku Theatre after years of playing in various rival companies. Here too he was entrusted with secondary characters, though on occasion he still operated the feet. But at least Eiza could be reasonably sure that one day he would achieve recognition as a principal operator. Not all puppet operators are so fortunate. There is the famous case of Yoshida Kanshi (1855–1930), the oldest member of the Bunraku company when he died, who was condemned to operate the feet exclusively for forty years. In 1929, the year before his death, various persons from the literary and artistic world presented him with fifty yen—about one month's salary—to console him for his unlucky career. Other men have never gone beyond operating the left hand. Eiza, however, after his first great success in 1907, at the age of thirty-five, quickly established himself as a master. Until his death he and Bungorō divided honors as the chief puppet operators. Both were known for their performances of the female roles, but whereas Bungorō excelled in colorful or even erotic parts, Eiza, probably as a result of his retiring disposition, was better suited to the long-suffering heroines of domestic tragedies.

Whatever role an operator assumes, he must observe its traditions, or if a new work, the traditions of similar parts in older works of the repertory. In addition, he is bound by the traditional appearance of the puppets. A puppet is at once an internal mechanism and an external presence. The operator tries not to let the audience become aware of the various armatures and strings which move the parts of the puppet's body, but he is powerless to change the external features: the head, the wig, the arms and legs, the costuming. A number of possibilities exists in each of these categories, but tradition has long since decided the proper appearance, say, for Matsuōmaru in "The

Village School" scene, and any attempt by the operator to change the accepted view of the role by using an untraditional head or wig would certainly arouse much controversy.

The puppet heads have been divided into different categories. One common division is into good and bad characters, in the following manner:

	Good	Bad
Old man	Kiichi, Masamune, Sadanoshin, Takeuji, Shiratayū	Shūto (father-in-law), Ōjūto Toraō
Old woman	Baba (old woman)	Bakuya
Middle-aged man	Kōmei, Bunshichi	Danshichi, Kintoki
Middle-aged woman	Fukeoyama (middle-aged heroine)	Yashio
Young man	Kembishi, Genta, Oniwaka Wakaotoko (young man)	Yokambei, Darasuke
Young woman	Musume (young woman) Shinzō (young courtesan) Keisei (courtesan)	
Clown	Matahei	Onoemon
Female Clown	Ofuku	

In addition to the above heads (some of which are known by variant names) there are heads for children, for various minor comic and eccentric parts, for the supernumerary characters operated by one man, and for the half a dozen or so special roles which have heads used exclusively for them. Some heads have several variations: the Bunshichi head, for example, depending on the role, may or may not be able to open its mouth; the female heads similarly are sometimes able to shut their eyes. The heads are known by the names of characters in famous plays of the past for which the particular heads were originally employed. Kiichi, for example, is the name of an old man in a play first produced in 1731. The same head is used today for such roles as Honzō in *Chūshingura* and Midaroku in "Kumagai's Camp."

In general, each head has a fixed personality, though some shadings exist. Kiichi outwardly shows a stern expression, emphasized by his eyes and eyebrows, but inwardly, we can sense, he possesses deep understanding. This head comes in two sizes, the larger used in the historical plays, and in both gentler and severer expressions, depending on the role. Two shades of coloring are used for Kiichi's face, expressive of slightly different personalities.

The most important head of all is that of Bunshichi, used mainly in the historical plays for middle-aged warriors, impressive figures tormented by a secret grief. Kumagai in "Kumagai's Camp," Matsuōmaru in "The Village School," and Takechi Mitsuhide in *Taikōki*, men of quite different circumstances, are all represented by the Bunshichi head because they share the same essential traits. Shadings in character or in social position are revealed otherwise by the use of appropriate wigs and the costuming, both of which can transform a given head considerably.

The possibility of moving the eyes, eyebrows, and mouth enormously increases the expressive range of the heads, though these movements can be resorted to only infrequently without weakening their effect or else becoming positively comic. For many roles, however, no such range of expression is needed. The young heroes of Chikamatsu's domestic tragedies, for example, exhibit relatively slight changes of mood in the course of a scene, and the heads used for them are accordingly immobile. However, it sometimes happens that different acts of the same play will call for a given character to be portrayed with different heads; thus, Jihei in "The Love Suicides at Amijima" is played with a Genta head in the first act (at the Kawashō Teahouse), but customarily, with a Wakaotoko head in the second act, the scene with his wife at the paper shop. The greatest variety of expression occurs in the villainous or comic parts, the least in the "good" female parts. The Fukeoyama (older woman's) head is equipped with a pin projecting from the lower lip which enables the operator to press the grief-stricken wife's sleeve to her mouth as she restrains her sobs.

The heads are often beautiful examples of carving and deservedly prized as objects of art. The Bunraku company formerly possessed a magnificent collection, many over a century old, but the fire of 1926 and the bombing of 1945 destroyed almost all the best heads. When the company was reorganized in 1946 it was necessary to borrow heads from private collections which had escaped the war. Most of the heads currently employed are recent, carved by a few men working in Tokushima, who also supply the larger puppet heads used in the Tokushima and Awaji theatres. These conscientiously executed heads have proved serviceable in production, but inevitably they lack the artistic excellence of the older examples.

The wigs used in Bunraku are important not only in distinguishing, say, a warrior like Kumagai from a nobleman like Matsuōmaru, but define the age of the characters more precisely than is possible with the head alone. In pre-modern Japan, hairstyles were unmistakably indicative of a person's age and status, and the difference in appearance between a woman of twenty and a woman of twenty-five can still be conveyed quite precisely in a puppet performance by the style of hairdo and the costume even if the head is the same.

Hands and (in the case of the male puppets) feet also vary considerably with the part. Nine commonly used types of hands, and another twenty-four more unusual varieties, have been distinguished. The fingers of the *tsukamite* ("grab hand"), for example, are all independently movable; the *takotsukami* ("octopus grab") permits additionally the movement of the wrist. Needless to say, these hands are appropriate to energetic male puppets, but would not be used for a young lover or for a woman. Most female puppets are equipped with hands which possess independent movement only of the thumbs and wrists; the hands used for old women, however, can exercise movement only of the wrists.

Legs and feet are less complicated; there are six principal varieties for the male puppets, and one each for female and child puppets. They vary depending on whether or not they will be fully visible and also on the size and strength of the character portrayed. Legs and feet are rarely used for the female puppets. In "The Love Suicides at Sonezaki," where it is essential that the heroine's foot be seen, a foot not connected to the puppet's body is pushed out from the puppet's skirts by the third operator at appropriate moments but discarded as soon as it is no longer needed.

In general, Bunraku heads and hands are allowed only the minimum amount of movement necessary. Unless there is some special reason for a character to open his mouth, for example, the head employed for the role will have a fixed mouth; the fewer the moving parts, the more attractive the head or hands. In certain roles, like the courtesan Akoya's in *Dannoura Kabuto Gunki*, the character plays a musical instrument, and specially designed hands are therefore employed. For a few plays also in which a woman in the course of the action reveals her true identity as a demon, a head has been contrived which splits horizontally, revealing a hideous demon's grin. The more grotesque heads, though remarkable examples of the carver's art, are rarely used, and connoisseurs of Bunraku are likely to prefer the Bunshichi or Fukeoyama heads, which symbolize the essence of Bunraku drama.

The operator manipulates not only the puppets but most props figuring in the action. If a sword, lantern or broom must be wielded by a character, the operator inserts his own hand in the puppet's sleeve and holds the object for the puppet, though in a few special instances puppet hands are used which are specially made to hold a brush, fan or drumstick. The props in Bunraku, for the most part identical to those used in Kabuki, are disproportionately large for the puppets. A movable stand is now commonly used to support props not moved much in the course of a scene, though formerly (as Eiza complained) it was customary for an operator to hold the object motionlessly from underneath, often for a quarter of an hour at a time.

The stage settings are designed to reveal immediately the category of play (whether historical or domestic tragedy), the class of society to which the characters belong (nobility, warrior, merchant), or else a particular landscape (riverside, street, forest) which dominates the scene. The conventions of Japanese architecture are invariably followed, but for practical reasons the characters are not required, say, to remove their footwear on entering a house; on the other hand, characters invariably seat themselves when they begin to talk, even if the action occurs in a street without benches or chairs. Such conventions are accepted easily, and any attempt at greater verisimilitude in the settings would only impede the free movements of the operators along the three passages across the stage or on the steps going down from one passage to the next. Occasionally use is made of the *hanamichi*, a raised passageway from the stage to the back of the audience that is an essential feature of Kabuki. In Bunraku the *hanamichi* calls excessive attention to the operators by suddenly exposing all three men to full view, an effect more curious than pleasing.

The presentation of Bunraku plays continues to change as the result of improvements in stage apparatus and shifts in taste. Puppet plays were originally performed out of doors in uniformly bright light, but it is now possible in the theatre to dim or extinguish the illumination, creating new effects. The use of foreign or modern plays has led to the use of new heads with the appropriate features and hairdos, and to trousers, tights, hoopskirts, and other articles of clothing much less successful than kimonos in filling out the rude framework of the Bunraku puppet. An increasing use of devices like the movable stand has made things so much easier for the operators that older members of the company remember nostalgically the difficult demands of the audiences of the past.

Despite such changes in plays and presentation, and a perhaps excessive desire of some members of the Bunraku world to bring the puppet theatre up to date, it remains essentially a traditional art learned, especially the manipulation of the puppets, by the traditional, unscientific methods of transmitting "secrets" from master to disciple over the years. It is a difficult profession to enter, and requires an immense amount of training before the beginner is qualified to appear before the public. No matter how conscientiously he performs when he finally has his chance, the critics are likely to reward his efforts by recalling wistfully the superior artistry of the great men of the past. But each chanter, samisen player, and puppet operator must feel satisfaction when he realizes that his very presence on the Bunraku stage means that he is continuing the traditions of generations of masters before him.

VI. THE GESTURES OF BUNRAKU

EVERY form of stage entertainment performed in keeping with long-standing traditions inevitably develops special, stylized gestures, instantly recognizable to connoisseurs, though not always to persons seeing them for the first time. When, for example, the prince in *Swan Lake* touches his hand to his forehead, the balletomane knows without explanation that the gesture means the young man is straining to catch a glimpse of the swan princess, though a rather similar gesture in a Nō play would signify that the character was weeping. Again, when the Italian operatic tenor places his right hand on his left breast, we may safely assume that he is in love, though the Kabuki actor making a similar gesture might intend us to realize that he is struggling to control over-powering rage. The gestures of the stage, when not directly imitative of universally recognizable phenomena (weeping with sorrow, shuddering with fear, and so on), are derived of course from the habitual gestures of the particular society of which the theatre is a part. The European or Japanese actor shakes his head laterally to signify "no"; the Indian actor makes the same gesture to signify "yes." Both are merely reproducing on the stage the normal daily gestures of their societies. In the puppet theatre, however, the reproduction of believable gestures is complicated by the necessity of reinforcing almost every word with appropriate bodily movements if the wooden figures are not to seem utterly lifeless.

The sculpted puppet faces are deliberately fashioned so that the expression can be markedly altered by moving the eyes, eyebrows or mouth, but these movements are employed relatively seldom, so as not to weaken their effect in the climactic scenes. Changes of expression normally come from the successive poses of the puppet's body. The texts themselves, with their frequent and violent shifts of emotion, favor the almost ceaseless, fluid movements. Without this flow of gestures, indeed, there would be little possibility of dramatic illusion in the puppet theatre.

Gestures performed by actors can be so restrained as to be almost imperceptible at times, yet retain their effect because of the unifying strength of the actor's personality. In the puppet theatre, however, the inability of the puppets to rival the subtlety of movement of a living person has led the operators to choose the opposite extreme: they create an illusion of life by simplifying and intensifying human gestures so as to make the audience feel it is witnessing a distillation of the emotions experienced by the characters on the stage. Nothing, then, can be casual or approximate; a repertory of clearly established gestures is employed to define each moment. Repeated performances of the same work tend to make the gestures almost automatic, and the identification between a puppet and the chief operator may seem unconscious, but a worthy performance requires complete concentration on every gesture. Because gestures form the visual center of the play, the range is far greater than in a theatre of actors, where other means are available.

Two varieties of gesture may be distinguished in Bunraku: the first is a stylized reproduction of familiar human movements, whether the manner of using the body to express grief or joy, or the way a woman sews clothes or plays a musical instrument; the second is not so much a reproduction of human attitudes as an extension of them which permits the operator to display the unique beauty of line that puppets can achieve. The former variety of gestures (known as *furi*) includes as many motions as living people perform; the latter variety (the *kata*) are relatively restricted in number. The creation of a definitive pattern of *furi* and *kata* for a given role is normally a long process, involving constant experimentation by successive operators until experts are agreed that the exact meaning of the text has been visually realized.

The movements of the Bunraku puppets do not constitute a gesture language in the sense, say, that the Kathakali dancers of India can mime every word of a sentence like, "Please come tomorrow at half-past twelve." Not only does the puppet move too slowly in the hands of its three operators for it to depict each word, even when delivered at the pace of the chanter's declamation, but the gestures are intended to underline with broad strokes the central aspect of an utterance rather than to reproduce each word. A choice must be made as to which part of a given phrase will be reinforced by gesture. If, for example, the text reads something like, "I shall be laughed at all over Osaka," the operator may suggest the character's distress at being mocked, or the action of mocking itself, or (with a sweep of the puppet's arm) the vastness of the city, or (if the action is taking place elsewhere) the direction of Osaka.

We cannot be sure of the successive stages undergone by the gestures of the repertory classics before they achieved their present, definitive forms a century or more ago, but we can observe today, especially when new plays are staged (or old plays are revived after a lapse of many years) the process of selection and refinement which probably occurred also in the past. "The Love Suicides at Sonezaki" (*Sonezaki Shinjū*) had not been performed by a Bunraku company for almost 250 years when it was revived in 1955, and no records survived of the *furi* which had originally been employed. The text itself afforded only meagre indications of the gestures intended by the author Chikamatsu Monzaemon. The best clues to the appropriate gestures for the different characters were provided by analogies with similar characters in other works of the repertory. It took considerable time for the operators to settle on the most effective *furi*. Initially, for example, the unhappy lover Tokubei narrated his woes in the first act from a seated position, in keeping with the familiar practice of the puppet theatre, but eventually the operator (Yoshida Tamao) decided that Tokubei's dejection would be more vividly suggested if he stood by a drooping willow as he spoke. Again, the play originally ended as Tokubei, his arm shaking with emotion, held his dagger poised over the throat of the kneeling Ohatsu, but in later performances Tokubei was variously made to drop the dagger in helpless despair, to stab Ohatsu and then himself, or to stab Ohatsu and then turn the point towards himself as the curtain was drawn. Such experimentations continued until the operators felt satisfied that the essential intent of the text had been realized. Nine years after the revival, in 1964, younger operators were given the chance to present their own interpretations of the roles, but they showed themselves disinclined to make innovations; the *furi* for "The Love Suicides at Sonezaki" had already become established. In the case of older works of the repertory, innovation by younger operators would be almost unthinkable.

A great performer who has demonstrated his mastery of the traditional *furi* may, however, choose to depart from tradition on the basis of his individual interpretation of a character. In this way variant traditions of *furi* have been created and preserved by different "family" lines. One well-known example of a variant tradition is found at the outset of the famous monologue from the "Saké Shop" scene in the play *Hadesugata Onna Maiginu*. Hanshichi's wife Osono wonders where her husband, who has run off with another woman, may now be. The great puppeteer Yoshida Bungorō had Osono go to the entrance of the saké shop as if to strain for a glimpse of her husband; she strikes an attitude of anxious reflection, one hand thrust in the bosom of her kimono. The effect of this pose is lovely, but critics objected that it made Osono seem less like a virtuous housewife than a courtesan. In the other tradition of performing the scene, exemplified by Kiritake Monjūrō, Osono pronounces the lines as she absent-mindedly dusts a standing lantern. This *furi*, though visually less charming than Bungorō's, evokes more successfully the character of the devoted wife who, even in the midst of her tormented worries, automatically wipes away the dust she has noticed on the frame of the lamp.

A psychologically true interpretation of each character is the chief goal of the operators, but they seek to embody in the performance not only the meaning of the words of the text but the moments of visual beauty they sense are implicit. This second requirement explains the use of the *kata*, spectacular poses which, unlike the *furi*, may have no direct connection with the text, and may not be necessary even in the general portrayal of a character. A scene without *kata*, even if dramatically effective, lacks something of the peculiar beauty of the art, for it fails to exploit the capacity of puppets to strike ravishing poses which are beyond the physical capacities of a human body. One unusually appealing *kata* is the *ushiroburi*, or "turning to the rear," of female puppets. The effect is to reveal the uninterrupted sweep of the kimono and the lovely undulant lines of the hems as seen from behind. No textual justification is needed for this *kata*, though obviously it fits more easily into certain scenes than others. During the course of Osono's monologue the two varieties of this *kata* are presented. The first (and more spectacular), the *ushiroburi* to the left, begins as Osono moves forward to the sharply accented rhythm of the samisen. She stamps with her right foot, at which point the chief operator, passing the stick for the right arm to the other operator, uses his left hand to move the body counterclockwise until it faces the rear. The other operator, hidden behind the figure, spreads out both sleeves to reveal the full beauty of the costume in an exquisite pose, only presently to touch the sleeves to the face in the gesture of weeping. In the other variety of this *kata*, the *ushiroburi* to the right, the chief operator, instead of entrusting the right arm to the second operator, himself takes the left arm also, and swings the puppet around clockwise to face the rear. This variation does not permit the spreading of the sleeves, but has a quieter, more pathetic quality.

The *kata* for male puppets naturally place great emphasis on the kicking and stamping of the feet with which male puppets are provided. Like the *mie* poses in Kabuki, these *kata* often epitomize by the violent angles of the body the powerful emotions of the character, but unlike the Kabuki *mie*, the Bunraku pose is not static. It consists rather of a series of movements rather like the climax of a dance. The Bunraku and Kabuki *kata* for the same work often differ considerably. In the Kabuki version of the head inspection scene from the "Village School" section of *Sugawara Denju Tenarai Kagami*, for example, the box containing the severed head is placed directly before Matsuōmaru. Then, depending on the variety of *kata* followed by the actor, he may lift the lid with both hands and stare at the head, or he may remove it with one hand, propping up his chin with the other to suggest his physical debility. In Bunraku, the box is placed to Matsuōmaru's right, and the play of gestures between him and the schoolmaster Genzō before the head is actually brought before Matsuōmaru affords a moment of dramatic conflict. Other *kata* for male puppets depend on such properties of the figure as the ability to open the mouth, lift the eyebrows, clench the fists, and so on.

The effect produced on Bunraku audiences by the *kata* for male and female puppets differs considerably, even when the movements themselves are similar. The female *kata*, though lovely to watch, may possess little dramatic significance; the male *kata*, on the other hand, usually occur at climactic moments, and are as appropriate to a particular character as the head or costume.

The movements making up a given *kata* were determined by the puppet operators of the past and are repeated faithfully today as a part of the discipline of the art, in much the way that elements of classical Western ballet are preserved intact, regardless of the work. The more naturalistic *furi* are also governed by long-standing traditions, not only in the basic interpretation of a role but in the details of the gestures. Even the most inconspicuous movements generally obey precedent, for in Bunraku there can be none of the unpremeditated or unconscious actions of people in daily life or of actors on a stage. One master of a century ago wrote a long series of poems (*waka*) offering advice to puppet operators, including:

fumidashi wa
otoko hidari ni
onna migi;
kore inyō no
sabetsu narikeri.

When they start to walk
The man puts forth the left foot,
The woman, the right;
This is how we distinguish
Male and female principles.

odoroki wa
kao shirizokete
ude wo dashi
kobushi wo chū ni
oku mono zo kashi

To express surprise
You should turn the face away,
Put forth the arms,
And raise clenched fists in the air
To achieve the best effect.

warau toki
otoko wa kata wo
souru nari
onna wa sode wo
atete utsumuku

When they are laughing
The man must throw his shoulders
Into the gesture;
The woman touches her sleeve
To her face and gazes down.

yō no naki
ningyō wa tada
tsuyu hodo ni
ugokasenu wo ba
tassha to zo iu.

The operator
Who does not move in the least
A puppet with no
Actions required of him
We call a master artist.

These and the other poems of the series indicate how clearly defined the idiom of the gestures had become. The audiences presumably were no less familiar with such conventions than the operators. But no matter how confining to free expression we may imagine the existence of established *furi* and *kata* to be, in practice there is always a considerable amount of variation from performance to performance. Such differences are due for the most part not to the relatively infrequent instances of an operator deliberately changing an existing pattern, but to the less conspicuous shadings given to the existing pattern by the temperament of the operator. This intrusion of the personality, despite formal patterns, may be found in all the traditional Japanese stage arts. The old saying had it, "Enter the mould, then break it!" by which was meant that a performer who had mastered the traditions could then break them to express his distinctive talents. The great puppet operators execute essentially the same gestures as the mediocre performers, but inevitably there are minute differences which are apparent to the audience and distinguish the true artist from the hack. Even the same man's manipulation of a puppet may vary in response to the atmosphere in the theatre or to a slightly altered tempo from the samisen accompaniment. The established gestures of the puppet theatre do not hamstring the operators and make them mere slaves of tradition; on the contrary, by providing a time-tested basic structure for the performance they enable the superior puppeteer to devote himself to the shadings and colorings of interpretation which are the truly interesting aspect of the art. When we go to hear a celebrated pianist interpret a familiar sonata we do not expect something almost unrecognizably different from previous performances, but rather a fresh attempt to achieve within tradition the ultimate interpretation of the work. With each Bunraku performance too we hope that the combination of tradition and individual talent will make an old masterpiece new again.

PLATES

1. *Yoshitsune Sembonzakura* (1747), by Takeda Izumo and ▷
others, is known especially for the "*Sushi* Shop" scene and the
"Journey" (*michiyuki*). The disinherited Gonta, profiting by
his father's absence from the *sushi* shop, arrives secretly and
calls his mother. (Danshichi head)

2. *Shōutsushi Asagaobanashi* (1832), commonly known as *Asagao Nikki*, contains many popular scenes. Here, Miyuki, separated from her lover Asojirō by a misunderstanding, plays a *koto* at a country inn to earn her living. She has gone blind from weeping over her griefs, as the closed eyes of the puppet head show. (**Musume** head)

3. "The Village School" scene from *Sugawara Denju Tenarai Kagami* ▷ (1746), by Takeda Izumo and others, is a great popular favorite. The evil Prime Minister, learning that the son of his hated rival is attending a village school, sends the nobleman Matsuōmaru to take the boy's head. Matsuōmaru, having identified the head of his own son as the one he had been commanded to take, rises to his feet and says he will resign from the Prime Minister's service. (Bunshichi head)

4. *Ehon Taikōki* (1799), by Chikamatsu Yanagi and others, describes the warfare of the sixteenth century. Jūjirō, the only son of the warrior Mitsuhide, staggers home badly wounded from the battlefield. Leaning on his sword, he describes the defeat. (Genta head)

5. *Chūshingura* (1748), by Takeda Izumo and others, is perhaps the greatest play of the puppet theatre. In the third of the eleven acts Enya Hanyan, taunted by the evil Kō no Moronao because he failed to offer the expected bribe, finally draws his sword and slashes at Moronao. (Moronao: Ōjūto head)

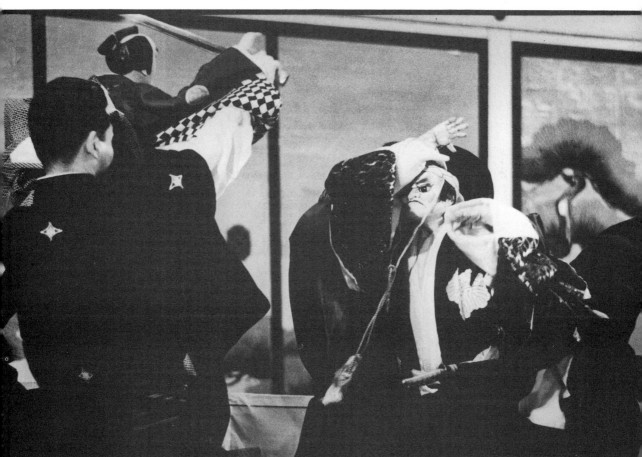

6 and 7. *Sonezaki Shinjū* (or "The Love Suicides at Sonezaki") was written by Chikamatsu Monzaemon in 1703. In the final scene, Tokubei and his sweetheart Ohatsu, a courtesan, journey to their death. (Tokubei: Genta head; Ohatsu: Keisei head)

(6) They pause a moment on a bridge and look down at the river.

(7) When they have reached the wood of Sonezaki, Tokubei holds his dagger poised over Ohatsu's throat. She urges him to kill her quickly.

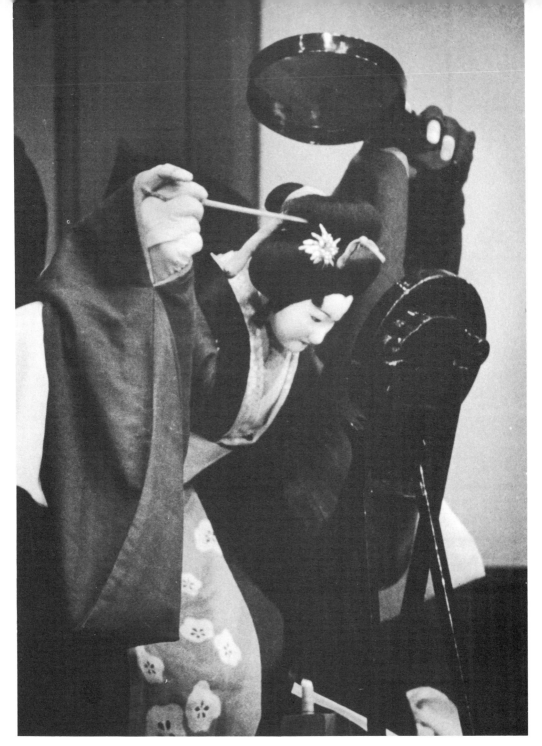

8. *Shimpan Utazaimon* (1780), by Chikamatsu Hanji, is frequently called "Osome and Hisamatsu" after the ill-fated lovers. The scene at Nozaki Village begins as Omitsu, a country girl who is Osome's rival for Hisamatsu's love, touches up her hair at word that he is on his way. (Musume head)

9. *Hadesugata Onna Maiginu* (1773), by Takemoto Saburo- ▷ bei and others, has a famous scene at the saké shop of Hanshichi, a young man who has deserted his wife Osono for the prostitute Sankatsu. Here, Sankatsu, carrying her small daughter, arrives at the shop entrance. (Keisei head)

10. Fukeoyama ("mature woman") head

This head is used for women of intelligence, passionately devoted to their children, and loyal to their husbands. Only the eyes move, but a needle is provided at the side of the mouth to catch the sleeve or hand towel in a gesture of weeping.

11. Ōdanshichi ("large Danshichi") head
First used for Watōnai in "The Battles of Coxinga" (1715), ▷
it represents warriors of violent temperament. The eyebrows and mouth move; the eyes move laterally.

12. The operator pulls one or more strings to make the eyes cross or (13) to lower the head and the eyebrows, or (14) to open the mouth in a shout of command.

15. The attention of the spectators is at times drawn from the stage to the chanter seated on a dais to their right, for the pleasure of seeing the range of expressions that cross his face. The samisen player seldom attracts attention to himself, though occasional virtuoso passages may make the audience applaud.

16. The operation of a three-man puppet, as seen from the wings, appears so unwieldy that it is hard to believe a dramatic illusion could be achieved. The chief operator, standing on high *geta*, holds the puppet above the floor level indicated by the top of the partition; the other two operators, less conspicuous because hooded and shod in low *zōri*, follow his leads almost instinctively.

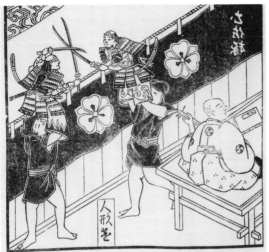

17. Behind the scenes at the puppet theatre of Yamamoto Tosa-no-jō, about 1690. To the left, concealed from the public by a curtain, the operators hold puppets above the railing. The chanter and samisen player, also out of the audience's sight, sit on a dais. Puppets not in use dangle from above. Each puppet was operated by one man.

18. Entrance of Temma Hachidayū's theatre in Edo, about 1685. A customer is paying the admission fee to the man seated on the platform. The man in black is the door manager. The entrance itself (under the sign) was made extremely small in order to prevent persons who had not paid from sneaking inside.

19. A group of Edo chanters of the 1690s during rehearsal. They beat time with their fans.

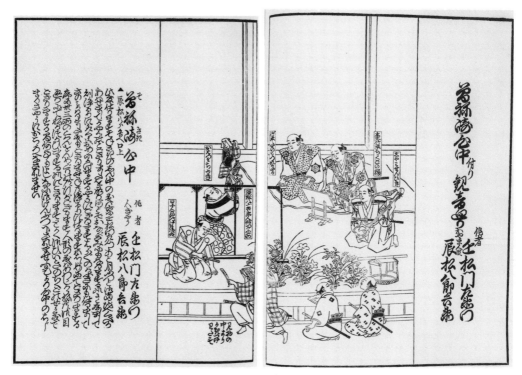

20. This stylized drawing of a performance of "The Love Suicides at Sonezaki" (1703) depicts the *michiyuki* scene. Tatsumatsu Hachirobei operates the puppet for Ohatsu in view of the audience; at the same time, the chanter Gidayū and his assistants are visible to the right. The curtain speech delivered by Tatsumatsu at the first performance (left) explains how Chikamatsu came to write the play.

21. An illustration of Chikamatsu's play "The Mirror of Craftsmen of the Emperor Yōmei" (1705), showing in stylized form the puppet operator Tatsumatsu Hachirobei and the chanter Takemoto Gidayū performing in full view of the audience.

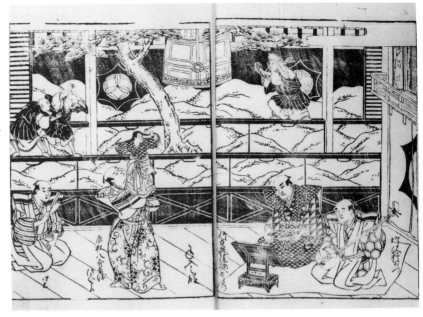

22. A performance in 1765 of *Ranjatai Nitta Keizu* by Chikamatsu Hanji, showing three-man puppets of the variety still used. The chanter and samisen player sit behind a bamboo blind stripped to the waist, no doubt because this performance took place in summer.

LIST OF PLAYS

Akoya no Kotozeme: See *Dannoura Kabuto Gunki.*

Amida no Munewari (阿弥陀胸割). Sixteenth century play by unknown author, no longer performed.

Asagao Nikki: See *Shō Utsushi Asagaobanashi.*

Ashiya Dōman Ōuchi Kagami (芦屋道満大内鑑) by Takeda Izumo. Five acts, of which the fourth (*Yasunauchi*) is most frequently performed. 1734.

Ataka no Seki (安宅関). Music by Toyozawa Dampei. A dance play adapted from the Kabuki work *Kanjinchō.* 1895.

Benkei Jōshi: See *Goshozakura Horikawa Youchi.*

Chest-Splitting of Amida: See *Amida no Munewari.*

Chikagoro Kawara no Tatehiki (近頃河原の達引) by Tamekawa Sōsuke, Tsutsui Hanji, and Nagawa Shimesuke. Three acts, of which the second (*Horikawa*) is frequently performed. 1785.

Chūshingura: See *Kanadehon Chūshingura.*

Daidairi Ōtomo no Matori (大内裏大友真鳥) by Takeda Izumo. Five acts. The play is not commonly performed at present. 1725.

Dango-uri: See *Ne mo Sayuru Haru no Usuzuki.*

Dannoura Kabuto Gunki (壇浦兜軍記) by Matsuda Bunkōdō and Hasegawa Senshi. Five acts, of which the third (*Akoya no Kotozeme*) is frequently performed. 1732.

Danshichi Kurobei: See *Natsumatsuri Naniwa Kagami.*

Date Kurabe Okuni Kabuki (伊達競阿国戯場) by Tatsuta Benji, Yoshida Kigan, and Utei Emba. Ten acts. 1779.

Date Sōdō: See *Date Kurabe Okuni Kabuki.*

Dōjōji: See *Kyōganoko Musume Dōjōji.*

Domomata: See *Keisei Hangokō.*

Ehon Taikōki (絵本太功記) by Chikamatsu Yanagi, Chikamatsu Kosuiken, and Chikamatsu Senyōken. Thirteen acts, of which the first (*Nijōjō Haizen*), second (*Honnōji*), sixth (*Myōshinji*), and tenth (*Amagasaki*) are still frequently performed. 1799.

En no Gyōja Ōminezakura (役行者大峰桜) by Takeda Geki, Yoshida Kanshi, and Miyoshi Shōraku. Five acts. 1751.

Futatsu Chōchō Kuruwa Nikki (双蝶々曲輪日記) by Takeda Izumo, Miyoshi Shōraku, and Namiki Sōsuke. Nine acts of which the second (*Sumō-mae*), sixth (*Hashimoto*), seventh (*Kyōran*), and eighth (*Hikimado*) are frequently performed. 1749.

Gappō's Daughter Tsuji: See *Sesshū Gappō ga Tsuji*

Go Taiheiki Shiraishibanashi (碁太平記白石噺) by Kino Jōtarō, Utei Emba, and Yō Yōtai. Eleven acts, of which the seventh (*Yoshiwara Ageya*) is frequently performed. 1780.

Goshozakura Horikawa Youchi (御所桜堀川夜討) by Matsuda Bunkōdō and Miyoshi Shōraku. Five acts, of which the third (*Benkei Jōshi*) and fourth (*Tōyata Monogatari*) are most frequently performed. 1737.

Hadesugata Onna Maiginu (艶容女舞衣) by Takemoto Saburobei, Toyotake Ōritsu, and Yatami Heishichi. Three acts, of which the third (*Sakaya*) is frequently performed. 1772.

Hamlet adapted by Ōnishi Toshio. 1956.

Heike Nyogo no Shima (平家女護島) by Chikamatsu Monzaemon. Five acts, of which the second (*Kikai-ga-shima*) is most frequently performed. 1719.

Hidakagawa Iriaizakura (日高川入相花王) by Takeda Koizumo, Chikamatsu Hanji, Takemoto Saburobei, Kitamado Goichi, and Nibudō. Five acts, of which the fourth (*Hidakagawa*) is most frequently performed. 1759.

Hiragana Seisuiki (ひらがな盛衰記) by Miyoshi Shōraku, Matsuda Bunkōdō, Asada Kakei, Takeda Koizumo, and Takeda Izumo. Five acts, of which the second (*Genta Kandō*), third (*Sakaro*), and fourth (*Kanzaki Ageya*) are frequently performed. 1739.

Honchō Nijūshi Kō (本朝廿四孝) by Chikamatsu Hanji, Miyoshi Shōraku, Takeda Inaba, Takeda Heishichi, Takeda Koide, and Takemoto Saburobei. Five acts, of which the third (*Kansuke Sumika*) and fourth (*Jusshu Kō* and *Kitsunebi*) are frequently performed. 1766.

Ichinotani Futaba Gunki (一谷嫩軍記) by Namiki Sōsuke, Namiki Shōzō, Asada Itchō, Namioka Geiji, Naniwa Sanzō, and Toyotake Jinroku. Five acts, of which the third (*Kumagai Jinya*) is still frequently performed. 1731.

Igagoe Dōchū Sugoroku (伊賀越道中双六) by Chikamatsu Hanji and Chikamatsu Kasaku. Ten acts, of which the sixth (*Numazu*), and eighth (*Okazaki*) are frequently performed. 1783.

Imoseyama Onna Teikin (妹背山婦女庭訓) by Chikamatsu Hanji, Matsuda Baku, Sakai Zempei, Miyoshi Shōraku, and Chikamatsu Tōnan. Five acts, of which all but the fifth are frequently performed. 1771.

Ise Ondo Koi no Netaba (伊勢音頭恋寝刃) original Kabuki play by Chikamatsu Tokusō (1796). Four acts, of which the third (*Aburaya*) is the only one performed. 1838.

Kagamiyama Kokyō no Nishikie (加賀見山旧錦絵) by Yō Yōtai. Eleven acts, of which only the sixth (*Zōri-uchi*) and seventh (*Nagatsubone* and *Okuniwa* scenes) are performed at present. 1782.

Kagekiyo Victorious: See *Shusse Kagekiyo.*

Kamakura Sandaiki (鎌倉三代記) probably by Chikamatsu Hanji. Nine acts, of which the seventh (*Kinugawa Mura*) is most frequently performed. 1770.

Kanadehon Chūshingura (仮名手本忠臣蔵) by Takeda Izumo, Miyoshi Shōraku, and Namiki Sōsuke. Eleven acts, all commonly performed. 1748.

Kasaneizutsu: See *Shinjū Kasaneizutsu.*

Keisei Hangokō (傾城反魂香) by Chikamatsu Monzaemon. Three acts, of which the first (*Tosa Shōgen Kankyo*) is most frequently performed. 1708.

Kiichi Hōgen Sanryaku no Maki (鬼一法眼三略巻) by Matsuda Bunkōdō and Hasegawa Senshi. Five acts, of which the third (*Kikubatake*) and fifth (*Gojō Ōhashi*) only are at present performed. 1731.

Kikubatake: See *Kiichi Hōgen Sanryaku no Maki.*

Kishihime: See below.

Kishi no Himematsu Kutsuwa Kagami (岸姫松轡鑑) by Toyotake Ōritsu, Wakatake Fuemi, Fukumatsu Tōsuke, and Namiki Eisuke. Five acts, of which the third (*Asahina Jōshi*) is most frequently performed. 1762.

Koharu Jihei: See *Shinjū Ten no Amijima.*

Koi no Tayori Yamato Ōrai (恋飛脚大和往来) by Suga Sensuke and Wakatake Fuemi. Two acts. An adaptation of *Meido no Hikyaku.* 1773.

Koinyōbō Somewake Tazuna (恋女房染分手綱) by Yoshida Kanshi and Miyoshi Shōraku. Thirteen acts, of which the tenth (*Dōchū Sugoroku* and *Shigenoi Kowakare* scenes) is frequently performed. 1751.

Kokaji (小鍛冶) by Kimura Tomiko. A dance play adapted from the Nō drama of the same title. 1941.

Kumagai's Camp: See *Ichinotani Futaba Gunki.*

Kuzunoha: See *Ashiya Dōman Ōuchi Kagami.*

Kyōganoko Musume Dōjōji (京鹿子娘道成寺). Author unknown. A dance play. 1810.

Love Suicides at Amijima: See *Shinjū Ten no Amijima.*

Love Suicides at Sonezaki: See *Sonezaki Shinjū.*

Madame Butterfly, adapted by Ōnishi Toshio. 1956.

Meiboku Sendai Hagi (伽羅先代萩) by Matsu Kanshi, Takahashi Buhei, and Yoshida Kakumaru. Nine acts, of which the sixth (*Goten* and *Yukashita*) is frequently performed. 1785.

Meido no Hikyaku (冥途の飛脚) by Chikamatsu Monzaemon. Three acts, all of which are commonly performed. 1711.

Mekura Kagekiyo: See *Musume Kagekiyo Yashima Nikki.*

Miracle at Tsubosaka Temple: See *Tsubosaka Reigenki.*

Mirror of Craftsmen of the Emperor Yōmei: See *Yōmei Tennō Shokunin Kagami.*

Modoribashi (戻橋). Author unknown. A dance play adapted from the "Modoribashi" scene in *Ōeyama Shutendōji.* Date of first performance not clear.

Mōjōzakura Yuki no Miyashiro (盲杖桜雪社). Author unknown. A dance play. 1884.

Moritsuna's Camp: See *Ōmi Genji Senjin Yakata.*

Musume Kagekiyo Yashima Nikki (嬢景清八島日記) by Wakatake Fuemi, Koku Zōsu, and Nakamura

Akei. Five acts, of which the third (*Hyūgashima*) is most frequently performed. 1764.

Natsumatsuri Naniwa Kagami (夏祭浪花鑑) by Namiki Sōsuke, Miyoshi Shōraku, and Takeda Koizumo. Nine acts, of which the third (*Sumiyoshi Hambe*), sixth (*Sabu-uchi*), and seventh (*Nagamachi Ura*) are frequently performed. 1745.

Nebiki no Kadomatsu (寿の門松) by Chikamatsu Monzaemon. Three acts. A revised version entitled *Futatsu Chōchō Kuruwa Nikki* is usually performed. 1718.

Ne mo Sayuru Haru no Usuzuki (音冴春臼月). Author unknown. A dance play. 1915.

Nigatsudō Rōben Sugi no Yurai (二月堂良弁杉由来). Author unknown. One act, four scenes, of which the last two scenes (*Tōdaiji* and *Nigatsudō*) are frequently performed. 1887.

Nijūshi Kō: See *Honchō Nijūshi Kō.*

Ōeyama Shutendōji (大江山酒呑童子). Author unknown. Sixteen acts. 1854.

Ohatsu Tokubei: See *Sonezaki Shinjū.*

Ōmi Genji Senjin Yakata (近江源氏先陣館) by Chikamatsu Hanji, Miyoshi Shōraku, Yatami Heishichi, etc. Nine acts, of which the eighth (*Moritsuna Jinya*) is most frequently performed. 1769.

Ōshū Adachi ga Hara (奥州安達原) by Takeda Izumo, Chikamatsu Hanji, Takemoto Saburobei, and Kitamado Goichi. Five acts, of which the third (*Sodehagi Saimon*) is frequently performed. 1762.

Oshun Dembei: See *Chikagoro Kawara no Tatehiki.*

Osome Hisamatsu: See *Shimpan Utazaimon.*

Osono's Monologue: See *Hadesugata Onna Maiginu.*

Otokodate Itsutsu Karigane (男作五雁金) by Takeda Izumo. Seven acts. This play is not performed at present. 1742.

Ranjatai Nitta Keizu (蘭奢待新田系図) by Chikamatsu Hanji, Takeda Heishichi, and Takemoto Saburobei. This play is not performed at present. 1765.

Rōben Sugi: See *Nigatsudō Rōben Sugi no Yurai.*

Sakaya: See *Hadesugata Onna Maiginu.*

Sannin Zatō: See *Mōjōzakura Yuki no Miyashiro.*

Sanyūshi Homare no Nikudan (三勇士名誉肉弾) by Matsui Shōō. Not currently performed. 1932.

Sembonzakura: See *Yoshitsune Sembonzakura.*

Sendai Hagi: See *Meiboku Sendai Hagi.*

Sesshū Gappō ga Tsuji (摂州合邦辻) by Suga Sensuke and Wakatake Fuemi. Two acts, of which the second (*Gappō-uchi*) is frequently performed. 1773.

Shigenoi Kowakare: See *Koi Nyōbō Somewake Tazuna.*

Shimpan Utazaimon (新版歌祭文) by Chikamatsu Hanji. Two acts, the first (*Nozakimura*) and second (*Aburaya*) are commonly performed. 1780.

Shinjū Kasaneizutsu (心中重井筒) by Chikamatsu Monzaemon. Three acts, of which the first (*Konya*) and second (*Rokken-chō*) are presently performed. 1707.

Shinjū Ten no Amijima (心中天網島) by Chikamatsu Monzaemon. Three acts, all commonly performed. 1720.

Shin Usuyuki Monogatari (新薄雪物語) by Matsuda Bunkōdō, Miyoshi Shōraku, Ogawa Hampei, and Takeda Koizumo. Three acts. This play is not commonly performed. 1741.

Shiraishibanashi: See *Go Taiheiki Shiraishibanashi.*

Shokatsu Kōmei Kanae Gundan (諸葛孔明鼎軍談) by

Takeda Izumo. Five acts. This play is not performed at present. 1724.

Shō Utsushi Asagaobanashi (生写朝顔話) by Yamada Kakashi. Five acts, of which the first *(Ujigawa Hotarugari)* and fourth *(Shimada Yadoya and Ōigawa)* are frequently performed. 1832.

Shunkan: See *Heike Nyogo no Shima.*

Shusse Kagekiyo (出世景清) by Chikamatsu Monzaemon. Five acts. This play is at present not performed. 1686.

Soga Heir : See *Yotsugi Soga.*

Sonezaki Shinjū (曾根崎心中) by Chikamatsu Monzaemon. One act, three scenes, all commonly performed. 1703.

Sugawara Denju Tenarai Kagami (菅原伝授手習鑑) by Takeda Izumo, Miyoshi Shōraku, Namiki Sōsuke, and Takeda Koizumo. Five acts, all frequently performed. 1746.

Summer Festival: See *Natsumatsuri Naniwa Kagami.*

Taijū: See *Ehon Taikōki.*

Taikōki: See *Ehon Taikōki.*

Tamamonomae Asahi no Tamoto (玉藻前曦袂) by Chikamatsu Baishiken and Sagawa Tōta. Five acts, of which the third *(Dōshun Yakata)* is most frequently performed. 1806.

Tamba Yosaku Matsuyo no Komurobushi (丹波与作待夜の小室節) by Chikamatsu Monzaemon. Three acts. A revision entitled *Koi Nyōbō Somewake Tazuna* is more frequently performed than this original. 1708.

Terakoya: See *Sugawara Denju Tenarai Kagami.*

Three Heroes, Glorious Human Bullets: See *Sanyūshi Homare no Nikudan.*

Tōkaidōchū Hizakurige (東海道中膝栗毛). Original story by Jippensha Ikku. 1919.

Tōkaidō Yotsuya Kaidan (東海道四谷怪談) by Tsuruya Namboku (originally a Kabuki play). Five acts. 1825.

Tsubosaka Reigenki (壺坂霊験記) adapted by Toyozawa Dampei and his wife Chika from an earlier work. One act. 1879.

Tsuri Onna (釣女) composed by Tsurusawa Dōhachi. A dance play adapted from a *kyōgen* bearing the same title. 1938.

Umegawa Chūbei: See *Meido no Hikyaku.*

Village School: See *Sugawara Denju Tenarai Kagami.*

Yōmei Tennō Shokunin Kagami (用明天皇職人鑑) by Chikamatsu Monzaemon. Five acts. This play is at present not performed. 1705.

Yoshitsune Sembonzakura (義経千本桜) by Takeda Izumo, Miyoshi Shōraku, and Namiki Sōsuke. Five acts, of which the second *(Tokaiya)*, third *(Konomi* and *Sushiya* scenes), and fourth *(Michiyuki, Yoshino,* and *Kawatsura Yakata* scenes) are frequently performed. 1747.

Yotsugi Soga (世継曾我) by Chikamatsu Monzaemon. Five acts. No longer performed. 1683.

Yotsuya Kaidan: See *Tōkaidō Yotsuya Kaidan.*

Yūgiri Awa no Naruto (夕霧阿波鳴門) by Chikamatsu Monzaemon. Three acts, of which the first *(Yoshidaya)* is frequently performed. 1712.

SOME RECENT BOOKS IN ENGLISH ON BUNRAKU

Adachi, Barbara. *Backstage at Bunraku*. New York: Weatherhill, 1985.

Brandon, James R. *Chūshingura: Studies in Kabuki and the Puppet Theater*. Honolulu: University of Hawaii Press, 1982.

Dunn, C. J. *The Early Japanese Puppet Drama*. London: Luzac, 1966.

Gerstle, C. Andrew. *Circles of Fantasy: Convention in the Plays of Chikamatsu*. Cambridge, Mass.: Harvard University Press, 1986.

Jones, Stanleigh H., Jr. *Sugawara and the Secrets of Calligraphy*. New York: Columbia University Press, 1985.

Keene, Donald. *Chūshingura (The Treasury of Loyal Retainers)*. New York: Columbia University Press, 1971.

SHORT BIBLIOGRAPHY

Bowers, Faubion. *Japanese Theatre*. New York: Hill and Wang, 1960. Mainly devoted to Kabuki, but contains also a general introduction to Bunraku and the translation of a scene from *Sesshū Gappō ga Tsuji* ("Gappo and his Daughter Tsuji.")

Chikaishi Yasuaki (近石泰秋). *Jōruri Meisaku Shū* (浄瑠璃名作集). Tokyo: Kodansha, 1950. Two vols. Scenes from the most celebrated *jōruri* plays, annotated with special attention given to performance on the Bunraku stage.

Engeki Hakubutsukan (演劇博物館), (ed.). *Engeki Hyakka Daijiten* (演劇百科大事典). Tokyo: Heibonsha, 1960-62. A six-vol. dictionary of the theatre; invaluable for the study of Bunraku.

Engeki Hakubutsukan (演劇博物館), (ed.). *Geinō Jiten* (芸能辞典). Tokyo: Tōkyōdō, 1953. A useful one-volume dictionary of the arts which includes articles on various aspects of Bunraku.

Inoue, Jukichi. *Chushingura or Forty-Seven Ronin*. Tokyo: Maruzen, 1937 (4th edition). A complete translation of the celebrated play.

Kawatake Shigetoshi (河竹繁俊). *Nihon Engeki Zenshi* (日本演劇全史). Tokyo: Iwanami Shoten, 1959. An exceptionally detailed general history of the Japanese theatre which includes much material on Bunraku.

Keene, Donald. *The Battles of Coxinga*. London: Taylor's Foreign Press, 1951. A complete translation of Chikamatsu's play *Kokusenya Kassen* (國性爺合戦), together with an introduction treating the history of *jōruri* and the background of the play.

Keene, Donald. *Major Plays of Chikamatsu*. New York: Columbia University Press, 1961. Complete translations of eleven plays, together with an introduction.

Kiritake Monjūrō (桐竹紋十郎) and Tsurusawa Seijirō (鶴澤清二郎). *Bunraku no Ningyō to Samisen*. Nagoya: Bunraku Kenkyūkai, 1944. Random recollections by a leading puppet operator and samisen player, valuable for personal glimpses of Bunraku, as seen from the inside.

Malm, William. *Japanese Music and Musical Instruments*. Tokyo: Tuttle, 1959. The best book in a Western language on the subject.

Miyao Shigeo (宮尾しげを). *Bunraku Ningyō Zufu* (文楽人形図譜). Tokyo: Jidaisha, 1942. An enchanting study of the Bunraku puppets, with drawings of every variety of head, hand, leg, prop, etc. Filled with odd bits of information which only a person deeply familiar with Bunraku could possess.

Miyake Shūtarō (三宅周太郎). *(Shimpen) Bunraku no Kenkyū* (新編文楽の研究). Tokyo: Sōgensha, 1947. Essays on performers and performances. Interesting especially for its picture of Bunraku immediately after the end of the war in 1945.

Mori Shū (森修). *Chikamatsu Monzaemon* (近松門左衛門). Kyoto: Sanichi Shobō, 1959. An excellent account of the career and artistry of Chikamatsu.

Oda Sakunosuke (織田作之助). *Bunraku no Hito* (文楽の人). Tokyo: Hakuōsha, 1946. An absorbingly written account of the career of the first Yoshida Eiza, together with a shorter essay on Yoshida Bungorō.

Ōnishi Shigetaka (大西重孝) and Yoshinaga Takao (吉永孝雄). *Bunraku*. Tokyo: Kōdansha, 1959. A large collection of Bunraku photographs, together with excellent short essays by various authorities on different aspects of the art.

Ozawa Yoshikuni (小澤愛圀). *Daitōa Kyōeiken no Ningyō-geki* (大東亜共榮圏の人形劇). Tokyo: Mita Bungaku Shuppambu, 1944. Despite the ultranationalistic title, this is a scholarly study of the puppet theatre in various parts of Asia.

Saitō Seijirō (齊藤清二郎). *Bunraku Kashira no Kenkyū* (文楽首の研究). Tokyo: Aterie Sha, 1943. A well-illustrated study of puppet heads by an authority.

Scott, A. C. *The Puppet Theatre of Japan*. Tokyo: Tuttle, 1963. A general introduction.

Shively, Donald H. *The Love Suicides at Amijima*. Cambridge: Harvard University Press, 1953. Complete translation of Chikamatsu's great play, together with an introduction.

Takemoto Tsunadayū (竹本綱太夫). *Denden Mushi* (でんでん虫). Osaka: Nunoi Shobō, 1964. An amusingly written autobiography and book of reminiscences by a gifted chanter.

Tanabe Hisao (田辺尚雄). *Samisen Ongaku Shi* (三味線音楽史). Tokyo: Sōshisha, 1963. The history of the samisen, its development, and its music. The author is a noted scholar of Japanese music.

Tsunoda Ichirō (角田一郎). *Ningyōgeki no Seiritsu ni kansuru Kenkyū* (人形劇の成立に関する研究). Osaka: Asahiya Shoten, 1963. A massive study of the puppet theatre in Japan up to the middle of the 17th century. The best work on the subject.

Utsumi Shigetarō (内海繁太郎). *Ningyō Jōruri to Bunraku* (人形浄瑠璃と文楽). Tokyo: Hakusuisha, 1958. An uninterestingly assembled collection of facts about Bunraku.

Utsumi Shigetarō. *Ningyō Shibai to Chikamatsu no Jōruri* (人形芝居と近松の浄瑠璃). Tokyo: Hakusuisha, 1940. A compendium of material relating to the puppet theatre in Chikamatsu's day and earlier.

Wakatsuki Yasuji (若月保治). *Ningyō Jōruri Shi Kenkyū* (人形浄瑠璃史研究). Tokyo: Sakurai Shoten, 1943. An excellent history of the *jōruri*.

Watsuji Tetsurō (和辻哲郎). *Nihon Geijutsu Shi Kenkyū* (日本藝術史研究). Tokyo: Iwanami Shoten, 1955. An important examination of materials available for study of Bunraku and Kabuki in their early periods.

Yokoyama Tadashi (横山正). *Jōruri Ayatsuri Shibai no Kenkyū* (浄瑠璃操芝居の研究). Tokyo: Kazama Shobō, 1963. A splendid study of the texts and literary qualities of plays by Chikamatsu and later dramatists.

Yoshida Bungorō (吉田文五郎). *Bungorō Geidan* (文五郎芸談). Tokyo: Sakurai Shoten, 1947. Recollections and opinions by the great puppet operator.

INDEX